WAR
AN ENQUIRY

A. C. GRAYLING

YALE UNIVERSITY PRESS
NEW HAVEN AND LONDON

VICES AND VIRTUES

Series editors Richard G. Newhauser and John Jeffries Martin

For information about this and other Yale University Press publications, please contact:
U.S. Office: sales.press@yale.edu   yalebooks.com
Europe Office: sales@yaleup.co.uk   yalebooks.co.uk

Set in Sabon MT by IDSUK (DataConnection) Ltd
Printed in Great Britain by Hobbs the Printers Ltd, Totton, Hampshire

Library of Congress Cataloging-in-Publication Data

Names: Grayling, A. C., author.
Title: War : an enquiry / A.C. Grayling.
Description: New Haven, CT : Yale University, 2017. | Series: Vices and virtues | Includes bibliographical references and index.
Identifiers: LCCN 2017000689 (print) | LCCN 2017010233 (ebook) | ISBN 9780300175349 (alk. paper) | ISBN 9780300226287 ()
Subjects: LCSH: War (Philosophy) | War—History. | War—Moral and ethical aspects.
Classification: LCC U21.2 .G674 2017 (print) | LCC U21.2 (ebook) | DDC 355.0201—dc23
LC record available at https://lccn.loc.gov/2017000689

ISBN 978-0-300-23445-9 (pbk)

A catalogue record for this book is available from the British Library.

10 9 8 7 6 5 4 3 2 1

War is a bloody, killing business. You've got to spill their blood, or they will spill yours! Rip them up the belly. Shoot them in the guts. When shells are hitting all around you and you wipe the dirt off your face and realize that instead of dirt it's the blood and guts of what was once your best friend beside you, you'll know what to do.

From General George Patton's speech to the United States Third Army, 1944

One cannot fight a war with one hand tied behind one's back.

Winston Churchill

War does not determine who is right, only who is left.

Attributed to Bertrand Russell

Mankind must put an end to war – or war will put an end to mankind.

John F. Kennedy, address before the United Nations, 1961

I hate war as only a soldier who has lived it can, only as one who has seen its brutality, its futility, its stupidity.

Dwight D. Eisenhower, address before the Canadian Club, 1946

You may not be interested in war, but war is interested in you.

Attributed to Leon Trotsky

Contents

Foreword
Richard G. Newhauser and
John Jeffries Martin

War has been a salient aspect of human civilisation for the last 5,000, if not the last 10,000 years. We should not normalise this. Even if war may have at times accomplished some good in the past, it has routinely been and remains the source of great harm and suffering. The combined death toll of the First and Second World Wars, for example, exceeded 100 million souls. But the terms of the debate have shifted. In the nuclear age war has the potential to destroy civilisation itself.

Through most of recorded history, ethicists have sought to limit both the frequency and the lethality of war. Yet, as A. C. Grayling demonstrates in this analysis of 'armed conflict between states or nations, or between identified and organised groups of significant size and character', moral reasoning about war has never been static but has rather continually sought to adapt to new social and political circumstances as well as to new technologies. Moral reasoning, that is, can best be understood historically.

Indeed, the central goal of the series 'Vices and Virtues', to which Grayling has now contributed the first two volumes, is to underscore the deep connections between historical change and ethics. This is true of a wide spectrum of moral subjects, from friendship and war to emotions such as anger. Moral concepts, this series argues, have neither fixed contents nor contours. On the contrary, their meanings shift as new historical circumstances and challenges arise; they are cultural constructions. The series does not seek to offer one model of how ethical thought is related to social, political and cultural change. Its goal rather is to open up a sense of the diverse ways in which moral reasoning is shaped by and shapes the worlds in which we live. War may be a reality, but this in no way diminishes the need to imagine a warless world – indeed, the two may go hand-in-hand.

The exploration of changes in moral thought, moreover, is not limited to the past. As Grayling makes clear, our ethical reasoning about war must continue to adapt to emerging forms of physical warfare. As the battlefield becomes increasingly automated, for example, how should we fashion a morality that guides us in the regulation of computerised weapons capable of making increasingly complex 'decisions' about when to strike and whom to kill? Yet it is above all the nuclear threat that requires a redoubling of our moral imaginations. The mere existence of such weapons poses an existential threat to humanity. If our species is to survive, we must bring an end to war.

Perhaps Grayling's most compelling and hopeful innovation has been his decision to juxtapose war not to peace, its customary opposite, but rather to friendship, the subject of his earlier book inaugurating the series. If war undermines the bonds between us, forcing each of us into a corner and leading us to seek the destruction of our enemies, friendship fosters these bonds, leading us to hope for the best for our fellow beings. To be sure, friendship is a category that, in general, we use for a few and not for whole societies. Yet Grayling does suggest in this book that our best hope to avoid war lies in our recognition that we are far less likely to fall prey to war if we can promote greater integration among peoples, along with 'mutual linkages of a practical and beneficial kind, and the elimination of boundaries between interests'. In short, the elimination of war would seem to require a kind of global friendship. The question remains open whether or not we human beings have the will to achieve this.

Preface

This book makes a pair with a previous book published by Yale University Press: *Friendship* (2013). In that book I discuss aspects of the most desirable of human relationships and, arguably, the most achieved of such, in the sense that it is where our best interpersonal bonds are to be found, as the mature form of the many different kinds of loves, family ties and comradeships there are. Discussion of friendship as an ideal was initiated by the philosophers of classical antiquity, beginning with Plato and then most famously Aristotle, who devoted two books of his *Nichomachean Ethics* to the subject, thus sparking a debate about friendship which persists to our own day and has had many distinguished contributors.

Friendship's opposite is enmity, and the fullest expression of organised enmity takes the form of war. At the very outset of looking at the phenomenon of war I must declare an interest: while being the closest thing to a pacifist that one can be without being a pacifist, and while abominating war, I think there are two sets of circumstances in which fighting a war is justified and can even be a duty. They are explained in the appropriate place below. But I emphatically think – as by far the great majority of us must – that war is an evil, a great evil, even in the two cases which I think justified; they too are an evil, though alas necessary ones.

As an evil, even in the rare cases in which it is justified, war raises urgent ethical questions, not least about what conduct is acceptable during hostilities. In *Among the Dead Cities* (2006) I examined the particular case of Allied mass bombing attacks on the civilian populations of Germany and Japan during the Second World War. My argument was that the Allied war against Nazism and Japanese aggression was justified – indeed, the Allies had a moral duty to defeat these evils since they were greater evils than the evil of a war to oppose them – but that this fact did not justify all the actions taken in pursuit of that aim. And this applied paradigmatically to indiscriminate aerial bombardment – which means attempted and enacted massacre – of civilian populations. This is an example of the difficult question that moral considerations prompt when one reflects on Winston Churchill's remark that 'One cannot fight a war with one hand tied behind one's back'. Moral scruples can dangerously hamper military efforts; in the darkest days of the Second World War, when Britain was alone in facing Nazi Germany, and the Wehrmacht was massing on the French coast in preparation for an invasion, it would have seemed suicidal to wring hands over which harms to the foe were acceptable and which not. And yet it is precisely in times of greatest emergency that such questions are most in need of clear and, one hopes, principled answers.

Thucydides wrote his account of the Peloponnesian War to illustrate the danger to individual and national morals posed by war. In the third year of that conflict, Mytilene on the island of Lesbos broke its treaty obligations to Athens and the Athenians decided to punish the Mytileneans by massacring them and razing their city. After a night's sleep they 'repented' and decided instead that it was too cruel to require that a city's whole population should suffer for the actions of its leaders. Twelve years into the war the island state of Melos, a Spartan colony, refused to submit to Athens; the Athenian generals who conveyed their city's demands to the Melian magistrates said to them – I paraphrase – 'Let us not waste words on fine sentiments about right and wrong. The plain fact is, they who have power do what they can, they who are weak accept what they must.' Thereupon Athens set about treating Melos and its citizens in the manner previously envisaged for Mytilene. Thus does war corrode and corrupt the moral sense, said Thucydides, and he wrote his book in part to illustrate that fact and to warn against it.

Arguments continue about the justification, if any, for the 'area bombing' strategy of RAF Bomber Command in the years 1942–45 over Germany, and the dropping of the atomic bombs by the US Army Air Force (USAAF) over Hiroshima and Nagasaki in 1945. In the 1977 First Protocol to the Fourth Geneva Convention of 1949, military attacks on civilian populations were outlawed. But the various aspects of 'collateral damage' – death and injury to civilians, the use of chemical, biological and nuclear weapons, the destruction of livelihoods, and imprisonment, rape and torture – are pressing problems because they remain a threat, and in far too many cases an actuality, in conflicts everywhere.

The means of harm in warfare have become ever more effective and dangerous, but although this is a matter of degree rather than kind, the greater harm threatened by advanced weapon technologies raises the perennial moral dilemmas in more acute form. Theodor Adorno, in his remark that humankind has become cleverer but not wiser over time, pointed to the spear's evolution into the rocket-propelled missile: our cleverness developed the latter, our failure to grow in wisdom keeps us engaged in arms races.

Thucydides wrote his book 2,500 years ago. Has any progress been made on the moral front regarding war? Has war changed for the worse, now that it is not only or even armies on the front lines, but whole populations? What will result from developments in military technology – the use of drones and robots, the displacement of battles into space? All this is premised on the assumption that wholesale nuclear conflict will not occur, but that war will continue as the deadly attrition of less wholesale conflict. For if global nuclear conflict were precipitated by one or other of the more local wars, discussion of war will have become – as the saying has it – merely academic.

In this book I survey the phenomenon of war, and canvass some points of view on its different aspects, more by way of contributing to discussion of them than in the belief that any of them are definitive. My themes are the history of war, theories of war, the causes of war and the effects of war, the efforts made from ethical and legal directions to limit both the occurrence and the harm of war, and finally some thoughts about the future of war. That is a broad range, so the word 'survey' at the beginning of this paragraph is apt. But a conspectus can be useful; most discussions focus on highly particular topics, and there are so many of these that the whole can be lost to view. And to see things clearly, we need to see them whole.

Introduction

Why do wars occur? Are they ever justified? Is any act permissible in the dangerous and desperate struggle to defeat an enemy? What, indeed, is war, and how does it differ from other kinds of violent conflict? What does history teach about the effects wars have on individuals and societies? Are these effects universally bad? And if they are not, does this consideration enter into the justification for war (as some indeed claim)?

These are the main questions that arise in connection with the phenomenon of war.

The first question – why do wars occur? – is the most complicated one to answer. It asks for the cause of war in the general sense of 'Why is war a pervasive and highly frequent feature of human history?' in contrast to queries about what caused this or that particular war.

The first question to ask about this first question, in its own turn, is: is it the right question to ask? It is tempting to think that it is a misleading question, for it appears to assume that there is a single answer that applies to all wars, perhaps framed in terms of generalities about human nature, the human condition, social structures, political ambitions or necessities, international arrangements, some combination of these – or perhaps all. One can imagine a critic of the question arguing that there are only causes of particular wars, that causes of one or some wars differ from those of other wars, that each war has its own unique set of causal factors. One can support such a view by the expedient of appealing to a different generalisation – that wars occur at different times in different places, so of course the prevailing conditions must by definition be different in each case.

However, this blanket rejection of the general question might be too quick. The pervasive and recurrent fact of war in history invites at least some speculation as to whether there is something generic about war in human affairs. The discovery that groups of male chimpanzees mount organised attacks on other chimpanzee groups raises the uncomfortable possibility that there is a genetic element involved – that, in short, human beings are programmed for socially organised violence. One has at least to consider that possibility along with others before rejecting the idea that there is a common underlying theme at issue, and that the historically more specific triggers for war are not the reasons but the excuses for it.

In asking the wholly general question 'What causes war?' it is helpful to note the following about the concept of causation itself. Few occurrences of any kind have single causes. Most things that happen are the outcome, as philosophers are quick to point out, of multiple factors, acting in concert to bring about the effect. Consider the example of a fire starting in a house. Among the causal factors are the presence of oxygen, the dryness of the structure and its furnishings, and something like a spark from a broken electricity wire or a dropped burning match. We are inclined to nominate the spark or the dropped match as 'the cause' of the fire, but although either of them is sufficient to cause the fire if the other necessary conditions are present – the oxygen, the dry materials – in truth all the factors are jointly required, because the spark or the lit match would not result in a house burning down if there were not enough oxygen or if the house and its contents were wet. The point is standardly put by saying that each factor by itself is necessary but not sufficient for the fire to break out; it is some appropriate combination of them which is sufficient for the fire – that is, that *makes* it occur.

Causal complexity would apply as much to the generic cause of war, if there is such a thing, as to the causes of historically specific wars. To unpick the co-operating factors that bring about specific wars might reveal whether there are underlying commonalities: either the discovery that there are, or the discovery that there are not, is of equal interest and importance.

Another point to be made at the outset is that whatever else one thinks about war, it has to be acknowledged that it represents failure – failure of diplomatic efforts, and failure in the ties of trade and cultural exchange which should in general make it difficult for nations to go to war with each other. When the shooting starts it is because the talking has stopped. There is something very crude indeed about war as a solution to serious differences between two or more parties, for it hands the argument over to killing and destruction as a form of settlement, leaving to killing and destruction the decision as to who will have the final say. It goes without saying that there is no guarantee such outcomes will represent the better moral case in the dispute. As Bertrand Russell said, 'War does not determine who is right, only who is left.'

There is scarcely any boundary, any border, in the world that was not drawn in the blood of conflict at some point in history. This compelling fact reminds us, if being reminded is necessary, of the importance of the fact that war is failure: if our national boundaries are in effect legacies of failure, we do well to consider how we might manage borders and boundaries better in the interests of peace.

Although this point embodies a truth, one has to remember and accept that not all parties to a war are responsible for the failure that it represents. War is sometimes forced on one or more of the combatant parties by the aggression or intransigence of another party. War is sometimes the last resort in the face of what would be a greater evil than the evil of war itself: in such cases, though there is certainly failure earlier in the process, blame for the failure does not fall equally.

Here is another question that deserves an answer: who has a right to pontificate on war? I sit in the safety of a largely peaceful country, having never served in the military, having never been a civilian caught up in the midst of full-scale military operations. A direct acquaintance with the business and experience of war might seem to be a credential that would benefit pontification. And so it would. But there is the general point that war and its harms are a concern for humanity at large, independently of whether these or those individuals or groups are directly embroiled: just being a member of the species is more than sufficient ground for taking an interest. And there is the more particular point that historians of war, and philosophers, might be thought to have something to contribute to the conversation; though they sit on the sidelines, that can sometimes be a point of vantage.

Introduction

These sidelines provide opportunities to learn from those who know. In my own case it has been a privilege to discuss with those who really know, at the Defence Academy of the United Kingdom at Shrivenham and the Royal College of Defence Studies in London. I am grateful to both institutions for the opportunities to learn from the senior military personnel there. They are highly impressive individuals, thoughtful and experienced, who have led in times of stress, who have seen what war means. From the unusual vantage of having been a commander in both peace and war, President Dwight D. Eisenhower, who commanded the Allied forces in the D-Day landings of 1944, said, 'I hate war as only a soldier who has lived it can, only as one who has seen its brutality, its futility, its stupidity.' As a patron of the United Kingdom Armed Forces Humanist Association I have had the further privilege to learn from active service personnel how the front lines of human experience deepen the sense of ethical concern that the realities of life, death and conflict raise.

There is the saying *verbum sapienti sat est* – 'a word is enough to the wise' – meaning that hints can be sufficient for instruction if one is attentive. It might therefore be pertinent to mention the following, very minor as they are in the way of experiences of conflict. As a child living in a part of Africa where an insurgency for liberation from British rule was in progress, I used to ride my bicycle to school among armoured cars and troops stationed at street corners. My father was a member of the civil guard, and slept with a revolver under his pillow. (He nearly shot me with it once, when I startled him early one morning after returning from a journey, he being in the house alone and expecting no-one.) The precautions were not otiose; there had been murders and violent riots, and the situation was tense. When the Katangese war erupted a few miles away across the border from where we

5

lived – the aircraft carrying UN Secretary-General Dag Hammarskjöld crashed even fewer miles away from us, killing all on board, almost certainly shot down – floods of bloodied refugees poured into our town, and we had numbers of them sleeping on the floor of our house. They had horror stories to tell. On one occasion my father's driver and I had to venture into the Katanga Pedicle, to Sakania, to fetch my parents from the railhead there, because the war had stranded them on their way back from Europe via Elizabethville: on that same road Congolese troops periodically machine-gunned convoys of refugees. I had to lie on the dusty floor of the car, under the back seat, in case we were attacked. Later, in Malawi as an apprentice journalist, I reported on some of the effects of the civil war in the early phase of Hastings Banda's rule. The London of my youth was still scarred with bomb sites in which the buddleia grew, and scraps of faded wallpaper curled down from the exposed walls of what had been upstairs bedrooms. In Sri Lanka I once rented a cottage near Trincomalee which was full of bullet holes; that was in a tenuous moment of truce in the midst of a frightful civil conflict.

Such in my case were a few hints and indications, a few minor brushes, serving as mere peepholes into terrible things, which led to sympathy for those who know the full reality of war; for even such minor hints make more palpable what the distancing of television news conveys only at third hand.

And yet even television news reports ought to be enough to impress upon everyone the need to think about this ugly phenomenon which blasts our history and our present, and how its evils are to be abated. If one is to dream of ending war, utopian as such a dream is, one has first to make some sense of it and to answer as many questions about it as one can – these being the questions asked at the opening of this Introduction.

A final introductory matter is the definition of the word 'war' itself. To be too prescriptive about this can lead to false distinctions. One standard working definition is 'a state of armed conflict between states or nations, or between identified and organised groups within a state' (this latter being 'civil war', usually the most uncivil of things). Better still might be 'a state of armed conflict between states or nations, or between identified and organised groups of significant size and character'. It is not clear whether the wars between warlord and insurgent groups in Afghanistan, Iraq and Syria that began in the first decades of the twenty-first century clearly fit into the second clause of the first attempt at a definition, but the second attempt captures them.

One meaning of the expression 'total war' is the unbridled use of any means possible to defeat an enemy, in disregard both of the 'laws of war' and effects on civilian populations. This means not just the enemy's civilian population, which is treated as an indiscriminate target of efforts to demoralise and paralyse its war effort, but of one's own civilian population, for example by conscripting its members into the war effort in factories, commandeering their property for resources, and submitting them to danger from enemy action. However, the expression is also used to denote the effort of a state to bend every sinew to war production and military endeavour – thus, the wholesale commitment of economic and population resources to defence or victory – without automatically implying a disregard of moral constraints. British efforts in the Second World War exemplify the latter; Soviet efforts perhaps denote both senses; neither the United States nor Nazi Germany committed themselves to 'total war' in the second sense, the former because it did not need to, and the latter (against Albert Speer's judgement) because Hitler wished to avoid the social breakdown that occurred in 1919 when over-concentration on war production had deprived the German population of such ordinary necessities of life as soap and blankets.

'Asymmetric warfare' is war between unequal combatants, for example between a conventional military force and a guerrilla force. This kind of war proves difficult for conventional militaries to win. Conflicts in Vietnam and Afghanistan exemplify asymmetric warfare.

For purposes of evaluating the ethical status of combatants there is an important difference between a war of aggression and a war of self-defence. On the face of it the distinction looks clear, but is blurred by the fact that some pre-emptive military actions might be defined as acts of self-defence, and wars of intervention, in which one power initiates hostilities against another in order to protect a third group from harm, might sometimes be describable as aggressive.

Some definitions of war include the idea of 'armed hostility', as in the Cold War. A phenomenon of the post-Second World War world was the near half-century of bristling opposition between major blocs – the NATO versus the Warsaw Pact led by the Soviet Union – between whom there occurred a series of localised proxy wars of the actual shooting kind. Korea, Vietnam, the Soviet incursion into Afghanistan, indeed dozens of shooting wars between 1945 and 1989, were proxies for the West–East stand-off in a variety of ways. In light of this, inclusion of 'armed hostility' in the definition of war is justified.

In light of the increasingly rapid technological advances to which the world has been subject in recent decades, the concept of 'cyberwar' has intruded itself into discussion of confrontations among states and non-state parties. Should this be fitted into the definition of war? It certainly figures in any assessment of the likely future of war and associated conflicts, as I mention in Chapter 6.

Nevertheless, the paradigm case of war is a major conflict involving actual violence of an organised and sustained military kind, aimed at forcing the enemy to the point where they cannot or do not wish to continue fighting. It is hard to think of a society which condones murder, yet in war the killing of other human beings is not merely taken for granted but enjoined and licensed as a necessity. But officially at least there are taken to be limits to what is acceptable in the use of force. These limits are frequently, perhaps usually, breached. Coercive measures such as internment, imprisonment, torture and rape, and the sequestration of resources necessary to the survival of enemy forces and populations, are too often encouraged or at least condoned while the state of emergency persists. It is said that the first victim of war is truth; a very close second is human rights.

War, then, is armed conflict between states or nations, or between identified and organised groups of significant size and character, and can include armed hostility which verges on actual conflict and which typically sponsors proxy conflicts. In all cases of actual conflict it licenses and promotes killing of enemy combatants and those in logistical support of them, accepts killing of bystanders as unavoidable 'collateral damage' on occasion, and enacts destruction of enemy materials from military assets to factories, buildings, towns and cities. It licenses detention and imprisonment without trial of enemy combatants and their supporters. All this is overtly sanctioned by the existence of a recognised state of war. It can further, in technically, officially, or putatively unsanctioned ways, mask individual murder, massacre, rape, torture, 'ethnic cleansing', looting, and other harms.

Fighting between armed groups does not count as war until such factors as the number of combatants and the nature of their organisation and practices as fighting forces places their conflict above what has been called 'the military horizon'. Clashes between spear-wielding members of different tribes, or gangland shoot-outs in (say) 1930s Chicago, are not war. The First World War is war. At some point in the difference between a tribal clash and the First World War, closer to the first than the second of these examples, lies a blurred boundary. That there should be a boundary is important; matters of legal and ethical significance are at stake in the difference. In a pub brawl crimes can be committed, but not war crimes and crimes against humanity, and the Geneva Conventions do not apply. A soldier on leave who kills someone in a pub brawl will be indicted for murder; yet he might have killed a number of people on his preceding tour of duty, as a matter of duty and in ways that earned him honourable recognition.

This point shows us something of the greatest significance. War, because in so many fundamental ways it constitutes a different universe from ordinary human experience, obliges us to recognise that in as many fundamental ways it constitutes a different moral universe too. That is a fact we all accept, whether we know it or not or like it or not; the example just given of the same soldier in the pub and on the battlefield proves it.

Can we hope that war might be expunged from human transactions? Eventually – if we survive as a species – it will be. In the meantime the more modest hope is that by understanding war in all its aspects, we can reduce its frequency, mitigate its horrors and lessen the burden of its consequences. Any step in that direction would be a step towards the good.

PART I

War in History
and Theory

CHAPTER 1

Ancient War

A survey of the history of war suggests that war-making falls broadly into two kinds, in one of which a certain sense of appropriate procedure, perhaps even chivalry or ethics, constrains what combatants do, and in the other of which the aim of winning justifies any and every act.

An example of the former is given by the case of the Duke of Sung in a battle in 638 BCE between the states of Chu and Sung. The Duke's minister of war saw that the forces of Chu were not ready for battle, and because they outnumbered the Sung troops he realised that it would be an advantage to attack them before they became organised. He asked the Duke's permission to attack, and was refused; he asked again, explaining his reasons, and was again refused. Only when the Chu forces were ready was battle joined. The Sung were defeated and the Duke himself wounded; asked afterwards why he had refused his minister's request, given the circumstances, the Duke replied: 'A gentleman does not inflict a second wound, or take a grey-haired man prisoner . . . Though I am but the unworthy remnant of a fallen dynasty, I would not sound my drums to attack an enemy who had not completed the formation of his ranks.'[1]

An example of the other kind of war-making is provided by General Patton's remarks to his troops in 1944, quoted as an epigraph to this book; by the view expressed by the Athenian generals at Melos, to the effect that the strong do what they like and the weak suffer what they must; and by the Mongols under Genghis Khan, whose military success owed itself in large part to a complete lack of interest in ethical niceties – victory was all, and the Mongols adopted the anything-goes approach accordingly. Fighters who do so have a great advantage over those who expect some proprieties to be observed. The Mongols would retreat in the face of counter-attack, which seemed cowardly to their enemies, but the retreats would be feints to draw their enemies into a trap. They gave no quarter to those they defeated, slaughtering the wounded where they lay and showing no mercy to non-combatants. They were not interested in heroics or refinements of any kind: 'victory is all' meant to them what it says.

Some military historians speculate that more restrained approaches to war-making have their roots in 'primitive' warfare, still observable among Amazonian and Papuan tribes today. (The term 'primitive' is used in this context by anthropologist Harry Holbert Turney-High in his study of the difference between 'submilitary' conflict and war as such.)[2] Among these peoples combat between opposed parties is tentative, with a good deal of posturing and hurling of insults rather than weapons, both sides keeping their distance and being reluctant to make close contact. Rituals and symbolic gestures play an important part, and casualties tend to be low if actual fighting occurs. In some cases conflict ends altogether if a single individual is wounded or killed, and in any case the opposing forces usually go home for supper after a day of shouting imprecations and dancing about – nimbleness in avoiding projectiles is regarded as an accomplishment.[3]

Anthropological studies of contemporary versions of 'primitive' warfare also show, however, that ritualistic confrontations are not the only form, and that more serious encounters often enough occur. Although the Yanomamo people of the Amazon indulge in ritualistic contests that adhere to set formulae, there can also be much bloodier fights, and in Papua New Guinea land transfer between stronger and weaker tribes can take the form of enforced displacement, murderous when resisted.[4]

It is obvious who is likely to have the upper hand in an encounter between the anything-goes warrior and the tentative ritual-observing warrior. It seems that, so far as the ethics of conflict goes, lessons were learned everywhere from the Mesopotamian civilisations' fatal encounter with invading charioteers from the Central Asian steppes; the futility of resisting them in any but their own unrestrained style taught hard lessons. The later success of Roman arms in the building of empire was due to the lethal combination of highly disciplined fighting with indifference to moral niceties when necessary. Caesar reports in his *Gallic Wars* that his troops made much slaughter among those they fought, slaying non-combatants who were manning the baggage trains and pursuing and killing fleeing enemy warriors, and he was prepared to be brutal if agreements were broken by subjugated tribes. At the same time he was lenient with those who submitted and kept their promises: the courtesies of war were reserved for situations where danger was past.[5]

Both forms of warfare, and the supersession of the more by the less decorous general form, are fully visible in history. But it is difficult to say when war itself began, and whether its earliest versions really did have the character observed among Papuans and Amazonians at their most ritualistic. Even the more plausible idea that hominin ancestors and relatives of *Homo sapiens* must at times have engaged in fighting is not unambiguously supported by evidence.[6] One of the skulls found in the 'Pit of Bones' (*Sima de los Huesos*) in Spain's Sierra de Atapuerca suggests a violent attack, because it has two near-identical traumatic punctures on the left forehead suggesting a repeated blow. The skull is 430,000 years old.[7] But it could have been an accident, or a crude effort at trepanning. A Neanderthal skeleton has been found which has the marks of a spear-thrust to its deceased owner's groin, another with an apparent spear-thrust to the right side of its chest, the latter dating back perhaps 90,000 years (Neanderthals were extinct by about 30,000 BCE). But again, both could have been hunting accidents.[8] The earliest traces of human record are cave paintings, some of which date back 35,000 years; they contain extremely little evidence if any – and even that little is ambiguous – of fighting between humans. The cave-art scenes in which darts or arrows appear to be in use are particularly doubtful, given that the bow-and-arrow weapon was not invented until the beginning of the Neolithic period around 10,000 BCE. Some cave art after this date depicts archery battles.

The picture changes after this date to more definite indications of war. Excavation of Jericho near the Dead Sea uncovered city walls of great height and thickness, dating back to 7000 BCE; the walls were 3.6 metres high (the height of two six-foot tall men, one standing on the other's head) and 1.8 metres thick at the base (one six-foot man lying horizontally). Within the walls was a tower also 3.6 metres high, but as it was placed on a mound it afforded a view over the top of the walls. Mighty walls and a tower plausibly imply a need for defence, and a degree of foresight and organisation probably predicated on a recurrent danger of war or attack. But some archaeologists alternatively suggest that the walls were a defence against flood water, and that the tower could have had ceremonial use.[9]

The loose coincidence of dates between fortification and advance in weapons technology nevertheless adds to this suggestiveness. Previously there had been spears, clubs and sharp-edged instruments serving as knives, used for hunting prey and skinning and butchering carcasses; but no doubt prehistoric humans and their hominin ancestors sometimes used these instruments on each other as well. Spears and stones could be thrown, putting distance between hunters and dangerous prey, and this distance would have been useful in a fight between hominins too. But the bow and arrow is a different order of thing. In considerably supplementing muscle-power by mechanical means it makes the weapon more lethal because more forceful and accurate, and safer too because it permits engagement with the target from a greater distance. Given that among our contemporary hominid relatives, the chimpanzees, male gangs form to launch murderous raids on other groups of their own species, it would be more surprising than not if our hominin ancestors did not sometimes do likewise, fighting over territory or resources, or even just because the others were 'other'. Such fighting is not war in the full sense of this term, but would of course be its precursor.

Although Jericho's walls, and the availability of weapons equally efficacious for hunting and fighting, together make it implausible to think that groups of people did not fight each other – and indeed make war on each other in the full sense of the term – before the historical record begins, all is surmise until then. John Keegan suggests that war-making as such – as opposed to skirmishing and brawling – began about 5,000 years ago, and principally as a result of the development of settled agricultural communities whose vulnerability to attack by nomads made both sides attentive to questions of weapons, fortifications and tactics.[10] Others place the origins of war very much earlier: Keeley rejects the 'myth of the peaceful savage' and, like Azar Gat, argues that humans have been fighting each other far longer than records suggest.[11] Indeed Gat makes the excellent point that the precariousness of prehistoric life would have given an evolutionary rationale to the practice of fighting in order to gain control over resources, so that the risks attached to it were outweighed by the advantage of having possession of land, animals, water, and (alas, but such were the realities) women.[12]

To anyone interested in the nuances of phrasing and naming, there seems to be no inconsistency in the idea that *the origins of war* lie very long in the prehistoric past in fighting between groups of humans, as Keeley, Gat and others argue, and for the reasons they identify; but that *war as such*, as an organised phenomenon lying above what Turney-High called 'the military horizon', requires a relatively advanced degree of social and economic sophistication, as we shall see shortly. No doubt the boundary between war and the conflicts from which it emerged is blurred, but a blurred boundary is still a boundary, and there is a difference to be marked here which is of use.

There is, however, a different but in fact more important question implied in these debates. It is whether human beings are genetically programmed for fighting and therefore for its more organised form as war. Is human nature inherently violent?

Or is violent conflict an artefact of social arrangements? Either way, is war inevitable? These questions are addressed in the next chapter.

The first actually recorded wars are those that occurred in southern Mesopotamia between competing Sumerian city-states between 3000 and 2500 BCE. The Stele of the Vultures records a battle in c. 2500 BCE between the cities of Umma and Lagash, in which the latter triumphed. It was fought between two organised armies, depicted as close-packed ranks of soldiers accompanied by solid-wheeled carts probably carrying dignitaries and supplies. The stele shows the ruler of Lagash, Eannatum, leading his army into the fray, and reports that he received an arrow-wound. But he survived to enjoy the victory, and the stele describes with relish how vultures feasted on the corpses of the enemy.

Sumerian warfare was evidently quite advanced; the stele shows troops in orderly formations wearing helmets, with a command structure and a supply train, and in itself bearing witness to a level of sophistication in which records are kept of significant military events. This places Sumerian war above Turney-High's 'military horizon', below which is fighting that is little different from the brawling of gangs without much – if any – plan, preparation, command structure, or idea of what is to happen when the fighting stops. The concept of the military horizon is a useful if controversial one for distinguishing 'war as such' from skirmishes, raids, and the 'primitive' formulaic confrontations described earlier.[13]

In Turney-High's view war as such (he calls it 'civilised war' to distinguish it from 'primitive' conflict) is characterised by 'adequacy of team work, organisation, and command working along certain simple principles'.[14] These principles have been invariant since the beginnings of the history of war; Turney-High cites examples and authorities to show that if one strips away considerations of armaments and dates, the essentials of battle are always and everywhere the same. Fighting involves *fire* (stones, arrows, bullets, shells, cruise missiles), *shock* (an infantry charge, cavalry, tanks, aerial bombardment), *mobility* (speed and effectiveness of manoeuvre), and *protection* (city walls, armour, helmets, trenches). By luck or judgement two or more of these might have been applied in combination by prehistoric groups of fighters, but in war as such their joint application is distinctively the product of planning and preparation.

As this suggests, among the main essentials of battle are organisation, co-ordination and the concentration of forces they enable, this latter most notably at critical points either offensively or defensively. Another essential is the integrity of tactical units, so that their members stick together, fight together, protect and aid each other, and divide tasks between them. Yet further essentials include co-ordination of firepower and mobility, correct utilisation of terrain, and clever use of intelligence and subterfuge. Equally essential are the simplicity of the plan of action, the advantages of surprise, and the proper exploitation of victory if gained. Turney-High calls these essentials the 'principles of war'.[15]

The overarching principle is organisation. Troops must be deployed in orderly formations for entering into battle, sustaining their part in it, and leaving it, whether in victory or defeat, the former to profit from victory fully, the latter to prevent worse loss by slaughter or capture while in retreat. It is essential for proper command that troops be organised, so that their leader can control their movements and position them suitably to the needs of the fighting.[16]

The basics of proper military organisation are the column and the line. 'Those people who do not avail themselves of these two simple sociologic devices are below the military horizon without argument', Turney-High prescriptively asserts; 'their fighting can be nothing but a scuffle, regardless of the amount of bloodshed, and cannot be called a war'.[17] The column is the formation in which troops get to the battle, the line is the formation in which they fight it.[18]

Taken together, these considerations say that what divides war from 'submilitary combat' is tactics. But there is another factor besides: the ability to sustain a campaign with organised and secure supply. It is a notable feature of Caesar's account in the *Gallic Wars* that he paid constant attention to supply and the fortification of encampments. The direction and nature of his campaigns was chiefly dictated by who had to be fought, of course, but how he went about the task was assiduously premised on considerations of supply.

Sumerian cities such as Umma and Lagash made war with each other probably for control of land and water resources, motives no different from those identified by Keeley and Gat in discussing the origins of war. With the appearance of Sargon of Akkad about 2300 BCE war takes on a different and more ambitious appearance. Sargon was not satisfied with local suzerainty, but sought conquest and empire. With a professional army, small by subsequent standards but obviously effective, he extended his rule from the Persian Gulf to the Mediterranean coasts of Syria and Anatolia, and eastward to Elam. The Akkadian dominion lasted nearly 200 years. It was not conquered by force of arms but by climate change and the attrition of chronic conflict between farmers and pastoralists, the latter driven by drought to seek pasture for their herds in the farmers' lands. At one point a wall more than 100 kilometres long was built between the Tigris and Euphrates to keep them out.[19]

The pharaohs of Egypt during the Middle Kingdom period, which lasted for about 250 years from the mid-twenty-first century BCE, had effective armies which fought their way into Nubian territory, thereby establishing Egypt's southern border. A chain of fortresses was then built to protect that border. In the eighteenth century BCE Hammurabi of Babylon achieved an empire similar in extent to the Akkadian and by similar military means. After this point both the Egyptian and Mesopotamian states began to employ new military technologies to which they had been painfully introduced by marauders from outside their world: the Hyksos, who conquered Egypt for a time, and the Hurrians and Kassites, who invaded Babylonia in the late seventeenth century BCE. The new technologies they brought included the composite bow – more powerful than the simple 'self' bow fashioned from a single piece of wood – and, most significantly, the chariot.

The advent of the chariot is described by Keegan as 'one of the most extraordinary episodes in world history'.[20] Solid-wheel carts, themselves a development from the sled, had been dragged by oxen or donkeys around the Middle East for centuries before the appearance of the chariot. But the chariot was a great advance, running light and fast on a pair of spoked wheels, drawn by expertly handled and trained horses, providing a highly mobile platform for an archer to shoot from or a warrior to leap from to fight on foot, and as quickly to leap back upon and dart out of harm's way. It gave armies equipped with chariots great superiority over armies without them.

Keegan points out that the advent of the chariot and composite bow depended on advances in the technologies of metalworking, leatherworking and woodworking, the chemistry of powerful glues, and the breeding and training of horses, all demanding refined skills and knowledge. The very nature of the horse suggests the chariot as against the heavy cart, which horses are not as good at hauling as are the patient ox or the donkey. Whereas a donkey can be controlled by reins attached to a noseband, a horse cannot be controlled without a bit. The invention of the bit was a big jump forward. Combine the bit with a light vehicle that a horse can pull, and the chariot invents itself.[21]

The speed with which a king could go to war in a donkey-drawn four-wheeled wooden cart, as depicted on the Standard of Ur in the third millennium BCE, was about two miles an hour. A Hittite war chariot could hurtle into battle at nearly ten times the speed. This was revolutionary. And it was not only the outcome of major technological developments, but it brought with it changes in the organisation of militaries and society itself; for the chariot was an expensive high-technology piece of equipment, manned by skilled personnel requiring a supporting team of grooms, wheelwrights, fletchers and others. If organisation is a defining principle of war, the armies of the second millennium BCE had advanced well beyond the 'military horizon'. It is one reason why Turney-High himself suggested that a principal driver of civilisational change was the art and technology of war-making.

The other major advance, the composite bow, was also important. It was fashioned not out of a single length of sapling as with the self bow, but was a laminate of horn, wood and sinew, capable of storing far more energy when drawn, and therefore delivering far greater power across greater distances. Like the chariot it required skill and time to manufacture, and much training and practice to master. Like the chariot too, it was therefore an expensive item. The composite bow may have appeared much earlier than the chariot, but when they were brought together they made a formidable combination. In the conquests of the Hyksos and Hittites they jointly exemplify the obvious truth that technological superiority is a major factor in the winning of battles and wars.

The chariot was the result of a meeting of influences among pastoralists occupying borderlands between wild steppes to the north of them and the civilised agricultural states – the states of Mesopotamia – to the south of them. Belying the Arcadian connotation of the word 'pastoralist', these folk were anything but pacific. They were more used to killing, butchery and blood than their sedentary farming neighbours, who had a variety of sources of nutrition other than meat available to them, and therefore left the task of meat preparation to specialists. The pastoralists – hardened nomads with no sentiment for the animals on whom their lives depended – not only had the sharp-edged implements necessary for the task of cutting throats and sinews, but also the anatomical knowledge and practice that enabled them to 'deal the lethal blow once, quickly and neatly' when dispatching their animals for meat and hides.[22] Moreover, from the techniques of herding they knew how to round up a flock, catch stragglers, cut off lines of escape, outflank, separate individuals from the mass and start a stampede – this last translating as panic and disorderly flight by a routed enemy. Their working lives gave them many of the aptitudes of the soldier who confidently knows what he is doing, is mobile and expert, and is trained in working seamlessly in concert with his comrades.

From these formidable people came the conquerors of the Egyptian Middle Kingdom and the Babylonian empire in the early centuries of the second millennium BCE. Those they conquered soon enough adopted the military technologies that the conquerors brought with them, and overthrew the invaders in their turn: the New Kingdom in Egypt was founded by the pharaoh Amosis in about 1565 BCE when he expelled the Hyksos, and the Assyrian empire was founded by Ashur-uballit in the first decades of the fourteenth century BCE when he defeated the Hurrians who had captured Mesopotamia.

It is easy to think that the chariot must have been a fighting instrument of great effect, combining mobility, shock value and an excellent firing platform for skilled archers. Curiously, there is disagreement among military historians about how they were in fact used.[23] There are illustrations from Egypt showing a pharaoh standing with drawn bow in a chariot behind galloping horses, and others showing a driver handling the horses while an archer operates at his side. Caesar describes British chariot-eers dashing about before their enemies' lines to confuse them, then plunging into the gaps thus opened in their ranks. Contrastingly, Homer's account of the Trojan War suggests that chariots were conveyances only, taking warriors to battle where they jumped down and fought on foot.[24]

One obvious possibility is that the nature and use of chariots evolved over time and at different rates in different places. Suppose, to take Herodotus's dating, that the Trojan War occurred in the thirteenth century BCE; the supposition that chariots at that time were merely conveyances does not fit especially well with the idea that Trojans were Hittites, whose chariot armies had been so successful, several centuries before, in overthrowing the Babylonian empire. But perhaps the Hittites' success with them resulted from their use not as fighting vehicles but as instruments of mobility, getting warriors to battlefields more quickly and in more rested condition than their foes; both are great enough advantages to explain much.

By the eighth century BCE, however, the chariot was at its height as a military tool, particularly in Assyrian hands. Keegan writes:

> It is not surprising if both the Egyptians and the Hittites were as yet clumsy charioteers and that the system had to wait until comparatively late in the development of Assyrian battlecraft before it achieved its full potential. By then it may well have become, as the scribes of Sargon and Sennacherib describe, a weapon of shock and terror, manipulated by the driver to charge at breakneck speed behind a team of perfectly schooled horses and used by the archer as a platform from which to launch a hail of arrows; squadrons of chariots, their drivers trained to act in mutual support, might have clashed much as armoured vehicles have done in our time.[25]

However the chariot was used, the sophisticated military organism that developed around it eventually had the effect of extending the reach of armies and therefore the ambition of their leaders. The Egyptian and especially Assyrian empires advanced their external boundaries and developed their internal organisation on the basis of what the chariot enabled them to achieve in war. They both maintained their power for centuries. By the eighth century BCE Assyrian armies could campaign hundreds of miles from their base camps, and move across their growing empire at speeds not surpassed until the nineteenth century CE. In parallel they developed most of the logistical techniques still used by armies today for the provision and security of supply, with depots, training camps and engineering and transport corps. They recruited soldiery from all over their empire, thus furnishing the army with a variety of skills and weapon types drawn from local tradition.[26]

The chariot was also the core of Chinese military practice in the late second and much of the first millennium BCE. The story of the Duke of Sung, told above, indicates that chariot warfare reintroduced something of the etiquette and restraint absent from the all-out war-making practised by Mongols and their like. Because chariots were expensive to build and operate they were the equipment of aristocrats, who brought their codes of behaviour to the fray. The same thing happened much later with knights of the medieval era, whose elaborate armour, great warhorses and accompanying retainers could only be afforded by the rich, who were *ipso facto* gentry and aristocracy (if they were not senior churchmen), and who likewise brought their courtly ways into the jousting lists and sometimes onto the battlefield.

Chariots were displaced by cavalry almost everywhere by the late classical period, except in Britain, where they were encountered by Julius Caesar on his first exploratory landing there in 54 BCE. This development was a result of successful breeding of horses with strong enough backs to carry a man. Until about the time of Troy, riders had to sit well back, almost over the horse's rump, so that it could bear their weight. That is a difficult seat for controlling a horse, in contrast to the forward sitting position which stronger backs allow. Moreover early horsemen were without saddles and stirrups, the latter especially making a great difference to a rider's activity in fighting from horseback with bow or sword.

Cavalry has several advantages over chariots. It is faster, more manoeuvrable, and considerably less expensive to set up and maintain. Cavalry can typically therefore be far more numerous than a chariot force, and since their shock value in a charge against enemy infantry is not much less than that of chariots, they offer an even greater advantage there too.

This swift and nimble horse-and-rider combination irrupted into the civilised world at the beginning of the seventh century BCE from the steppes of central Asia, in the feared form of the Scythians. They did not immediately displace chariots; Darius's Persian army still had them when defeated by Alexander the Great at the Battle of Gaugamela in 331 BCE. In that battle – leaving aside the infantry forces, where Persians greatly outnumbered Macedonians but were far less well trained and organised – Darius had 200 scythed chariots, 12,000 cavalry and 15 elephants, against Alexander's 7,000 cavalry. In his account of the battle Arrian tells us that Darius had the battleground prepared for his chariots, clearing away bushes and levelling the ground to give them an unimpeded field of action. In the event they were unimportant, the cavalry on both sides proving far more significant. During the struggle there were major cavalry battles on both wings, doubt- less not unacceptable to Alexander whose plan was to draw the Persians into attempts at outflanking his army on both sides, thus stretching their centre; and when a gap opened in it Alexander struck, his cavalry and the heavily armed Greek infantry phalanxes breaking through and causing Darius to flee. Alexander might have pursued and killed him, but had to go to the rescue of his own left wing instead, where the Persian cavalry were pressing his forces hard.

Keegan tellingly observes that the rulers of the Ottoman empire, which lasted into the first decades of the twentieth century, were until the very end wont to take their leisure in tents pitched in the gardens of the Topkapi palace in Istanbul, dressed in loose-trousered riding gear, surrounded by ornamental quivers and bows and wearing the archer's thumb-ring, memorials of their long-ago galloping ancestors of the steppes.[27] It was from the steppes that the Scythians had come, from them that the Xiongnu harassed Han-dynasty China between the third century BCE and the first century CE, and from them that the Huns invaded the Roman empire in the fifth century CE, having first, over the preceding couple of centuries, pressed upon the Goths of east and central Europe, causing them to threaten, and eventually to burst, the Roman imperial borders by their migrations.

The leader who united the various bands of Huns and led them against the declining Roman power was Attila (died 453 CE). The Huns were superbly skilled riders and archers, firing their arrows at full gallop, and carrying double-edged iron swords and daggers. Each owned a string of as many as eighteen horses (so Marco Polo reported)[28] and they were able to travel great distances in a day, changing mounts periodically. Some reports say that when on campaign they lived off the blood they nicked from their horses' necks; others say that they ate raw meat which they tenderised by placing it under their saddles. Their appearance was strange and frightening to Europeans, not because of their Asiatic appearance, which was familiar enough at the western end of the Silk Road, but because they practised cranial deformation on their infants, giving a peculiar elongated shape to the eventual adult head, on which a pointed cap was perched.

Although the westward penetration of the Huns was a significant factor in the eventual collapse of the Roman empire in the West, indirectly through their forcing other 'barbarian' peoples against and through the Roman borders, and directly by their assaults on Gaul and northern Italy, Attila – known as 'the Scourge of God' – was ultimately unsuccessful. He was defeated by the Romans and their allies at the Battle of the Catalaunian Plains in Gaul, and was repulsed in his efforts to reach Rome, though a significant outcome of his marauding in northern Italy was the founding of Venice by people who had fled to the islands of the lagoon to escape him. The fifth-century historian Priscus described him as a man 'born into the world to shake the nations', a lover of war, haughty and proud of spirit, whose reputation terrified people long before he appeared with his horse-borne army.[29]

The Hunnish empire did not long outlast the death of Attila. Almost as rapidly as they had appeared they disappeared again. One theory is that their complete reliance on the horse, the source of their military successes, was also their downfall; getting a resupply of mounts proved difficult after a time, given the high equine death rate that constant long-distance campaigning involves. As a comparison, Keegan points out that of the 500,000 horses taken by the British to South Africa in the Boer War of 1899–1902, nearly 350,000 died – only 2 per cent of them in battle, the rest from exhaustion, disease and malnutrition, at a rate of over 330 a day.[30] Something like this must have happened to the Huns. From the base they established in Hungary – itself insufficient in space and provender, as compared to the steppes, for raising large numbers of horses – the Huns' remounts would have arrived in as poor a condition as those they were replacing. So it was that after the last of Attila's sons was beaten by the Romans of the eastern empire in 469 CE, the Huns vanished from history.

But they were only the first. New bodies of horse warriors, made hard and fierce by nomadic life on the steppes of Central Asia, appeared in successive waves over the next centuries, conquering and occupying: the Bulgars west of the Black Sea, the Avars in Hungary, the terrifying Mongols, and eventually the Turks, who reached right to the walls of Vienna. These were people for whom the making of war was a way of life, a profitable one to which all their energies and preparations were bent. The entire male population was the army. For the most part they made war to maintain their war-making way of life – not to change or improve their lot, nor to acquire the advantages of the more civilised peoples whose cities they plundered. This at last changed when the Turks overthrew the eastern Roman empire in its descended form as Byzantium, but even then they could never quite relinquish the sense that they were horsemen and conquerors; the example given above, of the Ottoman court remembering its equestrian roots, demonstrates this.[31]

As early as the sixth century CE the steppe horsemen had established a dominion in their vast lands that touched on the borders of all the great centres of civilisation – China, India, Byzantium and Persia. By the eighth century they had met the new power burgeoning out of the Arabian desert: Islam. Of this, more below.

Three great chapters in the history of war have been bypassed so far in this account: the fifth century BCE Greek resistance against the then superpower of the world, Persia; the conquests of Alexander the Great; and the construction by military might and superb organisation of the Roman empire, after a perilous early encounter with its rival Carthage in the Punic Wars.

Darius I of Persia had extended his empire to the eastern shores of the Mediterranean, thereby bringing a number of Greek colonies under his sway. These colonies, collectively known as Ionia, revolted against his rule in the opening years of the fifth century BCE, with help from Athens and Eritria. Darius sent an army and navy – the latter supplied by others of his subjects, the Phoenicians – and defeated the Ionians, in 494 sacking their chief city Miletus and deporting its population to central Asia. Not content with subduing the rebels, Darius wished to punish the Greeks who had helped them; and at the same time he wished to extend his dominions to include their lands. But he had not reckoned with the character of the principal peoples among the Greeks – the Athenians and Spartans – whose attachment to the liberty of their city-state homelands was strong, and who, in their very different ways, had developed military hardihood and skill that enabled them to defeat the armies which Darius and later his son Xerxes – in vastly larger numbers – sent against them.

Darius did not expect to have difficulty in subduing the Greeks, and therefore sent only a modest army, some 20,000 men accompanied by horses and chariots, who landed at Marathon in September 490 BCE. The Persian strategy relied heavily on archery, cavalry and chariots, which meant that none of their forces were specialists in close-encounter infantry fighting. By contrast the Greek way of war was based on the tightly knit infantry phalanx consisting of heavily armed hoplites, each armed with a shield and a stabbing spear.

The Athenians at Marathon were outnumbered two to one by the Persians, and needed Spartan help, which the latter promised but could not deliver until the close of a religious festival that bound them at home. Despite the odds, the Athenians resolved on battle. Maintaining the integrity of their phalanxes they charged the Persian army and engaged it hand to hand, thereby rendering the archers and cavalry useless, and imposing their superiority as close-quarter fighters. Because the Persians were not trained for this they became disordered and scattered, suffering heavy casualties as they tried to flee. The Athenians lost 192 men, the Persians 6,400. When the Spartans arrived, too late to take part, they asked permission to inspect the Persian dead on the battlefield, and did so in wonderment.

The Athenians' bold strategy of charging the more numerous Persians was devised by their general Miltiades. His colleagues were doubtful whether they should fight that day at all, preferring to wait for the arrival of the Spartans. Miltiades argued passionately that attack was the right course. Herodotus gives an account of the debate and Miltiades' speech to the polemarch, Callimachus of Aphidnre, who had the casting vote in the council of generals, and which he gave in favour of Miltiades' plan.

Herodotus describes the attack:

> The distance between the two armies was just under a mile. When the Persians saw the Greeks coming on at speed they made ready to receive them, although it seemed to them that the Athenians were bereft of their senses, and bent upon their own destruction; for they saw a mere handful of men coming on at a run without either horsemen or archers.[32]

There was a doubtful moment when the Athenian centre was broken by the Persians, and fell back; but the fighting on both wings went the Athenians' way, and they were able to close on the centre in a pincer to attack the Persians who had passed between them on the inland side. Much of the slaughter that followed occurred as the Persians fled to their ships, seven of which the Athenians captured and set on fire.

The bulk of the Persian fleet escaped, and sailed as quickly as it could round Sunium in the hope of getting to Athens before its soldiers returned. But the Athenian troops were too swift for them, and were home and ready before the Persians arrived off Phalerum, at that time Athens' harbour. The Persians had no stomach for a further fight, so, Herodotus tells us, 'after resting on their oars for a time, they departed and sailed away to Asia'.[33]

The effect of this famous victory was to annoy the Persians even more. When Xerxes ascended the throne in 486 BCE he inherited Darius's preparations for another invasion of the Greek world, and was determined to subject the Greeks to thorough punishment. This time there was not going to be a small expeditionary force, but a full-scale invasion requiring careful planning. Indeed, the preparations took four years, not just in the amassing of an army which, with its accompanying entourage, amounted to a million people when it crossed the Hellespont in 480 BCE, but because it involved huge engineering works too, including two bridges across the Dardanelles, and a canal across an isthmus near Mount Athos in Macedonia to make a safer passage for the accompanying fleet.

The scale of the preparations also gave the Greeks plenty of time to get ready. Some of the northern Greek cities, those first in line for Xerxes' attentions, agreed to ally themselves with the Persian cause. Athens and Sparta were resolved otherwise. One of Athens' leaders, Themistocles, persuaded the city to devote the funds from a recently opened silver mine to building a fleet of triremes, fast and nimble fighting ships manned by 170 oarsmen and armed with a projecting ram at the prow. This fleet was to prove decisive.

In the great Persian host were 200,000 soldiers, and it was accompanied as it marched into Greece by a fleet of a thousand ships keeping in close contact offshore. In one of the most poignant and heroic episodes in military history, a force of 300 Spartans under Leonidas held the Persians at bay for three days at the pass of Thermopylae, all of them dying in the fight; while not far off at sea the Athenian fleet grappled with the Persian fleet off Artemisium, but inconclusively. Nevertheless the delay achieved by these actions gave enough time for the population of Athens to be evacuated, leaving an empty city to be burned by Xerxes when he arrived there soon afterwards.

The Athenian fleet under Themistocles withdrew to the island of Salamis in the Saronic Gulf. He there employed a subterfuge, getting a message to Xerxes by means of a pretended deserter, saying that there was to be a full evacuation of Greeks by sea that night, and that because he was secretly on Xerxes' side he advised him to send in his fleet to prevent it. Xerxes accordingly committed his ships to the narrow straits of Salamis, where their congested numbers and lack of manoeuvrability compared to the Greek triremes gave the latter a major advantage. The Persian fleet was destroyed, and Xerxes, watching the battle from a hill on shore, began to fear that he would be trapped in Europe. He left for Persia, instructing his lieutenant Mardonius to remain in Greece with part of the army to continue the war in the following year. At Plataea in July 479 Mardonius was defeated by the Greeks, himself dying in the battle, and simultaneously the Greek fleet destroyed what remained of the Persian fleet by attacking it where it lay beached at Mycale. The Persian assault on Greece was over; the classical years of Athens' greatness began.

There is no way of knowing where Athenian greatness might not have reached if a combination of circumstances, including its own hubris, had not led to the Peloponnesian War with Sparta (431–404 BCE), and the mistakes it made during the course of that war, most especially its disastrous expedition against Syracuse in Sicily (415–413 BCE). But in the event the greatness of Greek arms passed to its northernmost bearers, the Macedonians, first under King Philip II and then even more spectacularly under his son Alexander III, known to history as Alexander the Great.

Philip II had brought most of Greece under his authority, and was preparing an invasion of Persia when he was assassinated in 336 BCE, leaving the kingdom to the twenty-year-old Alexander. The youthful king proceeded with his father's plans, and over the course of the next twelve years established an empire that stretched from the Adriatic in the west to the Indus River in the east and the Nile in the south. His first objective was to defeat Darius III and take his empire from him, which he did in a succession of victories of which the battles of Issus and Gaugamela are the most famous.

Alexander crossed the Hellespont in 334 BCE with 50,000 soldiers, 6,000 cavalry and a fleet of 120 ships. His first victory was the Battle of the Granicus which gave him the city of Sardis and its wealth. From there he campaigned down the Aegean coast, liberating Greek cities from Persian rule, and then turned inland to Phrygia. At its capital Gordium he undid the celebrated Gordian Knot, so complex that no-one had ever been able to untie it. A prophecy had proclaimed that anyone who could do this would become King of all Asia. Alexander, intent on just that ambition, said that it did not matter how the knot was untied, and proceeded to hack it apart with his sword.

The first victory Alexander achieved over Darius himself was at Issus in southern Anatolia, from which the Persian king fled, leaving his wife, both his daughters and his mother to fall into Alexander's hands, along with his treasury. Darius regarded Alexander as a young upstart who deserved a whipping, and he rejected the advice of his best general, a Greek called

Charidamus, regarding how to deal with the Macedonian force. The latter, not realising that Darius understood Greek, thereupon made a few acerbic remarks about Persian stupidity, and Darius in anger had him executed. As events showed, this was a mistake.

Alexander himself was not above acting in anger, as shown by what happened when he besieged Tyre. The siege caused Alexander so much difficulty that when at last the city fell he slaughtered all its male inhabitants of military age and sold the women and children into slavery. A similar baulk at Gaza, where to add injury to insult he received a shoulder wound, prompted him to the same measures.

By this time Alexander was master of Syria and the Levant, and ready to push south into Egypt. There he was regarded as their liberator from the Persian yoke, and declared to be a son of the god Amun and fulfiller of a prophecy which said that a Greek king would save Egypt. He founded the city of Alexandria before turning his attention north-eastward again to resume the task of unseating Darius. Babylon, Susa and then Persepolis fell to him; while he was resting in the latter, after the famous Battle of the Persian Gates, a fire started which destroyed the city, to Alexander's subsequent regret. Plutarch attributes to Alexander a meditation on the question whether he should allow a statue of Xerxes to remain fallen, in punishment for his invasion of Greece, or whether he should set it up again, in recognition of the emperor's 'magnanimity and other virtues'.[34]

Darius was pursued through Media and Parthia by Alexander, only escaping capture because he was assassinated by one of his own kinsmen, Bessus the satrap of Bactria. After the murder Bessus assumed the titles Artaxerxes V and 'Great King of Persia'. Alexander gave Darius a royal burial, and claimed that he had been named by the dying Great King as his successor to the Persian throne. Viewing Bessus as a traitor and usurper, Alexander pursued him round large tracts of Central Asia and Afghanistan, and eventually Bessus was betrayed to one of Alexander's lieutenants, Ptolemy, who executed him.

Naturally enough, Alexander had to deal with occasional insurrections among the defeated Persians, for example in Sogdania, which rose against him as he was fighting Scythian horsemen who had unexpectedly appeared from the steppes. He was also faced with conspiracies among his own followers, some of whom were displeased by his assumption of Persian dress and court etiquette, including a requirement that subordinates should prostrate themselves on the ground before him. So little did this please his followers, who regarded this as an obeisance due only to deities, that he gave it up. But he adopted other oriental practices in preference to Macedonian ways, which his followers murmured at. And an incident that lost him favour with yet more of them was a drunken brawl in which he killed a man who was not only the brother of the woman who had nursed him as a child, but, more significantly, had saved his life at the Battle of the Granicus by severing the arm of a Persian satrap called Spithridates just as the latter was swinging a war hammer down onto Alexander's head.

Still hungry for more conquests, Alexander advanced towards India. He was met with fierce resistance, especially in eastern Afghanistan and the valley of Swat. Angered by the resistance he decided to make a punitive example, killing everyone in Massaga and reducing it to rubble. He founded his own cities instead, as was his practice; on the Hydaspes River he built two cities, one on either side of the stream, calling one of them Bucephala after his famous horse Bucephalus which had recently died.

But his desire to press yet further eastward towards the Ganges and the rich kingdoms that lay there was resisted by his army. Plutarch tells us that rumours spread among his soldiers to the effect that the Ganges was many miles wide and immeasurably deep, and that both its banks were lined with vast well-equipped armies – indeed that '80,000 horsemen, 200,000 infantry, 8,000 chariots, and 6,000 war elephants' were lying in wait for them. If such rumours were spread by agents of the Ganges kingdoms as a disincentive, they worked. Alexander's troops refused to go further.

Alexander failed to persuade them otherwise, so he marched down the Indus, sent his army back to Persia by land, and explored the shores of the Persian Gulf by sea. In Persia once more he dealt with problems that had arisen in his absence, executing recalcitrant or misbehaving officials. He attempted to reconcile his Macedonian and Persian followers by arranging a mass wedding between his men and Persian women. The marriages were not a success. Alexander was devastated by the death of his lover Hephaestion while the two were visiting the Persian treasury at Ecbatana, and not long afterwards Alexander himself died, on 11 June 323 BCE, in the palace of Nebuchadnezzar II in Babylon. He was aged thirty-two. Different accounts of his death are given by Plutarch, Arrian and Diodorus, who include the rumour that he was poisoned; all agree that the illness that carried him away followed yet another bout of drunkenness. In youth Alexander had been a pupil of Aristotle, but the philosopher had not, it seems, managed to teach him continence.[35]

The great conqueror's body was buried in a golden sarcophagus filled with honey, a more effective technique for preserving corpses than the elaborate mummification procedures of the Egyptians. This is an unsurprising attention to the dead king, employing out of veneration and respect two of the three substances that never decay (the third is amber, if kept from light). It is said that archaeologists once found a honey-filled amphora some 2,500 years old while excavating in Greece; the honey was still good, so they had it each day on their toast for breakfast; after a while they noticed something at the bottom of the jar, which when they investigated proved to be the body of an infant, whose loving parents had buried it thus to preserve it for ever. Such was the ambition for Alexander. The gold of the sarcophagus was of course eventually taken for coinage, and the glass coffin that replaced it was eventually lost after its removal from Alexandria, to which city it had been taken by Ptolemy although destined for burial in Macedonia. None of this is unsurprising either; not even the greatest of conquerors and kings can quite survive the attrition of time, as Shelley in 'Ozymandias' reminds us. Their exploits might survive, but their remains are a different matter.

It is said that it was humiliation at the hands of an invading Gaulish army that taught the Romans, at the beginning of the fourth century BCE, that they needed to improve themselves militarily. They had been applying the model of the Greek phalanx until then, but it had proved inadequate. The Gauls defeated a Roman force on the banks of the river Allia, occupied Rome, and agreed to leave only on payment of a large ransom in gold. The resulting changes made by the Romans in the organisation, equipment and fighting methods of their armies were the foundation of an empire greater than Alexander's, and far longer lasting.

The Romans replaced the thrusting spear of the Greek hoplites with a throwing javelin and a short sword for close combat. The armies were arranged into legions of 4,000 or 5,000 men, divided into maniples ('handfuls') of 120 soldiers who trained, fought, and lived together in units capable of independent action under their officers. Their training was rigorous, and the twin bonds of discipline and mutual loyalty made them highly effective.

Between the middle of the fourth century BCE and the late third century BCE Rome was engaged in conquering the tribes of central Italy, among whom the Samnites were most recalcitrant. It then turned its attention to the Greek colonies of southern Italy. Their eventual capture was an educative one for the Romans, because the colonists requested and received help from King Pyrrhus of Epirus, who arrived with a formidable army which inflicted several defeats on the Romans. The victories were however gained at great cost to Pyrrhus's own forces – hence the term 'Pyrrhic victory', for after a costly battle the king remarked, 'Another such victory and I will be lost.' He withdrew his forces, and southern Italy became Roman.

The immediate consequence was that Rome's southern frontier now lay against Carthage's Sicilian possessions. Carthage was the leading power in the Mediterranean, and its imperial expansion had established it in Sicily, Sardinia and on the southern shores of Spain. It had begun as a minor Phoenician trading post, for a time less important than nearby Utica. Legend attributed its foundation to a queen called Elissa, sometimes called Dido, at the end of the ninth century BCE, but its emergence into importance started after Alexander the Great's sack of Tyre in 332 BCE. A number of the wealthy Phoenician merchants of Tyre had been able to ransom themselves and take their families and businesses to Carthage.

There they soon flourished. They enslaved or displaced the native population of the coastal region, imposed tribute on neighbouring native tribes, and found their new location perfect for managing a trade that reached from the wealthy and thriving states of the eastern Mediterranean as far west as Britain. No other state rivalled Carthage's rule of the sea. Rome, still small and insignificant at that point, was of little interest to Carthage, but Carthage anyway imposed on it a treaty forbidding access to the trade of the western Mediterranean.

In the century after Tyre's destruction Carthage grew into a great city with splendid architecture and an immense harbour of 220 docks surrounded by a magnificent array of marble columns. In the city's suburbs were huge estates owned by rich merchants. It was a wonder of the world. It was inevitable that the expanding frontier of Rome would come not just to abut but to abrade the borders of Carthage's dominions. The result was a series of wars, the first of them the greatest naval conflict that the world had seen to that date.

Hostilities began in 264 BCE and lasted over twenty years. The Romans recognised that they would not be able to compete with Carthage without a navy, and therefore set to work to build one. Using Carthaginian warships as a model, but with ingenious additions and improvements that proved decisive, the Romans created a navy almost from scratch. In the span of two months in 261 BCE they built 100 quinqueremes – heavy ships each propelled by 300 oarsmen and carrying a full infantry maniple (120 soldiers) – and twenty lighter, faster triremes. The key novelty introduced by the Roman engineers was the equipping of each ship with a ramp (the *corvus*) that could be lowered onto enemy ships, allowing soldiers to rush across and fight as if on land.

Victory came neither quickly nor easily, however. Rome beat Carthaginian forces at the battles of Mylae in 260 BCE and

Tyndarus in 257 BCE, and in the following year launched an invasion fleet towards the North African coast. The result was a naval battle of epic proportions. Carthage's fleet intercepted the invaders off Cape Ecnomus, but lost 100 ships in the process, sunk or captured. Now unimpeded, the Roman fleet landed the army near Tunis, where it suffered defeat in its own turn, being annihilated by a massed charge of Carthaginian war elephants. The Roman ships escaped, only to be devastated by violent storms, hundreds of them sinking or being splintered to pieces on rocky coasts.

It took another fifteen years, until 241 BCE, for Rome to beat Carthage in the struggle for Sicily. It exacted a heavy war indemnity from Carthage, which now faced a different but no less dangerous problem. During the war it had levied a large army of mercenaries, whom they were now unable to pay because of the expense of the long war and the indemnity. The mercenaries rose against Carthage, waging a four-year struggle with it before Carthage's foremost general, Hamilcar Barca, succeeded in defeating them. While the Carthaginians were thus distracted Rome took Sardinia and Corsica from them.

That was the First Punic War. The second was ignited in 219 BCE when Hannibal, son of Hamilcar, attacked and captured the city of Saguntum, a Roman colony on the east coast of Spain. Both Rome and Carthage were expanding their holdings in Spain, so as had happened in Sicily their frontiers first encroached and then collided, with the added spice that Carthage, which had taken two decades to recover from the First Punic War, was eager for revenge, and intent on defeating Rome to ensure dominion of the Mediterranean world.

On the principle that only offence wins wars, Hannibal took his army from Spain and across the Alpine passes into northern

Italy, there defeating a Roman army on the shores of Lake Trasimene. In the anxiety, indeed terror, of the emergency Rome appointed Fabius Maximus Verrucosus as dictator.[36] Fabius was a leading Roman who had served as consul five times, and was twice appointed to the dictatorship, in 221 and 217 BCE. This second appointment followed the defeat at Trasimene. The apparent invincibility of the Carthaginian forces made Fabius cautious, indeed ultra-cautious, and he delayed pitched battle with Hannibal for as long as possible. The delay earned him the opprobrious nickname 'Cunctator' ('irresolute'), and the term 'Fabian' now applies to anyone who takes the long view on change or action.[37]

Perhaps, however, Fabius was right; for the hasty and fearful Romans dismissed him, sought battle with Hannibal again, and were disastrously beaten at Cannae in 216 BCE, losing nearly 50,000 men. But Rome refused to surrender, and now adopted the Fabian technique of a waiting game while Hannibal led his army around Italy, struggling to live off a largely hostile land, and unable to get resupplied from Carthage. His presence in Italy encouraged some cities to rebel against Rome, but the insurrections were quelled and Rome held firm.

Syracuse was one of the rebellious cities, and although recaptured it maintained a long enough resistance – two years in all – for a prominent citizen, the 'Eureka!' scientist Archimedes, to put several novel military technologies to work. He had catapult engines built, calibrated to different ranges, some of which fired hollow clay balls with incendiary material in them. He pierced the city walls with small loopholes at the height of a man, for archers to fire through. He constructed a giant grapple that could be lowered into the water to engage the underside of an enemy ship coming alongside the city's sea-walls, the grapple or claw then being raised to lift up the ship and heel it over. He constructed cranes that could be swung laterally outwards over the battlements from which boulders were dropped on ships and troops below. And he used great mirrors to reflect and focus the rays of the sun on enemy ships, in order to set them on fire.[38]

The siege of Syracuse began in 213 BCE and ended in 211 BCE. Both ancient and more recent historians suggest that a reason for the city's protracted resistance, apart from Archimedes' ingenuities, was the brutality of the Roman general Marcellus at Leontini, the first Sicilian rebel city to fall to him. Marcellus had 2,000 Carthaginian sympathisers beaten and then beheaded there in punishment. Fearing the same treatment, the Syracusans were determined to fight.

Hannibal's brother Hasdrubal led another Carthaginian invasion from Spain across the Alps into Italy in the hope of combining with Hannibal and at last defeating Rome. One of the consuls appointed that year, 207 BCE, by name Nero (an ancestor of the emperor who was said to have fiddled while Rome burned), defeated Hasdrubal at the Battle of the Metaurus after a brilliantly executed forced march, and an equally brilliant change of tactics during the battle which turned Hasdrubal's centre into a flank, enabling the Roman legionaries to effect much slaughter, either directly with the sword or by forcing the Carthaginians into the river where they drowned in large numbers.

One of Rome's greatest generals, Scipio Africanus – the epithet being awarded for his eventual victory over the Carthaginians on their home ground – had learned much from seeing action at the Roman defeat at Cannae, but more in consequence of gaining a string of victories over Carthaginian forces in Spain between 210 and 206 BCE. On his return to Rome he planned an invasion of North Africa, which was launched in

204 BCE. Because Hannibal was still stuck in Italy, because of the reverses in Spain, and because of the loss of Hasdrubal's army, Carthage at first offered a peace treaty. But then Hannibal managed to extricate himself and get back to Carthage with his army, thereby bolstering his countrymen's resolve. Accordingly the offer of peace was withdrawn. Hannibal and Scipio met at the Battle of Zama on 19 October 202 BCE, which, after a terrible and bloodthirsty struggle, the Romans won.

Two of the factors that aided Scipio's victory were a trick to deal with Hannibal's war elephants, and the fact that the formidable Numidian cavalry led by Masinissa, which had been with Hannibal in Italy, changed sides and fought alongside the Romans. Given that Hannibal's army was larger than Scipio's, this was a material boon. The combined heavy Roman and light Numidian cavalry were of higher quality than their opponent's mounted forces, a yet further factor; Scipio had learned to his cost at Cannae how effective Carthaginian cavalry could be, and took pains to ensure that his own were trained and equipped to outfight them.

The elephant trick was simple. Scipio knew that elephants can only charge in a straight line, dead ahead. Accordingly he arranged his forces so that they would open channels for the elephants to pass through, lumbering harmlessly to the rear of the main army where groups of skirmishers waited to deal with them. The tactic worked, as did another, which was to blow loud trumpets at the elephants right at the outset, which alarmed and confused a number of them, causing them to turn and trample back through the Carthaginian lines in a disorderly rampage, most notably on the left wing.

Scipio's success after a hard-fought day was chiefly owed to his cavalry's defeat of Hannibal's cavalry on the wings, enabling them to outflank the main army and assault its infantry from behind. The victory was so crushing that Carthage had no option but to sue for peace, and on the most humiliating terms. All its territorial possessions were sequestered, the city itself bankrupted, and it was forced to undertake never to mount military operations again without Rome's permission. This gave Rome its excuse for the Third Punic War of 146 BCE, when Carthage had to defend itself against a Numidian attack and did so without getting Roman permission first; so Rome attacked again, laying siege to the city and, on capturing it, destroying it completely. The Roman general who led that action was an adopted son of Scipio Africanus, namely Scipio Amaelianus.

The earlier Battle of Zama provided Rome with a different excuse, this time to invade and conquer Greece. The excuse was that Macedonian troops had fought in the battle on Hannibal's side. Rome had already taken action against Macedonia because of its alliance with Carthage, sending troops and ships to contain it on the Adriatic coast. A few skirmishes occurred, scarcely meriting the name given to them of the First Macedonian War, and a treaty was signed in 205 BCE which, among other things, stated that Philip V of Macedon would no longer aid Carthage. So when the fact or rumour came to Roman ears that there were Macedonians on Carthage's side at Zama, the trigger was pulled for a series of conflicts that resulted in Roman hegemony over Greece and the lands of the eastern Mediterranean. These were the second and more serious Macedonian War, the subsequent Seleucid War, and the Third and Fourth Macedonian Wars, which ended with the Battle of Corinth in the same year that Scipio Amaelianus obliterated Carthage, 146 BCE. After the Battle of Corinth, Greece became a Roman province.

In the following four centuries Roman armies extended, established and maintained an empire that stretched from Scotland to Syria and Palestine and Africa, bordered by the Rhine in the north and the African deserts in the south. The Gallic Wars, the civil wars that followed Caesar's assassination in 44 BCE and ended in Octavian's victory over Mark Antony at the Battle of Actium in 31 BCE (he was proclaimed emperor as Augustus in 27 BCE), and the consolidation of the empire's borders by the end of Trajan's reign in 117 CE, proclaimed the superiority of Roman military technology, training, equipment and practice – and the bureaucracy that maintained its great armies and territories by the superb efficiency of its organisation.

But in the later part of the empire's history in the West, from the third to the fifth centuries CE, pressure on its long borders from migration and invasion, by forces with new ways of fighting or with experience and knowledge gained from fighting Romans, together with the decline in the hardiness and military willingness of Romans themselves, cumulatively had their effect. An army of conquest is different from an army which defends borders or which has long periods of inactivity that allow its leaders to engage in politics, as happened with a succession of emperors and would-be emperors in this period, whom the armies of the empire made and unmade. The phenomenon of the decay and collapse of a great empire is an interesting and educative one, and well explains how a lifetime might be given to the study of it, as the example of Edward Gibbon shows.

CHAPTER 2

Medieval to Modern War

The thousand years between 500 and 1500, a period to which the extremely broad label 'medieval' is applied, was one of vulnerability in Europe to new and mobile forces such as Vikings, Muslim Arabs and steppe nomads, variously establishing themselves on the margins of the continent as conquerors. Viking states on the Atlantic coast and in the Mediterranean, Muslim states in North Africa and Spain, and Magyar and Bulgar settlements in east Europe, were chief among them. Each had their own military styles, and, in the case of Vikings and Muslims, cultural factors had a major part to play in them.[1]

The Scandinavians entered history as pirates and coastal raiders, but evolved into conquerors on some of the coasts of Europe. They were fierce, fearless fighters with a developed sense of personal honour and a hunger for posthumous fame. They gave no quarter in hand-to-hand fighting, and the shape and handling qualities of their ships enabled them to make lightning raids not only on coastal towns but up rivers like the Thames and Loire. They were not organised fighters, being likened to swarming bees rather than armies, but they made use of clever tricks that deserve the name of tactics – such as sailing innocuously past a coastal town, only to turn back swiftly and pounce when the defenders' guard was down.

Vikings were big men, who when entering a fight got themselves into a state of fevered excitement that made them near-impervious to pain and exhaustion, giving rise to the 'berserker' reputation they enjoyed. They used double-edged swords and battleaxes, and a combination of throwing and stabbing spears. Their long ships would appear suddenly and at speed, the warriors leaping from them and rushing at their victims even as they beached. On land their tactics were equally simple: they formed themselves into a wedge with their strongest and fiercest men to the fore, and charged. Because they paid no attention to sanctuaries and holy places, and had no chivalric hesitations about women and children, their attacks were terrible to those who suffered them.

In their early incursions the Vikings did not fight pitched battles army-to-army. Only later, when they had settled, did this occur, as in the Battle of Hastings (1066) when the Normans (from 'Norsemen', another name for Vikings) under William the Conqueror invaded England. By that time they had adopted the armour, weapons and tactics generally prevailing among their neighbours. At Hastings, the English under King Harold formed a defensive wall on the summit of a hill, and the Normans repeatedly and unavailingly charged them up the slope under a barrage of arrows. The English defence was solid for many hours, until it made a mistake; it broke ranks to chase the Normans as the latter retreated, yet again, down the hill, whereupon the Norman infantry and cavalry turned in amongst them and cut them to pieces.

The Muslim Arab conquests from the seventh century were partly a product of the mobility, speed and zeal of the Arab forces, and partly a product of the weakness of those they conquered. Byzantium and Sassanid Persia had just concluded an exhausting war with each other, their empires further weakened by a visitation of the plague, when the Arab attacks began on their southern and south-eastern borders.

The Arab forces of the Rashidun caliphate were well organised and introduced innovative modifications to what they had learned from the armies of their more advanced neighbours. One distinctive tactic was repeatedly to charge and then retreat from the enemy front under the protection of volleys of arrows, weakening the enemy by attrition. They used their cavalry to great effect, as at the victories won by Khalid ibn Walid at the battles of Walaja in May 633 and Yarmuk in August 636, respectively against Sassanid and Byzantine forces. The Battle of Yarmuk, one of Islam's most famous and decisive victories, was fought over six days on the plains south-east of the Golan Heights, and led to the permanent end of Byzantine rule in the Levant.

The Arabs' early advantage lay in their fine horses and horsemanship, and the logistical swiftness and mobility provided by camels. As their conquests spread so they acquired more horses and equipment from those they defeated, but also and most importantly more followers, by forced and voluntary conversion. The original Arab numbers were too few to sustain the far-reaching conquests they made in Africa and Spain, so the ideological aspect of their achievements was a key factor.

The success of Muslim arms was extensive. After overwhelming the Iberian peninsula, Muslim forces under Abdul Rahman Al Ghafiqi, governor of Andalusia, crossed the

Pyrenees and entered Aquitaine. They were met at Poitiers by Charles Martellus, 'the Hammer', King of the Franks. The Franks were the foremost military power in Europe at that time. The resulting battle, fought on 10 October 732, was a turning point; it brought an end to the advance of Islam in Europe, and laid the basis for Frankish power that reached its apogee later under Charlemagne.[2]

The Franks were outnumbered at Poitiers by an experienced and successful Saracen army under its formidable general, Abdul Rahman. But Charles had been thinking for a long time about how to defeat the Saracens, and had concluded that he needed to choose his ground carefully, achieve surprise, and employ some means of negating the Saracen cavalry. He succeeded in all three, taking Abdul Rahman unawares by marching across country so that his movements were unnoticed, and appearing before the Saracens with a large and well-equipped force along the summit of high ground which crossed the Saracens' line of march towards Tours.

Moreover, Charles had so picked his stand that the rising ground he commanded was pocked with woods, which placed the Saracen cavalry at a disadvantage. His own infantry was hardened and experienced, many of the men having campaigned with him for years. It was a cold October, too, which favoured the Franks, who were used to the weather; the Saracens were unused to it and disliked feeling chilly.

Despite the disadvantageous ground Abdul Rahman threw his cavalry at the Frankish phalanxes, who stood their ground solidly, repulsing the charges time and again. According to the *Mozarabic Chronicle*, 'The northern people remained as immobile as a wall, holding together like a glacier in the cold regions. In the blink of an eye, they annihilated the Arabs with the sword.'[3] Charles also used a tactic suggested by the Saracens' reputation for loving booty; he sent troops to harass the enemy's baggage guards, thereby threatening to capture the spoils accumulated on the Saracens' triumphant way through Aquitaine. When news of this reached the Saracen army, significant numbers of them hastened anxiously back to camp to protect their booty.

Indeed, reflection on the risk they were taking in campaigning so far from their warm Spanish possessions seems to have changed Saracen minds quickly. That night, secretly and swiftly, they departed as one man, taking their booty but leaving their tents standing, so that for some time Charles Martel thought they were still there. This was an occasion when, contrary to the practice alluded to in Longfellow's poem 'The Day is Done', they stole away without folding their tents in the night.[4]

The areas of the Middle East that fell to the Muslim Arabs in the early period of their conquests had been almost wholly Nestorian Christian, and the Levant was rich in sites holy to the Christians and their Jewish forebears and neighbours. The loss of these sites to Islamic conquerors, and the conquerors' continuing threat to the Christian empire of Byzantium, was a thorn in Christian sides. At the Council of Clermont in 1095 Pope Urban II therefore called upon all Christians to remedy the situation. It was a holy war he proclaimed; he promised remission of sins and eternal life to those who died in the endeavour. Prospects of land and plunder pre-mortem were just as alluring as the guarantee of post-mortem felicity to those who responded. A hundred thousand men pinned crosses to their tunics and set off in the direction of the Holy Land in answer to his call. This was the First Crusade.

Desertion, illness, the hardships of the journey and at last the fighting itself took a terrible toll. Less than half the original number reached Antioch to besiege it in October 1097. A mere 12,000 marched from Antioch, after it fell, in the direction of Jerusalem. They captured it, and the Christian occupation of the Holy Land began, with the establishment of a county, a principality and a kingdom in Edessa, Antioch and Jerusalem respectively. The crusaders set about fortifying their possessions, and two orders of knights, the Templars and the Hospitallers, came into being, dedicated to protecting the holy places and the Christians in them.

It took two decades for the Muslims to gather themselves in response, but they did so with a vengeance. At the Battle of the Field of Blood – *Ager Sanguinis* – Edessa fell to the Seljuks in 1144. A call for a second crusade made jointly by Pope Eugenius III and St Bernard of Clairvaux was answered by Conrad III of Germany, the first of the Hohenstaufen dynasty, and Louis VII of France, briefly the husband of Eleanor of Aquitaine. Conrad went overland via Constantinople and was badly beaten at the Battle of Dorylaeum in southern Turkey in 1147. The survivors of his army managed to combine with the French, who had travelled to the Holy Land by sea, and the two forces besieged Damascus. Quarrelling between them, and the poor arrangements made for the siege, resulted in the siege collapsing in 1148, bringing the Second Crusade to an ignominious conclusion.

The crusading conflicts were not always discrete large-scale events; fighting between Christians and Muslims was continuous, and occurred in the Iberian peninsula as well as the Holy Land. But the capture of Jerusalem in 1187 by the charismatic and formidable An-Nasir Salah ad-Din Yusuf ibn Ayyub, better known to

Western history as Saladin, galvanised the papacy and Europe's leading Christian monarchs to a third major crusade with the aim of recapturing the city. It was summoned by Pope Gregory VIII in a bull entitled *Audita tremendi*, which put the blame for the loss of Jerusalem on the sins of the Christian peoples. As with other crusade-summoning bulls, it offered plenary indulgences – that is, absolution from all sins – to any who died fighting for the cause and it promised crusaders protection by the Church of all their property and rights while they were away fighting.

Saladin had beaten the army of the Kingdom of Jerusalem at the Battle of the Horns of Hattin in July 1187, luring it away from its secure base at Sephorie and encircling it when it reached a waterless plateau near Meskana. In the night before the battle Saladin's men set fire to the plateau grass, the smoke from which irritated the dry throats and eyes of the Christian troops. By the next day, dehydrated and thirsty, bleary-eyed and smarting from the smoke, the crusaders were close to demoralisation. Some broke through the Muslim encirclement in their desperate effort to find water at the springs of Hattin, while a few surrendered to the Muslims, begging to be released from their misery by execution. Yet Saladin did not have too easy a victory; although surrounded, the Christians twice repulsed his attacks and pushed his forces back down the slopes of the plateau. When victory was at last achieved Saladin prostrated himself on the ground, so his son recorded, and wept for joy.

The Third Crusade was known as the Crusade of Kings, because so many monarchs led their armies to the Holy Land to recapture Jerusalem. They included the Holy Roman Emperor Frederick Barbarossa, Philip II of France, and Richard I (the Lionheart) of England. Frederick drowned in the Saleph River in Anatolia, and Philip quarrelled with Richard and went back to France, though he left most of his army with Richard's forces. Richard alone made an impression, capturing Cyprus, besieging and capturing Acre, and above all defeating Saladin at the Battle of Arsuf in September 1191, in the only major battle of the campaign.

Having learned from the crusaders' mistake at Hattin, Richard was assiduous in keeping his troops well supplied with water. He also kept close to the coast to be in touch with his accompanying fleet. Saladin attempted to lure the crusaders out of formation as they marched, by repeated feint attacks and withdrawals, but Richard ordered his columns to remain intact. Near the town of Arsuf a lucky accident delivered the victory into Richard's hands; the Hospitaller knights elected to disobey Richard's orders to maintain a tight formation, and launched an attack on their own account against the Ayyubids. At that moment Saladin's mounted archers, having decided that the crusaders would not break formation, had dismounted to better aim their arrows. The Hospitallers overran them and the Ayyubid right wing was driven back. Although angry with the Hospitallers for disobeying orders Richard saw the opportunity thus presented, and charged the Ayyubid centre with his English and Norman knights, breaking through it and driving Saladin and his forces from the field in flight. The crusaders lost 1,000 men, the Ayyubids 7,000. Richard pressed on to Jaffa and captured it.

With these successes Richard re-established control over most of the crusader lands, but he refused to besiege the holy city of Jerusalem and instead concluded a treaty with Saladin that restored the Kingdom of Jerusalem without the city itself, but with rights of access to it for Christian pilgrims and merchants.

The concept of the crusade had by this time lost its specific focus on the Holy Land, and had become an excuse for acquisitive war-making almost anywhere in Europe, against anyone whom a pope could be persuaded to describe as pagan. This included the Lithuanians, Prussians and Russians when convenient; Popes Celestine III, Innocent III and Honorius III all preached crusades against them.

Innocent III, despite such distractions as instigating the Albigensian Crusade against the Cathars of southern France, also raised a Fourth Crusade against the Muslims of the Holy Land. It was a disaster. It only reached as far as Byzantium, which it twice attacked, sacked and looted in 1200. The reason was that the crusaders had assembled in Venice with the intention of hiring a fleet there, but Venice's Doge, Enrico Dandolo, had another use for them, which was to help place the nephew of Philip of Swabia on the Byzantine throne, thereby enhancing Venetian influence in the eastern Mediterranean. The crusaders were unable to pay the money price demanded for a fleet, and so accepted the task of attacking Byzantium as, in effect, payment in kind. The crusaders, thus effectively turned gangsters, were finally stopped by the Bulgars at the Battle of Adrianople in 1205.

History in the service of piety can even make failure a cause for canonisation. Louis IX of France is the outstanding example, leading two failed crusades – the seventh and eighth – in 1248 and 1267 respectively, neither of which reached the Holy Land itself, both foundering in Egypt. At the first of them Louis was captured by the Mamluks of Egypt, and had to be expensively ransomed. At the second he accidentally drank contaminated water soon after arriving on the North African coast, as did many of his army, and with them died before the endeavour could get started. In recognition of his personal religious fervour and ambition to recapture Jerusalem for the cross, he was elevated to sainthood in 1297.

Like a river with a many-mouthed delta, crusading in the thirteenth, fourteenth and even fifteenth centuries diversified into many forms and places. Its chief legacy was to enrich the Italian port cities of Genoa and Venice, and to drive a deep wedge between Latin Christianity and Western Europe, on the one hand, and Orthodox Christianity and Islam, on the other hand, because of the cruelty, greed and vandalism that increasingly characterised the Latin Christian crusaders during this period.[5] The crusader states they had established in Asia Minor, the Holy Land, Greece and the Baltics, collectively known as 'Outremer' and sometimes described as the first European colonial experiments, did not last long; they had ceased to exist by the fourteenth century. But the conflict between Christendom and Islam that had reached its first apogee at the Battle of Poitiers in 732 was still not finished. The great naval Battle of Lepanto in 1571, the last fought by oared galleys and at which Cervantes was wounded and lost the use of his left hand, ended Muslim designs on the north coast of the Mediterranean, while the repulse of the Ottomans before Vienna in 1683 and at the decisive Battle of Zenta in 1697, were until recently seen as the culminating events in a thousand years of conflict between the two faith blocs. The troubling words here are 'until recently'.

Contemporary with the crusades was the conquest by the Mongol leader Genghis Khan and his descendants of nearly a quarter of the land surface of the planet. For the most part the activities of the Mongol hordes had little impact on events in Europe and the Mediterranean until the late thirteenth century, when Genghis's successors began to threaten the borders of the Arab world and Eastern Europe.

Mongol success was primarily based on the nomadic horse-manship skills already noted in connection with the Huns and other steppe peoples. But it was not just that the tough little ponies and their fierce, hardy, indefatigable riders were as one, or that the skills of herding had almost direct application to skills of mounted warfare, but the Mongol warriors were also superb archers, handling powerful composite bows which they could fire with accuracy at a gallop. Unlike the Huns they had the stirrup, which made archery from the saddle even more effective.

None of this, formidable as it is, would have given the Mongols their outstanding successes had it not been for Genghis's leader-ship. This extraordinary individual, born in 1162, was the son of a minor chieftain. His name was Temüjin; 'Genghis Khan' is a title, which can be translated as 'Ruler of the Universe' or at least 'Very Great King', and which he assumed after establishing an uncontested grasp of power. He was an astute politician as well as a highly intelligent war leader. First, he made the Mongols into a million-strong unified nation out of a loose arrangement of dispersed wandering tribes, centralising leadership and reorgan-ising the tribes' social structure by abolishing titles of chieftain-ship and the former inviolability of kinship. He turned the entire adult male population into an army arranged in units of tens, hundreds and thousands, the composition of the units cutting across tribal boundaries; and he appointed his most trusted comrades, or – if different – the best warriors, to command them, thereby further marginalising traditional leaders.

He was not only a war leader. He introduced a writing system, banned slavery and the practice of selling and kidnap-ping women for wives, made cattle rustling a capital offence, exempted the poorest from taxation, established freedom of religion, introduced a census of the population, and accepted the international system of immunity for foreign ambassadors.

But it was as a war leader that Genghis Khan achieved most. Although his warriors were natively skilled in horsemanship and the handling of their weapons, he obliged them to practise those skills constantly. He trained them in techniques of cavalry warfare that were subsequently adopted by most armies elsewhere, for example the trick of a cavalry charge seeming to falter and retreat in disorder, only to regroup extremely quickly and turn back on pursuers who themselves had become disordered in the heat of the chase.

Yet further to this, he was an assiduous student of warfare in all its forms. He learned from his enemies constantly, and was careful to capture and make use of engineers and craftsmen who made weapons and horse furniture. This made the Mongols not merely a swift-moving horde of merciless 'monsters', as one medieval chronicler called them,[6] but skilled at sieges too; they could rapidly fill deep moats with sandbags; build siege engines, towers and rams; and deployed catapult engines which could be dismantled into small parts for transport by horseback, but when assembled could fire incendiary bombs or the rotting carcasses of animals and people into walled cities.

But the reputation of mercilessness was also assiduously cultivated, because Genghis understood the value of psychological warfare, for a frightened enemy is a weaker enemy. He made good use of the Mongols' fearsome reputation therefore, which they enhanced by their actions; when they captured Samarkand in 1220 – it gave up without a fight – they massacred the entire population and piled the victims' heads into a huge pyramid outside the city, as a signal to everyone that the Mongols meant business.

Genghis began his wars in 1209 with an attack on the kingdom of Xi in north-west China, laying siege to the capital Yinchuan and forcing its ruler to submit and pay tribute. He then invaded the Chin kingdom of northern China, which had its capital at Beijing, then called Zhongdu. He campaigned across the kingdom for three years before besieging the city itself in 1214. A truce was agreed, with the Chins agreeing substantial tribute; but when the Chin court took itself south to Kaifeng in search of safety, Ghenghis took this as a breach of agreement, so he launched an assault on Zhongdu and destroyed it.

In 1219 Genghis turned his attention westward and attacked the Khwarezm empire, which included most of today's Turkmenistan, Uzbekistan, Afghanistan and Iran. The *casus belli* was that the Sultan of Khwarezm had entered a trade treaty with the Mongols, but when the first Mongol caravan arrived in his territories its merchants were murdered and their goods stolen. Ambassadors sent by Genghis to complain were also murdered. Retribution was devastating; Bukhara, Samarkand and Urgench were among the cities destroyed, and the Mongols spent six years preying on the wealth of the empire before Genghis returned to Mongolia.

When Genghis returned home in 1225 it was with the intention of resolving various problems that had arisen, as inevitably happens, while he was campaigning abroad. One was that Xi had refused to honour its obligation to supply troops for his Khwarezm campaign. In 1227 Genghis took a force south-eastward to punish the kingdom, and en route was thrown by his horse, sustaining an internal injury. Despite this, he continued with the campaign, dying of the injury on 18 August 1227, just before the city of Yinchuan was sacked.[7]

At the time of Genghis's death the Mongol empire stretched from the Caspian Sea to the Sea of Japan. He had conquered more territory than any other war leader before or since, though a considerable portion of it – the steppes of Siberia in particular – was a vast emptiness. It was now the turn of his descendants, not least among them Ogedei Khan and Kublai Khan, to continue the tale.

Ogedei's forces penetrated into central Russia, then the Ukraine – with a more than usually gruesome siege of Kiev – and further into Eastern Europe, defeating Polish and Hungarian armies at the Battles of Liegnitz and Mohi respectively, within days of each other in April 1241. These victories opened the way to the rich pastures and cities of central and Western Europe. Had it not been for Ogedei Khan's death immediately afterwards, obliging all the Mongol chieftains to return to Mongolia with their forces to participate in the arguments over his successor, the history of Europe, indeed of the world, would have been different.

While Kublai Khan, grandson of Genghis, was serving as governor of a southern Mongolian province and campaigning in western and south-western China, he developed into an avid Sinophile. He was born in 1215, and in 1260 succeeded his brother Mongke as khan of the empire after a civil war with another of his brothers, Ariq Boke. The civil war was the beginning of the fragmentation of the empire, though this process was furthered by the fact that Kublai's overwhelming interest was China, which kept him there and in its neighbourhood for the rest of his life. Between 1271 and 1279 he succeeded in unifying all China under his rule, establishing the Yuan dynasty with himself as its emperor.

In China itself Kublai suppressed the native Han aristocracy, which was resentful of his rule. Like his grandfather he was not merely a warrior, but a reformer; he opened hundreds of schools, built ports, rebuilt the Grand Canal to promote internal trade, and established a paper currency. But his military ambitions had not waned. After making Korea a vassal state he invaded Japan, Vietnam and Burma, exacting tribute from them all.

In the western reaches of the Mongol empire he had more difficulties, because his subordinates and relatives were at war with one another there. These territories had become increasingly autonomous as the Golden Horde or Kipchak Khanate, founded by another grandson of Genghis called Batu, son of Ogedei. Nominally the ruler of these western dominions was an 'ilkhan' or 'obedient khan' answerable to the Great Khan, but the fractious internal politics of the region made control of it difficult. At one point two of Kublai's sons were kidnapped and held prisoner as pawns in the civil war afflicting the region. The problems were all the greater because the khanate was also at war with its southern Muslim neighbours, in part a legacy of the invasions of the Middle East by Hulegu Khan in 1258, when the Mongol army, which was heading for Egypt, captured Baghdad and destroyed it, indulging in an orgy of murder. Some estimates say that half a million of its inhabitants were slaughtered by the Mongols.[8]

The empire of the Mongols did not long survive the second generation of Genghis's descendants. Tradition decreed that a khan should apportion his lands among his sons, a practice which instantly weakens a dominion and is a source of internecine conflict. This was the fate of the Golden Horde. Another and equally decisive factor was 'the besetting inability of horse peoples to translate initial conquest into permanent power'.[9] But before the Mongol presence faded, it sent one last major tremor through its time.

Hulegu Khan was ambitious to conquer Egypt. He sent the Mamluk sultan of Egypt, Qutuz, a message demanding his submission. It is a not inaccurate summary of the nature of Mongol conquest:

> You cannot escape from the terror of our armies. Where can you flee? What road will you use to escape us? Our horses are swift, our arrows sharp, our swords like thunderbolts, our hearts as hard as the mountains, our soldiers as numerous as the sand. Fortresses will not detain us, nor armies stop us. Your prayers to God will not avail against us. We are not moved by tears nor touched by lamentations. Only those who beg our protection will be safe. Hasten your reply before the fire of war is kindled. Resist and you will suffer the most terrible catastrophes. We will shatter your mosques and reveal the weakness of your God and then we will kill your children and your old men together.[10]

The crusaders, still at that time hanging by a thread to bits of the Holy Land and faced with the power of Islam all round them, regarded the approach of the Mongols with more hope than fear. It would serve them well to have their Muslim foes fighting a mighty enemy on a second front. So hopeful did the crusaders become that they began to think of the approaching Mongol horde as a relief sent by God, some even confusing Hulegu Khan with the legendary Christian king, Prester John. The same enthusiasm and hope prompted Armenian Christians to send volunteers to Hulegu's army.

Hulegu crossed the Tigris into Mesopotamia in early 1258, swatting aside the army of the Abbasid caliph Al-Muztasim and accepting the surrender of Baghdad. This was the event described above, when the Mongols massacred many of the inhabitants, perhaps as an act of psychological warfare to unnerve the cities that lay on their forward path to Egypt.

Aleppo shared Baghdad's fate because it resisted, but the citizens of Damascus surrendered well in advance of Hulegu's approach and survived. The crusaders had been delighted at first with the apparent collapse of Muslim power, but as the Mongols drew nearer to the Holy Land itself – by now under the command of Hulegu's lieutenant Kitbuga – the crusaders became anxious, and withdrew behind their castle walls. They sent an embassy to Sultan Qutuz in Egypt, proposing an alliance against the Mongols. This was a considerable departure, given the hardships that the crusaders had experienced at the hands of the Ayyubids' founder, Saladin, from whom the Mamluks had recently assumed the rule of Egypt. But because the Egyptians were equally nervous about the Mongols, an agreement was reached, and an Egyptian army under Sultan Qutuz and the formidable Mamluk general and kingmaker Baybars, entered the Holy Land as the crusaders' allies, and camped near Acre.

Kitbuga sent an embassy demanding the surrender of the crusaders and Egyptians. Baybars killed them. This was an intentional provocation, guaranteeing a fight. The Mongols marched into Palestine from Syria and met the Egyptian army at the Spring of Goliath, Ain Jalut, on 3 September 1260. It was a ferocious battle, and it ended in the Mongols' total defeat. Kitbuga himself was killed and the survivors of his force were scattered. The Mongols never returned to the Middle East.

Baybars used a tactic that the Mongols should have recognised: feint attacks and retreats to draw the enemy into an ambush, where the bulk of the Egyptian forces lay in wait to surround them. The Mongols fought desperately to break out, and nearly did so at one point in the encirclement, but Sultan Qutuz, seeing this, led his reserves into the fray shouting '*wa islamah!*' ('oh Islam!'). His charge, and the work of the Mamluk cavalry, completed the victory. It was the first ever major setback to Mongol arms, and its psychological impact was a crucial factor in the decline of Mongol power.

Keegan suggests that when Hulegu wrote his challenge to Sultan Qutuz before his Middle Eastern campaign began, he underestimated a principal factor in Muslim military success to that date: religious fervour.[11] This does not quite fit with the ease with which Hulegu defeated the Abbasid Muslims in the preceding campaign, and it underestimates the independent factor at work in Mamluk Egypt – the Mamluks themselves, and their commander and soon to be ruler, Baybars.

Mamluks were slave soldiers of Muslim rulers, drawn mainly from among Circassians, Georgians and Abkhazis, and thus Turkic in origin. They were made to convert to Islam, trained as warriors, and then set free, but under oath to serve their masters. They thus formed an elite warrior caste, and inevitably came to wield great influence in the Islamic world, some overthrowing their masters and rising to be sultans, others taking office as beys and emirs. From their origins in the ninth century they lasted as a key element in the Middle East until the nineteenth century. After the defeat of the Mongols at Ain Jalut, as just described, the Mamluk Sultanate of Egypt and Syria came into existence following Baybars' murder of Sultan Qutuz and seizure of his throne. It was the Mamluks who finally ejected the last of the crusaders from the Holy Land in 1302. Their sultanate lasted until 1517, when it was overthrown in its turn by the Ottomans.

The Mongols were, however, not yet done; they had more terrors to offer in the form of the rampages – there is no more apt term – of Timur, otherwise known as Tamerlane. Born in 1336, he became leader of the Barlas clan in the Khanate of Chagatai, named after one of Genghis Khan's sons. Timur idolised Genghis, and was ambitious to recover his idol's empire. When he had made himself master of the Chagatai Confederation he asserted his authority over the rest of the Central Asian steppe, and then invaded Persia and Mesopotamia to the south, and the Golden Horde in Russia to the north. He employed terror as a principal tactic, leaving pyramids of skulls wherever he went, and in some cases burying thousands of his victims alive. Inadvertently he prolonged the existence of Byzantium by fifty years, by defeating the Ottoman sultan Beyezid I at Ankara in Anatolia. He invaded India, repeating his atrocities there. His genius as a military commander was only checked by the Mings who repulsed his attempts to invade China.

To the rest of the world Timur looked little better than a bloodthirsty hooligan; some estimates say that he caused the deaths of 17 million people.[12] And in one sense there is no doubt that he was. But he was also a patron of architecture and the arts, liked to discourse with philosophers and poets, and he was idolised by his followers. He was a Muslim, and claimed to be punishing his fellow-Muslims for their lack of piety, sending a message to Damascus saying, 'I am the scourge of God, appointed to chastise you.' By the time of his death he had restored much of Genghis Khan's empire, apart from China, and left a line of notable descendants: he was the grandfather of Ulugh Beg, the famously learned ruler of Central Asia from 1411 to 1449, and thrice-great-grandfather of Babur, founder of the Mughal empire in India, which lasted from 1526 to 1857.

To the modern eye there is something exotic, majestic or both about the warriors and armies of medieval times. Illustrations of Mamluk fighters, of armoured Christian knights on warhorses, of ranks of archers, are at once familiar and remote. The Hundred Years' War between England and France (1337 to 1453) belongs to that era, and is perhaps its apogee.

France was the greatest kingdom of that age in Europe, a rich prize, over which what was in effect a family feud raged for its possession, because the royal houses of both England and France laid claim to it by inheritance.

When Charles IV of France died in 1328 his sister Isabella claimed the throne for her son, Edward III of England, because she was debarred from inheriting it in her own right by a Salic Law, introduced just twelve years earlier, removing females from the line of succession. The French said that she could not pass on a claim that she had not inherited, so her nephew Philip VI became king. When the French sent aid to the Scots in Edward's wars with them, Edward determined to revive his claim to the French throne, and the Hundred Years' War began.

English victories at Crécy (1346) and Agincourt (1415) are credited to the firepower of the English longbowmen; the French revival achieved by Joan of Arc in 1428 started a legend, but did not yet result in a French victory, for Henry VI was crowned King of England in Westminster Abbey on 5 November 1429 and King of France in Notre Dame in Paris on 16 December 1431.

By 1450 the French had driven the English out of most of the country's provinces, and as English power on the continent waned so the allegiance of its allies faltered, most significantly that of Burgundy. The Battle of Castillon in July 1453, a French victory, was the last major engagement of the war, although officially it did not end until the 1470s. At home in England the long and expensive series of struggles with France had caused a rift among the great aristocrats, who were now seriously falling out among themselves and taking sides in a civil war which, from 1455 onwards, was to be known as the Wars of the Roses.

A major significance of the Hundred Years' War was the change it brought to feudalism as a social system, and to military practice and technology. At the beginning of the war the opposed armies consisted of feudal levies, in effect citizen armies whose military training consisted in an obligation – in England anyway – to indulge in regular spare-time archery practice. By the end of the war armies were bodies of professionals, artillery and firearms had begun to appear, and government had become more centralised to cope with the administrative needs of equipping, fielding and supplying armies, and raising taxes to pay for them.

When the war began the knight in his armour on his equally heavily armoured horse was the pinnacle of the fighting machine. Almost immediately the drawbacks of this would-be machine became apparent: it was expensive, unwieldy, and hardly able to move once the ground became muddy and churned. Shedding armour was the first desideratum to create an effective cavalry. This lighter cavalry, known as hobelars, were used in pursuits and as skirmishers. In any case Edward III made his knights dismount and fight on foot in close formation with the archers, so that their horses became a means of transport only. It had been shown that the longbow was devastatingly effective against heavy cavalry, and the early battles of the war taught quick lessons. What could not have been foreseen is that the end of the knight in armour as a fighting entity also meant the beginning of the end of the nobility as a political entity.

A telling fact is that the technology of artillery had advanced so far during the course of the war that whereas at Agincourt the French cannon did little more than create noise and smoke, untroubling to the English archers who brandished two fingers to show that they could still draw their bows, at Castillon it was a decisive factor, blasting down the English defences. Almost at the same time the Ottoman Turks were blasting down the walls of Constantinople with cannon in their final overthrow of Byzantium.

By the middle of the sixteenth century the cannon and the hand-held gun were standard. Ways of casting cannon to make them lighter and more manoeuvrable, more accurate, with greater range, and at the same time safer for their operators (older cannon sometimes exploded in the cannoneer's face), had been achieved in France in the 1490s. Muskets were replacing bows and crossbows, and likewise had become more effective. The nature of war had changed.

There is added significance in this. From the time of the classical Greeks and Romans, what Victor Davis Hanson calls 'the Western way of war', meaning direct face-to-face, hand-to-hand combat aimed at outright victory, had prevailed in contrast to the more elusive stand-off style of the Middle East and the steppe, in which warriors preferred launching missiles at the enemy from a distance, and darting in for a brief encounter before quickly withdrawing.[13] The Greek phalanx of hoplites engaged with their enemies at close quarters, seeking a decision; the Roman legions did the same.[14]

Homeric battle seems to have involved both this and single combat between champions, but by the classical age the latter had been abandoned. Man-to-man combat was seen as honourable by the much later knights of the medieval age of chivalry, who deprecated stand-off means – such as the crossbow – as cowardly because they allowed an untrained man to kill a knight from a distance without fighting him. Some knights executed bowmen when they caught them, on the grounds that their behaviour was sneaking and treacherous.[15] But medieval contests between champions were limited to the jousting field. European warfare since the Greeks is all Greek; commanders in Western wars since then have always sought the decisive battle.

Artillery and guns reintroduce distance, but they do not alter the Western way of war. A musket ball could penetrate armour at more than 200 metres; a square of musketeers, working in combination with resolute pikemen, can repulse a cavalry charge. The new weapons had rendered many of the old techniques and weapons obsolete, though as Turney-High and other military historians point out, the fundamentals of warfare such as organisation, supply, the column and the line, the combination of fire, shock, mobility and protection, remained invariant.

It was only in Japan that the old ways – with beautiful swords so sharp that the touch of their cutting edge felt like a breath of air, and with techniques of samurai combat that depended on a long discipline of training and an entire philosophy and social system – were completely preserved long past the time that anything like them had been abandoned elsewhere. This was made possible by the exclusion of foreigners and all things foreign, including guns, from the Japanese islands. The Ashikaga shoguns had in fact made use of guns and gunpowder in taking power in the sixteenth century, but thereafter they banned them to protect the samurai way, which persisted until the Meiji reformation of the nineteenth century. It was an extraordinary hold-out.

Cannon and muskets, together with advances in ship-building and navigation, were key to the globalising spread of

European power in the first as in all successive phases of colonisation from the fifteenth century.[16] They overpowered native populations, then defended the coastal forts established by colonisers to keep other colonisers out, and armed the ships that fought off rivals. They ensured the success of the first steps of the imperial adventure from the beginning; they helped Portuguese mariners defeat their Muslim counterparts in the Indian Ocean, enabling the Portuguese to establish themselves at Goa, Hormuz and Malacca, after which they established their first Far Eastern station at Macao.

Serious war-making thus spread to the seas in a manner and volume that far outstripped any previous maritime conflicts, from Salamis and the naval battles of the Punic Wars right up to Lepanto, for now purpose-built men-o'-war capable of delivering broadside cannonades were centrally involved in capturing and protecting overseas possessions, and guarding the merchant shipping that passed between them and home shores.

Later naval conflicts – such as the Anglo-Dutch wars of the seventeenth century – were yet more ambitious in scope; they were fought for control of the seas themselves, not just particular routes across them, and the development of naval power was pivotal to the growth of Britain's empire. Accordingly the Royal Navy is the chief example of what a navy was and meant in the period between the seventeenth and early twentieth centuries.

Henry VIII had begun the process of establishing an English navy in the early sixteenth century, and it was strong enough to withstand – with help from the Dutch and the weather – the Spanish Armada in 1588. But it was in the age of Pepys a century later, at the time of the Anglo-Dutch wars themselves, that it began to achieve supremacy. It played a key role in all subsequent wars until the Boer War of 1899–1902, and served emphatically both as the British Isles' home defence as its 'wooden walls' and as the guardian of empire abroad. Its part in the Napoleonic Wars was significant, Nelson's victories at the Nile, Trafalgar and elsewhere keeping the focus of Napoleon's endeavours on land. In the nineteenth century the Royal Navy's size and firepower met a self-imposed 'two power standard', that is, the ability to outfight not just the next most powerful navy in the world, but the next *two* most powerful navies *combined*.[17]

The Royal Navy's role in defending the home shores and projecting power to distant quarters of the world rapidly diminished from the Second World War onwards. In 1940 it was the Royal Air Force that prevented an invasion of the British Isles, though in the Battle of the Atlantic the Royal Navy's defence of the convoys was vital.[18] In the contemporary world, ships have primarily become missile platforms and floating airfields, as the US Navy shows, though for a multiplicity of military housekeeping tasks it is hard to see how frigates and minesweepers could be dispensed with. But the days of the great battleships and cruisers are long over.

The advent of gunpowder weapons was contradictorily contemporary with the Renaissance admiration for classical examples of the theory and practice of war. By this I mean that just as the Renaissance was mining classical literature and examples to inform its military thinking, so the development of gunpowder weapons was undermining the utility of doing so. A signal example is given by Machiavelli and his *Art of War*, published in 1521.

Machiavelli's views rested on characteristically Renaissance assumptions to the effect that nature, human nature and the fundamentals of the human condition are everywhere and always the same, underwritten by unchanging universal laws. States and kingdoms might differ from one another in their customs, he wrote, but underneath it all 'The world has always gone on in the same way.'[19] This, among many other things, implied that a study of classical military literature would teach us what we need to know of military science. Machiavelli accordingly drew upon the best models, among them Xenophon's *Hellenica* and *Anabasis*, Polybius's *Histories* – in which a detailed account is given of Roman tactics in the Macedonian Wars – and Vegetius's *De Re Militari*. The two former works illustrated the effectiveness of the Greek phalanx and its methods, while the two latter described the sophistication of Roman military organisation and technique.[20]

What was distinctive about the Greek and Roman militaries was that they were citizen armies whose soldiers fought for patriotic reasons. The contrast between them and the mercenary armies standardly employed by Italian city states in Machiavelli's own day made him emphatic in his conclusion that the only workable military form is a citizen militia. *Condottieri* – mercenaries – were not only treacherous, greedy and unreliable, and as great or greater a danger to their employers as to those they were hired to fight, and use of their forerunners in late antiquity had been part of the cause of the classical world's own downfall. During his fourteen years as Secretary to Florence's Office of Ten (1498–1512) Machiavelli had occasion to deprecate the unreliability of mercenaries, and it prompted him to persuade the government of *gonfaloniere* Piero Soderini to allow him to establish a Florentine militia. It was a highly unpopular plan with Florence's aristocracy, but it was justified by events; Florence defeated Pisa in the war between the cities in 1509.

Citing Polybius's example of Rome's Macedonian battles, Machiavelli argued that tightly knit but manoeuvrable and co-ordinated squares of infantry armed with swords and shields would repulse cavalry and overcome looser formations of pike-bearing infantry. He was right; but he was putting forward his theories at just the moment when history was making them inapplicable. The advent of gunpowder weapons was the reason.

In the sixteenth century's Wars of Religion in France, the independence war of the northern provinces of the Spanish Netherlands, and the wars of the seventeenth century, especially the Thirty Years' War and the English Civil War, muskets and cannon came increasingly to dominate the battlefield. Maurice of Nassau, Prince of Orange, had a musket drill manual written in 1607, carefully detailing several dozen sequential steps to be followed by musketeers as they loaded, lit and fired their weapons. The necessity for this was in large part to protect the musketeers from themselves; if the man next to you applied a match to his powder, and a spark from it lit your powder before you were ready – and if further sparks ignited other unready muskets nearby – the result could be disastrous. Everything had to be done in lockstep.[21]

Sweden, meanwhile, which under its king Gustavus Adolphus was a major presence in the seventeenth century, had become pre-eminent in the art of artillery. Mathematicians and scientists such as Galileo had contributed to the theory of ballistics, and the continuing creativity of engineers and metal founders was constantly improving the manoeuvrability, accuracy and range of cannon. The Thirty Years' War, in particular, did much to change the nature of armies. In the early years of the war it was still the practice with most armies to disband at the end of the fighting season, with a new army recruited at the beginning of the next – the fighting season being the summer. As the war wore on, the national armies of France, Sweden and the United Provinces of the Netherlands, and the armies levied by such mercenary captains as Tilly (1559–1632), von Mansfeldt (1580–1626) and the famous Wallenstein (1583–1634) became standing armies. Instead of sending men home, the 'mercenary captains' took them into winter quarters as Caesar had done with his legions, and the men drilled and practised throughout the off-season.[22]

The combination of musketeers and pikemen proved a formidable one in the seventeenth-century wars. By the end of that century the invention of the bayonet had, however, rendered pikes obsolete. At the same time, armies began to be uniformed, a mark of their increasing professionalisation and the standardisation and efficiency which the supporting bureaucracy behind them required. The manufacture of weapons, the payment of soldiers, the logistics of supply and transport, the provision of barracks and medical services, and much more, required a formidable bureaucratic structure. It was matched by the greater organisation of military life and training itself. In the sixteenth and seventeenth centuries, especially in the mercenary armies of Tilly, Wallenstein and others, there had been a great deal of raffishness and hooliganism, for such were the kind of men that fighting for pay on anyone's side attracted. What it was like to have an army of this kind trample into your farms and villages to take up quarters there is well described in the opening scenes of Voltaire's *Candide*.

By the eighteenth century, soldiers were drilled and disciplined, trained in the use of their weapons, clad in uniforms with insignia of rank for officers and non-commissioned officers, and subject to stern punishment for stepping out of line. Infantry, artillery and cavalry had fallen into set patterns of interaction: muskets were effective only up to about 100 metres, if that, though fired in volley they were lethal at closer quarters. Well-directed artillery could make a serious dent in infantry formations, if they were manoeuvred to the battlefield and positioned correctly in time, but cavalry could neutralise artillery if it reached the guns before they were ready to fire. Indeed this became the primary use of cavalry, apart from pursuit of retreating enemy and occasionally attacking infantry if the latter's formations had been sufficiently broken by artillery.[23] As a result the battles of the eighteenth century took on a static, formulaic and indecisive character. Keegan describes the most notable battles of the eighteenth century, Blenheim (1704), Fontenoy (1745) and Leuthen (1757), as 'notable rather for the number of casualties suffered among the docile ranks of the participants than for any permanency of outcome achieved'.[24]

To break the stalemate, armies began to introduce irregular forces, in the hope of gaining a sharper edge. In the nineteenth century the reach of imperialism provided any number of exotic irregulars to enliven at least the appearance of the battle line: Sikhs and Gurkhas for the British, Jäger from the Tyrol for the Austrians, Zouaves from North Africa in the French army – these latter adding a particular sartorial spice – though in Keegan's view they added little to military effectiveness except in small local conflicts.[25]

Training and the drill ground certainly had a positive effect in such circumstances as, for example, British victories over Indian troops and, later, Zulus in southern Africa. But a factor that Machiavelli had noticed in preferring citizen militias to armies of professional mercenaries now came into play in a slightly different and much more potent form. In the wars of the

American and French revolutions, sentiment and belief in the rightness of the cause being fought for gave far more of an edge to military effectiveness than any admixture of irregulars could achieve. Indeed, sentiment of this kind can, and in these cases did, outweigh the effects of the drill ground altogether. In such circumstances an army of paid regulars fighting far from home, most of its members scarcely aware of where they are or why they are there, is not a match for people determinedly fighting for their homes and land. Of course there are plenty of examples to the contrary – imperialists appropriating other people's lands, as the Spanish did in Central and South America, and as the British did in Africa, India, Australia and elsewhere, for example, had great advantages in military method and technology, and these told despite the zeal of the victims in protecting their own. But in the rebellion of Britain's Thirteen Colonies in north America, and in the belief of France's *sans culottes* that aristocrats and the 'legitimate' monarchs of Europe were intent on putting down their revolution, an order of fighting spirit existed that made a material difference to the wars in question.

Accounts of the battles of the nineteenth century – Waterloo, Balaclava, the bloody battles of the American Civil War – do not read very differently from accounts of earlier battles. At Waterloo the infantry squares of the British held out against artillery bombardment and repeated cavalry charges, at Balaclava the vulnerability of cavalry against ready artillery was tragically demonstrated in the infamous 'Charge of the Light Brigade'. At Gettysburg, with cavalry battles unfolding to the south and east of them, General Robert E. Lee's Confederate infantry charged the Union infantry drawn up on Cemetery Ridge in what came to be known as 'Pickett's Charge'. The charge was repulsed with staggering loss of life; in all about 50,000 men died in this, the bloodiest battle of the Civil War; the infantry attacks of the First World War seem to reprise something of the same suicidal tactic of infantry charging in line abreast towards the mouths of guns.

The nineteenth century was not without auguries of what was to come when the twentieth century's two world wars, fought by huge armies, navies and air forces across the globe, had brought their tens of millions to the grave by the middle of the century. These were the guerrilla tactics of Pashtun and other tribesmen, and of Boer farmers, against British imperial forces in Afghanistan and South Africa respectively. In recent times this kind of warfare – asymmetrical warfare – has become the norm. Large armies and nuclear weapons still exist, and states still square off against each other threateningly – at the time of writing there is chronic bristling along the contiguities between India and Pakistan; North and South Korea; China and Japan; Russia and its neighbours, especially Ukraine; and Iran and Saudi Arabia, all of which, except the last, have taken the form of outright shooting war in living memory, and in every one of these except the last, the arsenal of at least one of the hostile states includes nuclear weapons.[26] These are alarming facts.

And, again at the time of writing, the immense military power of the United States remains embroiled in difficult situations where the asymmetrical nature of its fights is such that the Goliath of its forces is expensively (in lives and material terms) tied down by Davids with their slingshots in Afghanistan and the Middle East. The difficulties faced by US military endeavour are in part the result of changing views of war and military effort, and in part Washington's sensitivities about public opinion regarding its military activities overseas. This latter is the result of the United States' bitter experience of defeat in the Vietnam War. Vietnam placed a large dent in public preparedness to countenance the 'body bag' factor, so that when military action begins to go wrong or to get expensive in casualties, as in Iraq following the second Gulf War of 2003, American public opinion takes fright, and opposes 'boots on the ground' interventions. This hampered US efforts in Syria during the frightful civil war that followed the short-lived 'Arab Spring', which began in Tunisia in December 2010 and spread to other Arab countries. The government of Bashar al-Assad in Syria did not fall, as several other Arab governments did, but brutally sought to repress the uprising, with the result that a multi-sided civil war began, into which other players – Daesh (the so-called 'Islamic State'), various rebel forces as opposed to each other as to Assad, Russian allies of Assad, Kurds, Turks (the two latter conducting their own side-war in the process), the United States, Britain and others – all became involved in a terrible mess of violence, a drunken pub brawl writ very large, in which the victims were children and civilians generally, and from which millions of terrified and desperate refugees flooded into neighbouring countries and Europe.

As this suggests, the nature of war and thinking about war has changed since 1945. It is of interest to step back and take note of how thinking about war has evolved since the seventeenth and eighteenth centuries, resulting in the practical (and impractical) applications of which the immediately foregoing paragraphs speak.

CHAPTER 3

Theories of War and War's More Recent History

The distinctive feature of the Enlightenment, with its roots in the scientific revolution of the seventeenth century, was the determination of its *philosophes* to apply the successful methods of the natural sciences to the social sciences, politics and society. Scientific methodology – empirical observation disciplined by mathematics – had spectacularly proved itself, from Copernicus through Galileo to Harvey, Gassendi, Roche, Huygens, Boyle, van Leeuwenhoek, Newton and others. The process had at first been difficult and even dangerous – the Inquisition was still burning people at the stake for scientific views in the first decades of the seventeenth century – but the Church's Canute-like efforts did little to hinder the advance of science, and by the middle of the seventeenth century that advance was unstoppable.[1]

The scientific spirit of the time reached into military thinking also, not surprisingly given the major conflicts that wracked the period. In his scholarly study of military theory from the Enlightenment onwards, Azar Gat cites a number of works written before and leading up to that period, chief of them the works of Raimondo Montecuccoli, Duke of Melfi, a Field Marshal of distinction in the army of the Holy Roman Empire, who fought throughout the Thirty Years' War and afterwards, achieving his greatest victory at the battle of St Gotthard in 1673 over the Ottomans.[2]

Montecuccoli was an intellectual as well as a soldier, and a remarkably well-read one. Among influences ranging from Aristotle to his contemporary Francis Bacon, one of the chief was Justus Lipsius, the sixteenth-century humanist scholar responsible for championing a revival of Stoicism. In his *Treatise on War*, Montecuccoli examined the causes of war, preparations for it both political and logistical, alliances, recruitment and command, the conduct of war and the achievement of a favourable peace at its close – which was, he said, the aim of war in the first place.[3] He recognised that gunpowder weapons had changed the nature of war, but held that the fundamental principles of war remained as they had always been. In his memoir of fighting the Turks in Hungary he wrote, 'Disregarding the invention of artillery, which has somewhat changed the forms of war, the rest of [its] rules remain correct and valid.'[4]

It was Montecuccoli's belief in these universal principles, and in taking a scientific attitude to warfare based upon them, that recommended itself to his eighteenth-century successors. He believed in the interrelationship of practice and general rules, the latter derived from the former and then applied to guide further practice. His treatise self-consciously modelled itself on a mathematical treatise, first setting out principles and then demonstrating their use in action.[5]

The eighteenth century saw a great increase in the number of books on military matters. Something like thirty books on the art of war had appeared in Montecuccoli's time; in the next century there were nearly 200. Although the century had wars which brought to prominence individual military leaders of genius such as the Duke of Marlborough in the War of Spanish Succession (1701–14) and Frederick the Great of Prussia in the Seven Years' War (1754–63), it was not the wars themselves that promoted the outburst of theorising, but the belief – or perhaps hope – that the methods of scientific enquiry could make war a more exact, predictable and therefore winnable exercise if its general principles could be precisely identified and applied.

This is a characteristically Enlightenment view. It is of a piece with the 'grand project' aim of the *Encyclopédie* (1751–72) edited by Denis Diderot and Jean le Rond d'Alembert, which was to 'set forth as well as possible the order and connection of the parts of human knowledge . . . to contain the general principles that form the basis of each science and each art, liberal or mechanical, and the most essential facts that make up the body and substance of each'.[6] Their project too was expressly empirical: 'All our direct knowledge can be reduced to what we receive through our senses; whence it follows that we owe all our ideas to our sensations.' This emphatic empiricism, with its rejection of doctrines of innate ideas and, more importantly still, of knowledge acquired by way of revelation, was a profound challenge to the great institutions of Church and of a monarchy said to rule by 'divine right'.[7]

The scientific style of thought directly influenced military theory. Gat writes:

At the height of the French Enlightenment, military thinkers incorporated the all-encompassing outlook of the period into the military field. War, they complained, was ruled by 'arbitrary traditions', 'blind prejudices', 'disorder and confusion'.

All these had to be replaced by critical analyses and systematic schemes which the men of the period understood in definitive and universal terms, largely overriding circumstantial differences and historical change. The organisation of armies and conduct of war would thus become an orderly discipline with clear theoretical tenets.[8]

Perhaps the most celebrated of the many treatises which the spirit of the age produced was the Comte de Guibert's *Essai général de tactique* (1770).[9]

Because Enlightenment thinking represented such a profound challenge to orthodoxies, it immediately generated a Counter-Enlightenment. One of the most powerful Counter-Enlightenment movements is Romanticism. A distinctive feature of Romanticism – to generalise and simplify for brevity – is to oppose the idea that *reason* should be the ultimate authority over our ideas and actions, but instead that such authority should be accorded to the richer and more attractive dimensions of feeling, emotion, sentiment, the mysterious, the religious, the poetic. We would indeed not be without the poetry and music that this view sponsored, but I think many would agree that we could well do without its political and social applications, in which nationalism, the dangerous cant of *Blut* and *Volk*, racism, eventually Fascism, are among the chief expressions.

Among Enlightenment theoreticians of war themselves there are auguries of their own rejection by Romantic opponents. Guibert had eloquently argued, in the 'Preliminary Discourse' to his treatise, that the polities of his own day lacked the sterling qualities of the city states in classical times, with their republican virtues embodied in the people, while the Europe of his own time was, he said, corrupt and effete, tyrannical yet weak.

Hope lay in the example afforded by Frederick of Prussia, in the form of that monarch's 'enlightened despotism'.[10] The admiration felt by Enlightenment thinkers for the Prussian king was extended to the institutions of his country – including its military institutions – and to Frederick himself as a theoretician of war, indeed the leading such theoretician in the German world. He circulated his writings to his officers, and established military schools and officers' academies. This was an expression of the idea that, as military theory is a science, a formal training in its various departments is a necessity.

The Enlightenment was also a period in which mechanisation of industrial processes was beginning, and the idea of the greater power of mechanical over human things was infiltrating military thinking. Adam Heinrich Dietrich von Bülow provides an example. Some of his views, as exemplified in what he says about battlefield manoeuvres, were conventional, but other aspects were radical. He wrote copiously, but his most famous and controversial book was *Geist des neuern Kriegssystems* (1799), in which he argued that the introduction of firearms should be recognised as the most significant development in warfare ever. The volume of firepower on the battlefield replaces the courage and skill of individual soldiers, he said, so the chief determinant of military success is the sheer number of soldiers on the field.[11] That fact, as it happened, provided one of the motives for nineteenth-century armies to grow in size. In von Bülow's view it increased the necessity for thought about systems of supply, not least of ammunition for the gunpowder weapons that now dominated, so depots, transport, lines of communication, and the relationship between one's own and the enemy's, suggested itself as a subject for study – one's own depots and supply lines required protection while the enemy's provided a target. Von Bulow went so far as to suggest that geometry held the secret to a perfect science of strategy, for it showed how the relationship between an advancing army and its supply bases, focused on the enemy located at the vertex of a triangle so framed, would determine the success of an attack, and perhaps even render fighting itself unnecessary. In one way this was an extreme version of the eighteenth-century military focus on manoeuvre, which saw armies marching about, fortifying themselves and avoiding pitched battles if possible.[12]

But Bülow himself saw that the reason for the success of French arms over Austrian arms in the campaign of the year 1800 had to do with something other than geometry, namely, the new political order in France and the associated moral spirit that animated French soldiers. In any case Napoleon's methods had nothing to do with triangles and anxieties about logistics. His fast-moving armies supplied themselves from conquered territory, and his aim in engaging his enemies was very Greek: it was to win a decisive victory, so destructive of the opposing army that those whose army it was had no option but to surrender.[13] These were the novelties that the French Revolutionary and Napoleonic Wars introduced, and the military thinkers of the time strove to take account of them on Enlightenment lines.

Antoine-Henri Jomini (1779–1869) was a practical soldier who saw in the examples afforded by the victories of Frederick the Great at Leuthen, and by Napoleon in Italy, a 'key to all the science of war', namely, *concentration of forces at the crucial point*. At Leuthen Frederick had attacked one wing of the enemy with the bulk of his forces, and Napoleon employed the same tactic in his Italian campaign, in both cases complete victory being achieved.

As always, however, there is no single 'key' to guaranteed success, and Jomini recognised the importance of other factors, such as disrupting the enemy's lines of communication, supply and retreat. But the principal aim is always to bring the enemy to battle and to destroy its forces.[14] The 'general principle' for achieving this is:

> that the decisive points of manoeuvre are on that flank of the enemy upon which, if his opponent operates, he can more easily cut him off from his base and supporting forces without being exposed to the same danger . . . If the enemy's forces are in detachments or are too much extended, the decisive point is his centre, for by piercing that his forces will be more divided, their weakness increased, and the fractions crushed separately.

The examples Jomini cited were battles Napoleon had won, for these were precisely Napoleon's tactics; thus for Jomini Napoleonic methods and the universal principles of war were one and the same, which, he said, had been applied ever since the time of Scipio and Caesar.[15]

Jomini was established as the leading theoretician of war when, like an artillery shell, the posthumous publication of Carl von Clausewitz's *On War* in 1832 exploded on the scene, criticising Jomini and all Enlightenment military theories. Most people remember Clausewitz as arguing that war is an extension of politics 'by other means', but for Jomini himself and his contemporaries Clausewitz's novelty came from his rejection of the idea that there are universal principles of war. The reality of war, the role of 'moral forces' (sentiment and will), and the specific circumstances of a given battle, cannot, Clausewitz said, be reduced to rules.

In this rejection of the idea that there are universal principles that can be tabulated and applied to order, there is a similarity to themes in the emphatic criticism of Frederick of Prussia by Georg von Berenhorst (1733–1814), whose *Reflections on the Art of War* (1796) argued that war does not proceed by rules but by 'unknown and uncontrollable modifications of the human spirit . . . in an environment saturated with will-power and emotions' – and with blind chance playing its part.[16] Frederick's Prussia was seen by Berenhorst as by other Counter-Enlightenment thinkers as a 'bureaucratic, lifeless, "machine-like" state' predicated on a 'French rationalistic orientation'.[17] Prussian troops were brutally treated, endlessly and mechanistically drilled, to be regarded merely as cannon-fodder on the battlefield; this, in Berenhorst's view, was utterly to miss the point of the psychological aspect of war, which was won or lost on the moral sentiment of the combatants.

In Clausewitz the focus of attention was, similarly, shifted from questions about principles of war to the idea of freely expressed talent and creativity in the particular circumstances of battle. A general's plan of action, he said, is an expression of his personality, not the outcome of a formula; and he reinterpreted the military genius of Gustavus Adolphus of Sweden and Frederick the Great of Prussia in this light. He poured scorn on the idea that great generals can be manufactured in military academies by studying a science of war; 'we find many men who proved themselves able military leaders, yes even military leaders of the first order, without having had any military education', he wrote.[18] Personality and its qualities are what matter in a general; like Berenhorst he thought the same applies to each soldier and to an army as a whole.

The focus on psychology, on the motives and feelings that animate what people do and how they think, is a Romantic trope, and makes Clausewitz a creature of his time, influenced by German Romanticism in its rejection of Enlightenment ideas about the overriding authority of reason.[19]

One of the principal characteristics needed by a great war leader, Clausewitz said, is audacity. But this does not mean leaving the business of war to caprice. He wrote of the importance of careful preparation of forces, inspection of terrain and information about enemy dispositions. The main objectives of strategy are of two kinds, either the achievement of limited aims, or the destruction of the enemy's military power and the capture of its resources. The latter requires concentrating operations against the enemy's main army or a significant part of it; offensive operations must be carried out with the utmost vigour, and aimed at the decisive point in the enemy dispositions. Speed and surprise, and concentration on the battlefield rather than less immediately important objectives such as lines of communication, give great advantages.[20]

He famously said that war is 'not merely a political act, but also a real political instrument, a continuation of political commerce, a carrying out of the same by other means'.[21] This much-quoted dictum was, however, no more than that; he did not dilate upon it or explore its implications, but let it stand as self-evident. More influential, in fact, have been his definitions of war as 'a clash of wills' and as 'an act of violence intended to force our opponent to perform our will'. In the middle books of *On War*, where the focus is Napoleonic warfare, he talks of crushing the enemy and disarming it, lending weight to the interpretation of the Clausewitzian view as being that war should be *total*, its object the annihilation of enemies; and of this therefore as the founding principle of Prussian military effort in the later nineteenth century and Hitler's way of war-making in the Second World War. Some commentators point out that in revisions to

the text of the book – Clausewitz never completed it; his manu-
scripts were edited and published by his wife after his death – he
modified the impression that he was committed to the idea of
war-making as a Mongol-like obliteration of enemies, but that
he had a more nuanced view where limited war-making has a
place too, as more naturally associated with the idea that war is
an extension of politics and diplomacy.

As the remarks in the two preceding paragraphs show, *On
War* is a hybrid: both a manual of warfare and an account of the
philosophy of war regarding its purpose and character. Indeed,
on one view, Clausewitz's main purpose in the book was to make
people better judges of what war is about, so that they can better
understand how it should be conducted. One of the dominating
ideas in his theory is that of the 'trinity' of three interacting
forces that together drive what happens in real war. He wrote:

War is not a mere chameleon, because it changes its nature to
some extent in each particular case. However it is also, when
regarded as a whole and in relation to the tendencies that
dominate within it, a remarkable trinity – consisting of:
primordial violence, hatred, and enmity, which are to be
regarded as a blind natural force; the play of chance and
probability, within which the creative spirit is free to roam;
and the element of subordination, as an instrument of policy,
which makes it subject to pure reason.

The first of these three aspects mostly concerns the
people; the second, mostly the commander and his army; the
third, mostly the government. The passions that are to blaze
up in war must already be inherent in the people; the scope
that the play of courage and talent will enjoy in the realm of
probability and chance depends on the individual character

of the commander and the army; but the political aims are the business of government alone. These three tendencies are like three different codes of law, profoundly rooted in their subject and yet variable in their relationship to one another.[22]

Clausewitz likened the interrelations of these factors to the magnetic toy in which a pendulum hangs between three magnets which make it oscillate among them in what mathematicians now call 'deterministic chaos', deterministic because we fully understand the forces acting on the pendulum, but chaotic because, in the technical mathematical sense, tiny variations in initial conditions will have a 'butterfly effect' of large differences in outcomes.

In Clausewitz's view a military genius is one who, in addition to possessing the creativity and audacity required for the role, these being innate personality traits, must also be calm and not given to panic, must have a strong constitution enabling him to bear the hardships of the campaign, and must have the ability to see both what lies on the other side of a hill, and through 'the fog of war' (Clausewitz's phrase), that is, to grasp the circumstances of the battlefield and to see through the uncertainty and confusion of the battle. He cites the example of how Napoleon waited and waited for exactly the right moment to launch his decisive attack at Austerlitz, even though his forces were under dangerously mounting pressure.

Clausewitz's reputation was made for him by the fact that Helmuth von Moltke the Elder cited him as his inspiration in devising his own theory of war, reforming the Prussian military, and being victorious against Austria in 1866 and France in 1870–1 respectively. In what appears as an application of Clausewitz's concept of 'total war', von Moltke wrote:

> The days are gone when, for dynastic reasons, small armies of professional soldiers went to war to conquer a city or province, and then sought winter quarters or made peace. The wars of the present day call whole nations to arms . . . the entire financial resources of the state are devoted to military purposes.[23]

The ideas governing the Prussian-German military outlook in the nineteenth century influenced the militaries of the other great powers, not least in adopting the 'cult of the offensive'. This was the view that the attacker has great advantages over the defender, and that instead of waiting for an enemy to help himself to this advantage, one should launch the first strike. No doubt this doctrine was one of the precipitating factors of the First World War. Classic examples of it are the offensive plans prepared by the French and Germans before 1914; Marshal Joseph Joffre's plan for an attack into Alsace-Lorraine; and the Schlieffen Plan for an attack through Belgium and down towards Paris, with the intention of outflanking the French armies to their north. Adolf Hitler was likewise a proponent of the first-strike view, as his respective invasions of Poland, France and Russia between 1939 and 1942 show. The Japanese attack on Pearl Harbor in December 1942 is yet another instance.

The result of the 'Battle of the Frontiers', as the opening phase of the 1914–18 war is called, was a repulse to Joffre's forces, and a failure by Helmuth von Moltke the Younger to execute the Schlieffen Plan properly – for he initiated a version of it which required all of Germany's military force, but with only 80 per cent of it available because the rest had been sent east to mount a defence against an anticipated Russian invasion. And this led to the stalemate of the trenches, because the weakness of the Schlieffen thrust was resisted by French and British forces before it reached Paris, and Joffre's retreating armies were able to regroup behind the Marne and push the Germans back. The war then ceased to be a mobile one until the summer of 1918.

Critics of Clausewitz blamed the First World War on his theories. Basil Liddell Hart said that Britain should not have allowed itself to get embroiled in a war such as he took Clausewitz to have conceived it – a war of mass armies each seeking a deci- · sive battle to end a short conflict.[24]

During and after the First World War strategic thinking changed again, and dramatically, to take account of the new technological realities of mechanised and aerial warfare. The experience of bombing during the First World War persuaded military theorists that air power was to be a major part of the future of war. As a result, a great deal of thought and preparation went into this completely new subject.[25]

In Britain in 1918 the air forces of the army and navy, respectively the Royal Flying Corps and the Royal Naval Air Service, were combined into the Royal Air Force, and a dedicated Bomber Command was set up within it. The air force had grown from almost nothing at the beginning of the war to a force of 300,000 men by its end, during which time 50,000 aircraft of all military types were built. In addition to reconnaissance, bombing of enemy lines and fighter scraps, Britain underwent its first serious experience of bomber raids, delivered by Zeppelin airships in 1915 and 1916 and giant Gotha bombers in 1917. The damage and the 1500 deaths they caused were light in comparison to the massive air raids of the Second World War, especially those delivered by the Western allies on Germany and later Japan, but they were sufficient to cause a great deal of panic in the civilian population and a great deal of speculation among military theorists and governments alike.

In the decades after the war, even though air forces in most countries were being rapidly reduced in size, military theoreticians accordingly dwelt on the question of air warfare, and diplomatic initiatives among the major powers sought for international agreements limiting or even banning military use of aircraft, especially for bombing.

The first of the theoreticians, in order both of time and significance for bombing theory, had formulated his views before 1914, after he had seen just three aircraft and before he had himself flown in one. This was Giulio Douhet, an Italian officer who was put in command of a fleet of nine aircraft sent to Libya for the war against the Ottomans, and was therefore in charge when three aerial firsts were scored: the first aeroplane reconnaissance in combat conditions in October 1911, the first bombing raid on 1 November 1911, and the first aircraft shot down (by Turkish rifle fire) a week later.

Douhet was then given command of the Italian army's newly formed aviation battalion. He repeatedly asked for purpose-built bombers, but was denied them. Eventually he commissioned a bomber aircraft on his own initiative from the aero designer Gianni Caproni. Because he had done this without permission, he was relieved of his command and sent to an infantry regiment. His military career ended when he was court-martialled and imprisoned for a year for writing an article that said the Italian army was facing disaster because of its many deficiencies. (He was right; the disaster soon came, at Caparetto in 1917 where, in its worst-ever defeat, Italy's army lost 300,000 men – dead, wounded or captured.)[26]

Released from military duties, Douhet devoted himself to writing about the future of war. His book *The Command of the Air*, published in 1921, became a classic. The theory it advances was adopted, in all essentials, by RAF Bomber Command under Sir Arthur Harris's leadership in the Second World War.

The core of Douhet's thesis is that bombing should target the civilian population of an enemy state in order to break its morale, so that it will oblige its government to seek peace. Terror, material destruction and privation caused by shortages of food and other necessities are the keys. 'Take the centre of a large city and imagine what would happen among the civilian population during a single attack by a single bombing unit', Douhet wrote.

> I have no doubt that its impact on the people would be terrible . . . What civil or military authority could keep order, public services functioning, and production going under such a threat? . . . A complete breakdown of the social structure cannot but take place in a country subjected to this kind of merciless pounding from the air. The time would soon come when, to put an end to horror and suffering, the people themselves, driven by the instinct for self-preservation, would rise up and demand an end to the war.[27]

This thesis might well be called the Douhet–Trenchard thesis, for when Sir Hugh Trenchard took command of the RAF bombers in 1918, he set about building a force that would put just such a view to work. The British members of the Inter-Allied Aviation Committee indeed anticipated Douhet: '[the effect of bombing civilian targets] would be that the German government would be forced to face very considerable and constantly increasing civil pressure which might result in political disintegration'.[28] The war ended before Trenchard could implement the policy, but in thinking about how to conduct a war against Britain's traditional enemy, the French, he adhered to it: the French civilian population should be bombed in this event, he said, because 'I feel that although there would be an outcry, the French in a bombing duel would probably squeal before we did.'[29] He believed that wars would be short if civilians were bombed, and argued that this meant there would be no point in attacking industrial targets. As with Douhet, the entire focus of his thinking was the 'moral [i.e. morale] effect': 'The nation that would stand being bombed longest would win in the end ... The end of war is usually attained when one nation has been able to bring such pressure to bear on another that public opinion obliges the government to sue for peace.'[30] This further entails that it is essential to strike first, before the enemy can do the same to one's own civilians: another example of the 'cult of the offensive'.

On no known empirical grounds, Trenchard claimed that the ratio of moral to material effect created by bombing is 20:1. This supported the belief that national character is the key to answering the question 'Who would win a bombing duel?' Naturally Trenchard and most of his colleagues felt that this gave the British an advantage over any possible Continental adversaries, not just the French. One senior British officer claimed that in the First World War 'casualties affected the French more than they did the British. That would have to be taken into consideration too, but the policy of hitting the French nation and making them squeal before we did is a vital one – more vital than anything else.' The assumption underlying such views was sometimes expressed in openly racist terms; J. F. C. Fuller claimed that the people who panicked most during Gotha raids on London in 1917 were 'East End Jews'. In the 1920s the ease with which Iraqi and Afghani tribesmen were kept in order by British bombing seemed to confirm the efficacy of bombs when dropped on those who 'lacked moral fibre' – a failing universally attributed by the British to those they colonised. Notably, Arthur Harris served in the Middle East in command of a bomber force at that time, and his Douhet–Trenchard outlook was shaped by the experience.[31]

During the 1920s the RAF was striving to keep its existence separate from the Royal Navy and the Army, both of which were trying to reassimilate it. Trenchard, now chief of the RAF, needed arguments to persuade the government to keep as a separate force what had been reduced, for economic reasons, from being the world's largest air power to a few squadrons. The bombing argument was crucial to his case. Trenchard had powerful support from the military historian Liddell Hart, who argued in 1925 that bombing would make wars shorter and cheaper, and would save lives overall: 'When it is realised that [strategic bombing would inflict] a total of injury far less than when [a war is] spread over a number of years, the common sense of mankind will show that the ethical objection to this form of war is at least not greater than to the cannon-fodder wars of the past.'[32] He even claimed that a war would end all the more quickly with fewer lives lost if gas were used: 'gas may well prove the salvation of civilisation from the otherwise inevitable collapse in the case of another world war'.[33] His view implied that the threat of gas attacks from the air might prevent war altogether – an argument standardly deployed by those in favour of nuclear deterrence.

Trenchard was so impressed by these views that he had Liddell Hart's book sent to all his senior colleagues and the newly founded RAF staff college at Andover. Liddell Hart himself, however, later completely changed his mind; in 1942, after experiencing the effects of bombing, he wrote:

It will be ironical if the defenders of civilisation depend for victory upon the most barbaric, and unskilled, way of winning a war that the modern world has seen . . . We are now counting for victory on success in the way of degrading war to a new level – as represented by indiscriminate (night) bombing and indiscriminate starvation.[34]

By 1928 Trenchard found it expedient to modify at least the expression of his views, because doubts were arising about the ethics of the bombing weapon. In a memo to his fellow service chiefs he conceded that it is 'contrary to the dictates of humanity [to carry out] the indiscriminate bombing of a city for the sole purpose of terrorising the civilian population'. But he maintained that it was legitimate to target the morale of munitions workers and stevedores loading military supplies. Why should the maker of a gun be less a target than one who fired it? 'Moral effect is created by bombing in such circumstances but it is the inevitable result of a lawful operation of war – the bombing of a military objective.'[35] In these words was developed the official fig leaf that throughout the Second World War was used to justify 'area bombing', that is, indiscriminate bombing of civilian populations. It does, however, raise a legitimate question: what is a 'military objective'? In a modern war, the armaments factory is on the front line; are not the workers, their homes and families, those who supply them with bread and milk, on the front line too?

The British government took their military theoreticians seriously on the question of the effects of bombing. In 1939 the following preparations were made for London: it was estimated that there would be 250,000 dead in the first three weeks of bomber attacks, with 3 to 4 million refugees flooding into the surrounding countryside. It predicted 3 million psychiatric cases caused by terror. It estimated that 50 per cent of London would be destroyed in those first three weeks. The mathematicians had been busy too, calculating the number of casualties per ton of bombs dropped; they estimated a monthly need for 2.8 million hospital beds and 20 million square feet of coffin timber. As part of these preparations the Ministry of Health, bureaucrats to the last, printed an extra million death certificates for distribution to local authorities.[36]

The British government was convinced not just by the theoreticians' words, but by empirical evidence from places of conflict. The Italians bombed Addis Ababa in 1936; in 1937 the Japanese bombed Nanjing and the German Condor legion in Spain bombed Guernica. In the attack on Guernica 1,000 people were killed and 70 per cent of the town destroyed. Spain was close to home, so deep shock was caused by eye-witness accounts of screaming Stuka dive-bombers unleashing a mayhem of thunder, fire and death with bombs, and machine-gunning people as they ran into surrounding fields. The Nanjing atrocities – vastly greater but on the far side of the world and ignorable as a quarrel between Orientals – had nowhere near the same impact. But, as another report of the devastation of air power, it increased fears everywhere. The fact that these attacks occurred in 'ideal bombing conditions' – no air defence, in broad daylight – made no difference. The bodies and the ruins spoke too loudly for sceptical voices to be audible.

In response, the British government decided to strengthen fighter defences against bomber attack. Plans were afoot at the same time for a bomber force, including the heavy four-engined bombers that came into service later, when Sir Arthur Harris was chief of Bomber Command, which officially came into existence with that name in 1936. But the urgent need for fighter aircraft pushed bomber development into second place. Moreover, at that time Bomber Command's directive stated that it existed only to provide tactical army support and to mount attacks on enemy airfields, not to be a Douhet-style anti-morale weapon. Its orders were 'to do nothing that might be construed as an attack on civilians and so to give the enemy an excuse to do likewise'.[37] The motive was not ethics but anxiety at the thought of retaliation.

So great was the desire not to provoke enemy bombing attacks that a subcommittee of the Committee on Imperial Defence was convened to examine the bombing question, and it suggested that a public offer should be made to Germany to refrain from bombing its industrial Ruhr region, and likewise to refrain from imposing a naval blockade which, as in the First World War, would cause hardships to German civilians, in the hope that Germany would reciprocate with restraint in the matter of bombing.

American thinking about air power was different. Its aim was also to cause an enemy collapse, but not by direct attacks on civilians. It focused instead on the targeting of key nodes of the enemy economy, to disrupt supplies required by the population, and therefore undermine their willingness to keep supporting the war effort. The theory was devised by officers at America's leading air academy, the Air Corps Tactical School (ACTS).

The premise of this theory was that the economic functioning of a state at war would be vulnerable to a relatively small number of bombers dropping a relatively small tonnage of bombs on carefully selected targets, snapping vital threads in its 'industrial web'. The principal objectives would be electricity, transport and oil. Failure in their supply would quickly cause civilian distress; the belief was that an enemy would surrender within six months if just fifty-four such key targets were destroyed. The plan's architects recognised that the strategy required accurate bombing, and accurate bombing required control of the air, so it specified aircraft factories, and sources of raw materials for aircraft manufacture such as aluminium and magnesium, as supplementary targets.

The belief supporting this view was that popular will is what sustains a war effort, and that therefore:

> The ultimate object of all military operations . . . is to destroy the will of the people at home . . . the loss of the morale in the civilian population is far more conclusive than the defeat of the soldier on the battlefield . . . Air forces are capable of immediate employment towards accomplishing the ultimate aim. They can be used directly to break down the will of the mass of the enemy people.[38]

Another ACTS lecture described the 'industrial web' thesis:

> Modern warfare places an enormous load upon the economic system of a nation, which increases its sensitivity to attack many-fold. Certainly a breakdown in any part of this complex, interlocked organisation must seriously influence the conduct of war by that nation, and greatly interfere with the social welfare and morale of its nationals.

The audience is asked to consider what would happen if 'section after section of our [the US] great industrial system [ceased] to produce all those numberless articles which are essential to life as we know it'.[39] A third lecture suggested another example: if

New York's water supplies were interrupted, the city would soon have to be evacuated because of thirst, the danger of fire and the failure of sanitation. If bombs destroyed railway bridges, food shortages would quickly follow and make the city 'untenable'. If power stations were destroyed the resulting lack of electricity 'would cause refrigerated food to spoil'.[40]

Given what people can bear in real as opposed to imagined wartime conditions, it is clear that the unwitting premise of those last remarks is that what would bring a quick end to a war is a population's effeteness, its inability to do without refrigerators and plumbed sanitation. The lecturer seems to have forgotten completely that the majority of his fellow human beings elsewhere in the world lived permanently without either refrigerators or indoor plumbing. As bombed civilians of the Second World War everywhere proved, human beings are – short of an atom bomb attack, which is the only form of bombing that definitively works – much hardier than these theoreticians allowed.[41]

Such arguments were not alone in persuading the US government to produce a bomber arm. They also had the memory of a practical demonstration given by the United States' first and most enthusiastic proponent of bomber war, General William 'Billy' Mitchell. In 1921 he sank six surplus-to-requirement warships from the air in a demonstration that radically influenced US thinking about air power thereafter.[42] Mitchell was later court martialled and cashiered because of intemperate remarks he made about colleagues who disagreed with him. But by that time the Air Corps Tactical School was producing air theorists of its own, who had arguments that Washington's War Department could not ignore.

Received wisdom in the United States was that America was so far from potential major enemies that it was safe from bombing. The only risk it faced was from an enemy navy. Air power theoreticians argued that bombers, as Mitchell had shown, were the surest defence against enemy navies. This entailed the need for precision bombing. The US Army Air Force (USAAF) accordingly developed one of the first accurate bombsights, the Norden sight, and was so jealous of it that it refused to share it even with allies. Happily for the air theorists, enemy ships and 'industrial web' targets require the same bombing precision, so they could offer Washington a persuasive twin-track case.[43]

And that was key. The constrained economic conditions in 1930s America made the idea of 'selective attack' attractive because it was relatively cheap. Moreover liberal sentiment in Roosevelt's United States would not easily tolerate 'mass slaughter of civilians'. The generals who commanded the American air endeavour in Europe in the 1940s, H. H. 'Hap' Arnold and Ira Eaker, stated in their jointly authored book *Winged Warfare* – published just months before American entry into the war – 'Human beings are not priority targets except in special situations. Bombers in far larger numbers than are available today will be required for wiping out people in sufficient numbers by aerial bombardment to break the will of a whole nation.'[44]

The Army-Navy Board of the US government's War Department in Washington was sceptical about the airmen's claim that bombing could bring victory by itself. In a report to the president it asserted instead that 'only land armies can finally win wars'. So it assigned the USAAF a lesser role, that of supporting ground and sea forces by gaining air superiority, weakening the effectiveness of the enemy forces, reducing the capacity of the enemy economy and (at the bottom of the list) undermining civilian morale. This meant that American air units remained under the operational control of land forces, which the American fliers had hoped to escape. By mid-1943, however, they had gained their independence.

When the USAAF arrived in Britain their plans encountered reality. European weather – low cloud, rain, patchy mist, dense fog, hazy days, abrupt and unpredictable alterations between sunshine and showers – would by itself have made precision daylight bombing difficult, but there was the additional and infinitely worse nuisance of enemy anti-aircraft guns and fighter planes. The Norden bombsight required a long, straight, steady run of many miles with the bomb-aimer in clear visual command of his target, extremely hard to achieve in European weather and war conditions. So although American bombers were meant to attack military and industrial targets only, and to avoid civilian casualties, any city with a population exceeding 50,000 came to be regarded as a legitimate target because likely to contain military and industrial assets. As a result the USAAF not only carpet-bombed by default when 'blind bombing' (through cloud, at targets picked out by radar), but even when they could see what they were doing. The Americans' increasing acceptance of this tactic over Europe reached its logical conclusion in Curtis LeMay's XXI Bomber Command campaign over Japan.[45] Even here efforts were made to justify area bombing as targeting war production. Claiming that Japanese military manufacturing was carried out as a cottage industry, with components of equipment being manufactured in the civilians' small wooden houses, LeMay said after the firebombing of Tokyo on 9–10 March 1945, 'There are no innocent civilians . . . The entire population got into the act and worked to make those aeroplanes or munitions . . . men, women, and children.'

None of this theory or practice had been taking place in a vacuum. Efforts had been made at the Hague Conferences of

1899 and 1907 to outlaw bombardment from the air (in 1899, before heavier-than-air flight, conference delegates were thinking of bombs flung from balloons; Zeppelins proved this concept). These attempts to prevent the sky turning into another theatre of war intensified after it had already become so. Sir Edward Grey, British Foreign Secretary from 1905 to 1916, believed the accumulation of armaments by all powers in the years before 1914 was a major cause of the war.[46] The fourth of Woodrow Wilson's Fourteen Points stressed the need to limit armaments. Throughout the interwar years efforts were indeed made to limit weapons of all kinds, including air power.

Some success in reducing navies was reached in 1922, and, if only rhetorically, it was an important moment when the Kellogg–Briand Pact of 1928 renounced war as an instrument of policy.[47] The Clausewitzian allusion is unmistakable. But the question of air power proved more difficult to resolve. An effort to devise rules for air war was made at the Hague conference of 1922–23. Britain, France, the USA, Italy and Japan took part, neither Germany nor Russia being in a position to attend. Articles were drafted but never signed, nevertheless showing a clear understanding of the bombing threat.

Failure on this and all peace fronts prompted the League of Nations to call a conference of all its members to discuss disarmament – or, more modestly, arms control. A preparatory commission sat from 1925 to 1932 trying to find a basis for discussion. When the plenary conference began in February 1932 there was general agreement among the attending powers that air attacks on civilians were a violation of fundamental principles. But political realities quickly baulked further progress. France did not wish to limit its forces, fearing Germany. Germany said that unless all other parties disarmed to its own level as required by the Treaty of Versailles, it would take itself to be justified in rearming until equal to the other powers. During one of the conference's many adjournments Hitler came to power, and withdrew Germany from the conference. The conference was abandoned in 1937.

When the conference began, with calls from various countries for abolishing submarines and for limiting battleship firepower, Italy and Japan called for the outlawing of aerial bombardment. France wanted bombing to be forbidden beyond a radius of a given number of miles from front lines – which assumed that there would be front lines, as in 1914–18 – but the British were determined that there should be no repeat of trench warfare. Both Britain and, more modestly, France had far-flung empires, parts of which needed occasional bombing in the interests of policing, so neither wanted an outright ban. The conference contemplated banning offensive weaponry but permitting defensive weapons, only to realise that what counted as either was of course a matter of perspective: submarines for Germany were defences against British naval blockades, while for the British they were offensive weapons threatening Britain's sea trade. Bombs invited the same dilemma.

At one point it was suggested that flight itself should be banned altogether, since even civilian aeroplanes could be used to drop bombs. The former British prime minister Stanley Baldwin was profoundly anxious about bombing. He though it threatened the destruction of civilisation and a radical proposal was needed to deal with it. He suggested 'the total abolition of all military aviation'.[48] Sir Anthony Eden, after replacing him as representative at the conference, instead suggested strict limitations on when bombing would be permissible, and anyway a prohibition against bombing civilians. The RAF suspected that

Eden desired a complete ban; the RAF chief, Sir John Salmond, wrote to him with 'deep misgivings' about the British proposals, saying that in circumstances where a country is fighting for its life it would be 'inconceivable' that it would not use bombing to defend itself. Although Salmond was opposed to bombing civilians – 'no military advantage is likely to accrue to a country which employs its bombing aircraft to terrorise rather than to disarm its opponent', he wrote, he insisted that bombing was a necessary weapon, and that British efforts at the conference should go instead to defining what a 'military target' is, for without a definition belligerents would resort to indiscriminate bombing.[49]

Disillusioned by the conference's lack of progress, Stanley Baldwin made a famous speech on 10 November 1932: 'The bomber', he said, 'will always get through . . . The only defence is offence. You have to kill more women and children more quickly than the enemy if you want to save yourselves.'[50] These remarks offended the RAF, who felt themselves accused of wishing to bomb women and children, whereas – so its leaders adamantly believed – bombing would make wars shorter and therefore less costly in life overall, and the threat of it might even perhaps deter war altogether.

In the event bombing only proved really effective in the form of atom bombing, involving complete devastation of everything within the range of its effects, and with years of lingering problems for recovery afterwards. All those who had theorised and worried about the effects of bombing were right – but only for this extreme case. The same applies to the deterrence effect: only the threat of this degree and kind of destruction is (has so far been) a disincentive to war between parties equipped with nuclear weapons. This is 'MAD' – the wonderful acronym for 'mutually assured destruction'. Thus the one, sole, single vindication there has ever been to date for the bombing theorists' views is the USA's atom bomb assault on Japan. Bombing of less effect never fulfilled the theorists' predictions, whether of hope or fear: the Second World War proved that point conclusively.

The threat of MAD aside, in the industrial age both the practice and theory of war has diverged widely from preceding theory and practice. Linkages have been readily drawn between modernism in art and architecture, the 'machine aesthetic' and technology, Fascism and National Socialism, and conceptions of mechanised warfare – the tank, the aeroplane, the submarine, advanced battlefield weaponry, the technologies of radar and navigation, jet aircraft, missiles, atom bombs. Note that all these things were in existence and in play before the first half of the twentieth century was over.[51] But to begin with, the idea of the machine at war was intended to provide hope for a way out of the twentieth century's opening experience.

The horror of the First World War gave the first impetus to a determination to avoid the attritional stalemate of static trench warfare, and – much more importantly – to reject the nineteenth-century belief in all-out war, aimed at achieving swift victory in decisive battle by a nation at arms employing the tactic of massed attack. This was the doctrine of those who admired Napoleon and who contemplated the German victories of 1866 and 1870–71. That doctrine was associated with Clausewitz, whose theories Liddell Hart and others blamed for the horrors of the First World War.

According to Liddell Hart, the only person to foresee that Clausewitzian doctrine would result in attritional stalemate was the Polish financier Jan Bloch, who recognised that modern weapons, and in particular the machine gun, would lead to deadlock. He made his prediction in a lecture delivered in 1901 to the Royal United Service Institution in London. Within months of the outbreak of hostilities in 1914 he was proved right. As Liddell Hart puts it:

> Although armies had neglected the machine-gun, the comparatively few of these weapons that were available sufficed to turn the charging lines of infantry into swathes of corpses. Flesh and blood could not stand against this grim Reaper, and the common sense of soldiers, revolting from the common non-sense of military doctrine, led them to dig themselves in the ground before they were buried in it. A trench was at least preferable to a certain grave.[52]

Liddell Hart said that generals should have studied the bloody battles of the American Civil War, for they would have seen that even worse slaughter must follow upon the refinement of armaments that had been made between 1865 and 1914 if the same battle tactics were used. But they did not in advance see 'the resisting power of entrenched machine-guns and barbed wire. And [they were] equally slow to lose their faith in the power of numbers – of human tonnage.'[53] But when they grasped the reality, they hoped that the antidote would be the tank. 'Although hampered and opposed by military conservatism, and immature in design, the new armour-carrying machine proved its power. By German confession it was the decisive military factor in the tide-turning battles of July and August 1918.'[54]

Most Army officers thought the First World War tank was a one-off ad hoc solution to a problem that would not be allowed to recur, namely, the bogging-down of infantry in trenches. Those thirty-ton behemoths, moving at two or three miles an hour – walking pace, hence accompanied by infantry – that crushed barbed war and machine-gun emplacements, and which at Cambrai in 1917 successfully surprised the German trenches whose occupants had been given no prior warning by the usual several days' artillery barrage, could now be dispensed with. But Liddell Hart, an infantry specialist, was converted to belief in the tank's future by the man who had organised the Cambrai attack, Colonel J. F. C. Fuller, especially when a lighter and much faster tank – eleven tons only, and capable of more than 20 mph – became available in 1923. The concept of mechanical warfare had come into its own. So far as tanks were concerned, the Panzer divisions of the Second World War illustrated their potential. Their vulnerability was fuel: when in February and March 1945 over a thousand Wehrmacht tanks massed on the Baranov bridge-head on the Vistula in an effort to stem the Russian advance, they were immobilised for lack of fuel, and were overrun.

What the faster tank reintroduced was armoured mobility, which had been lacking since 'gunpowder and his own stupidity had finally deprived the mounted mail-clad knight of his para-mount position', and since cavalry had encountered the breech-loading rifle.[55] Army thinking was soon converted to the idea of mechanised war-making, and in 1929 the British War Office 'raised a landmark in the history of armies by issuing the first official manual of mechanised war'.[56]

Early ideas about tanks and their use were as primitive as the tanks themselves. Liddell Hart thought of them as knights in armour on wheels – or, more accurately, armoured infantry on wheels, for he was especially enthusiastic about the small one-man or two-man Carden-Loyd tanks which could replace the slow-moving highly vulnerable infantryman, covering the ground much faster, not needing to stop to fire, protected by its armour, and in numbers able to surprise the enemy and disperse its defensive fire.[57]

It is clear that, just a decade after the end of the First World War, the desire to escape its form was still hampered by expectations about its manner, that is, that at some point one's soldiers would need to charge an enemy front. But it was also the immediate ancestor of the doctrine of 'manoeuvre warfare', at the other end of the spectrum from static warfare. The thinking that led to the Wehrmacht's *Blitzkrieg* tactics and the Red Army's 'Operational Manoeuvre Groups' developed before 1939.[58] Mechanised manoeuvre reached a high point in the speed and mobility provided by helicopters as used by the US military in Vietnam, Iraq and Afghanistan, offering swiftness, surprise, flexibility, the ability to locate and deliver a strike at an enemy *Schwerpunkt* or key point, and getting troops in and out of a critical location accurately and quickly. The helicopter gunship as now equipped is itself a formidable weapons platform. But as the Abrams MI tank showed in the Gulf War of 1991, where it was especially effective, and in the Iraq War beginning in 2003 – though to a lesser extent in confined urban areas and not at all in the mountainous terrain of Afghanistan – the tank remains a highly significant battlefield armament.

The new military theories passed through an intermediary stage, embodied in the 'Airland' doctrine developed by the US military when contemplating a war in Europe against the Soviet Union during the Cold War. That was a strategy still premised on the idea of a struggle between armies and air forces; the fear always was that when one side began to lose, its nuclear buttons would be pushed. But a further change in mindset was concurrently in process. This was the idea of containment, of limited war, of succeeding by economic attrition rather than battlefield attrition. Limited war ideas went hand in hand with high-technology means for conducting them: satellite spying, drones, long-range precisely targeted missiles. Containment – close to or allied with appeasement – was tried in the 1930s, and failed; but the idea has not been abandoned. Limited high-technology conflicts are current, with US military engagement at various locations in the world, and to a slightly lesser extent the post-colonial interventions that Britain and France engage in.

But the chief contemporary challenge is how to deal with asymmetrical warfare, guerrilla warfare, the kind of conflict which it is very hard for conventional military forces to win or even control, as Afghani tribesmen have demonstrated against the might of three great military powers in succession: the British in the nineteenth century, the Russians between 1979 and 1989, and the Americans since 2001.

Not all asymmetrical conflicts prove intractable. In Malaya and Kenya during the anti-colonial insurgencies of the 1950s British forces succeed by the use of drastic means, as exemplified by 'Operation Anvil' in which the Kenyan capital Nairobi was sealed off by the military and 'cleared' of all suspects, thousands being incarcerated in detention camps, and mass deportations taking place to 'reserves' in the countryside. Forests were bombed, and measures were taken to isolate Mau Mau fighters from sources of support in rural communities. In both Kenya and Malaya 'villagisation' was practised, with large populations housed in townships which were in fact detention camps writ large, surrounded by wire fences and watchtowers.

As these examples suggest, asymmetric warfare is as rich as conventional war, if not in some ways richer, in the possibilities of war crimes and human rights abuses.[59] Thinking about war in the new landscape of diverse, diffuse, non-conventional and multi-party conflicts (as in the Syrian conflicts involving competing rebel groups, Daesh, Kurds, Turks, Americans, Russians and forces loyal to Bashir Assad, all messily at odds with one another) now involves having to think even more about 'collateral damage', human rights questions, and – very acutely – the problem of post-conflict settlement. Questions also arise about the justification of military action which has a policing intention, as with the intervention in Kosovo in 1998–99, or which have irredentist ambitions, as Russia's interventions in the Crimea and Ukraine from 2014.

The complicated mixture of regional conflicts, new military technologies, the role of religion, Chinese and Russian irredentism, and the anxiety of most of the Western major powers to avoid all-out war, makes thinking about war a more complicated matter than ever. Containment and limited war, and the increasing use of technology and its devices to take the place of military personnel on or above the battlefield, is the norm at time of writing. If the first decades of the twenty-first century set a pattern, this norm appears to make conflict a chronic rather than an acute condition: the larger wars of the early twenty-first century, in Afghanistan and the Middle East, have been longer than the First and Second World Wars put together.

There is an optimistic, although paradoxical-seeming, set of considerations to add here. In the period since the beginning of modern times – that is, since the sixteenth century CE – there has been a decline in the number of wars between major powers. There were twenty-two such wars in the sixteenth century, six in the twentieth. Because of the increase in the power of weaponry, however, deaths in battle have increased dramatically in the same period. According to Levy and Thomson:

If we examine major battles, which admittedly are not representative of all wars, deaths per war more than doubled between the fifth century BCE and the fourteenth century CE, more than doubled again between the fourteenth and early nineteenth centuries CE, and then increased by as much as a factor of 10 between the early nineteenth and twentieth centuries.[60]

At the same time, on the basis of compelling empirical data Steven Pinker has shown that the number of those who have died violent premature deaths, as a percentage of population, has declined throughout history, and the decline has been steepest since the eighteenth century – the period of the Enlightenment.[61] Absolute numbers of war-related deaths have risen; the world has been growing more peaceful; these two facts are not inconsistent. But the relevant fact is that war still happens. That is an aspect of history which has not yet come to an end.

PART II

The Causes and Effects of War

CHAPTER 4

The Causes of War

The previous chapters' sketch of the history of war and of views about war-making left largely implicit the question of why those wars occurred, but entirely ignored the more general question – if it is a question at all – as to what is the cause of war: that is, why is war a pervasive and recurrent phenomenon in history?

To provide insight into why any individual war occurred, one would need a detailed historical examination of the circumstances in which it arose. In the outline given in previous chapters we only see *kinds* of reasons. They include: competition leading to conflict over resources such as territory, water, women and slaves; raiding by nomads on settled people to expropriate supplies; wars of expansion, involving conquest of territories and peoples to gain wealth, power and aggrandisement. And of course there is the other side of this coin: wars of defence against aggressors and invaders; desire for revenge or restitution, including irredentism; and religious and ideological wars. The list of reasons is various and long. As *explanations* for why any given war occurred – though they are not automatically, if indeed very often, *justifications* for that war happening – these reasons are familiar enough, and do the work of explanation adequately. Some writers add to this list, as a further and even less appetising explanation, the notion of 'love of war for its own sake', as noted in Chapter 1 in connection with the Huns, Mongols and others for whom war was a way of life and an end in itself as a central aspect of their society's economic activity. In these cases the idea of manhood might be implicated in the imperative to make war, a way of achieving status by killing an enemy.

But is there something deeper that lies behind this variety of motivations, explaining in its turn why other means are not chosen for resolving or adjusting resource questions, or achieving the ends implied in some of the above list? One obvious suggestion is that humans are, or at least the male human is, innately violent; that war-making is built into human nature. Another and very different suggestion is that the way human societies are organised is the reason why war occurs. The first suggestion is a pessimistic one, in that if war is an expression of something natural or genetic in human beings, and not, as the second more optimistic suggestion has it, an accident of the way humans do things socially and politically, then we seem to be doomed to war – and eventually to be doomed by war. The second suggestion offers a way out, for it suggests that culture or politics is the cause, and could be within the power of intelligence to change.

There is much that has been said about both suggestions and others in between. I survey these ideas as follows.

In all discussions of war there is a ready and natural association between the concept of war and the concept of violence as a human propensity. Some distinctions and questions are required here. War is of course violent: blowing up people, vehicles, buildings, whole towns and cities, and killing and injuring people – both deliberately as when opposing combatants are targeted, and unintentionally as in 'collateral damage' – are violent events. But a group of generals sitting round a planning table inspecting maps, submariners watching plots on an ASDIC screen, politicians considering military options in response to a crisis, are not behaving violently. Neither are troops loading lorries, air force personnel refuelling aeroplanes, sailors scrubbing decks. Violence occurs at the sharp end of conflict, sporadically and intensely, and a commonplace of soldiers' reminiscences is that war consists of a great deal of boredom punctuated by episodes of terror and chaos.

The trope 'war is violent' easily slides into 'war is the expression of violent propensities in human nature'. As these remarks show, much of war is calm and deliberate, boring and routine. Something like the violence of a saloon bar brawl occurs when enemies come face to face, but even when one sees footage of fighters firing on enemies from rooftops or ruined buildings, say, the violence in train is not a matter of those fighters' being in a crimson rage, of 'feeling violent' or behaving as a saloon brawler does: they are aiming deliberately, protecting themselves, working in concert with others, and whatever may be their sentiments about the enemy whom they are seeking to kill, their hatred, contempt, fear or indifference does not make them act as a saloon brawler does. Indeed it would almost certainly be fatal to them if they did so. Unquestionably, shooting to kill another human being is an act of violence. But the connection between violent feelings, rage, the need to attack, hit, gouge, bite and kick – the emotions of the saloon brawl – are far from being the apparently overriding emotions of warfare, except in hand-to-hand combat.

There is furthermore the question of trauma that the violent events of war cause in those who experience them. I deal with this in the next chapter, but it is relevant to anticipate that discussion by asking: if human beings are naturally violent, why does violence upset them, mark them, even derange them psychologically? Perhaps most people are capable of anger and aggression under provocation that is severe enough, but at the same time most people are not naturally murderous. It has been suggested that in conscript armies, such as the Kitchener armies of the First World War, only about 20 per cent of the drafted soldiers were effective – in the sense that they actually pointed their rifles at the enemy and fired to kill – and that effective soldiers had a similar psychological profile to recidivists in prison, in having scant remorse for past actions, and being little affected by the memory of occurrences which would upset most people.

These thoughts at least suggest that to locate the cause of war in the human emotional capacity for violent feelings and actions is not a straightforward matter. Ethological studies of chimpanzees show that bands of males fight each other much after the manner of a saloon bar brawl, chiefly for territorial and resource reasons.[1] As mentioned in Chapter 1, anthropological studies of stone-age tribes show that conflict for the same kinds of reasons can result in fighting, though confrontations are often gestural and symbolic rather than actual, and sometimes fighting stops as soon as blood is drawn. Both kinds of conflict are organised, both do or can involve actual violent behaviour just as when opposing soldiers fight hand-to-hand; but they do not count as *war*, for which something non-violent seems to be required, namely, an accumulation of social, material and conceptual structures that contribute to the organised and orchestrated series of events that is war as such.

The fact that this is so – that war has a major non-violent component – of course makes it worse. Cold calculation aimed at destruction and death seems even less excusable than the outburst of rage that makes someone throw a punch in a saloon bar. A significant point accordingly offers itself. This is that 'the origin of war' only partly lies in the human capacity for moving from emotions prompted by disagreement or rivalry to threats and actual fighting, for what is required in addition is a sufficient degree of relevant social organisation.

And evidently the level of organisation in question has a reciprocal relationship to war-making. War both invites and requires organisation. Societies might get organised because of the experience of conflict or danger, as a response to it or the threat of it; a society needs to get organised in advance of going to war, as preparation for it. Social organisation does not of course by itself lead to war; inducements to war in competition and rivalry, threat or interference, duties of alliance and more, are the proximate causes of individual wars. But without a pre-existing level of organisation of the relevant kind, it is not war that a state or group engages in. It might come close; it might be an insurgency or rebellion, or an act of cross-border hostility perpetrated by a non-state agency. But the level of organisation of a state or state-like agency (such as, and typically, the contending parties in a civil war) is in those cases lacking. Manufacturing weapons, training soldiers, stockpiling resources: this goes on apace in peacetime.

The suggested point therefore is this. Organisation is best done calmly. War, in being a deliberate thing, would not on this view be a straight linear descendent of human propensities to physical expressions of anger, hostility, or a natural tendency to violent behaviour. Of course, violence on the individual or small-group level, of the bar-room brawl variety, might prompt astute leaders of such groups to begin organising in order to gain an advantage over other groups, and such organisation would be the seed of the immense logistics of full-blown inter-state war. If this were right, the answer to the question, 'What is the origin of war?' would be: war originates when societies reach a degree of organisation sufficient for creating both the reasons and the capacity for warfare, which accordingly prepares them to treat certain threats, problems, needs or opportunities, as a trigger for engaging in it.

If this in turn were right, it would shift the emphasis, when we ponder the origins of war, from matters of human psychology and its frailties to other matters, and arguably to two principal ones: to questions of *competition* over topics of importance to the contending parties, and to *difference*s in culture and belief where the differences are perceived as unacceptable or threatening.

I return to these points below. Whether or not they have a place in explaining the origins of war, once war is a fact of history we see that its organisational aspects are part of the fabric of states and societies. Training of personnel; construction and mainte-nance of barracks, airfields and naval dockyards; the manufac-ture of uniforms, weapons, ammunition and other equipment; scientific and technological research for their improvement; logistical arrangements; the financing of a continual state of military preparedness and advancement of capability – all this is institutionalised, and the sheer expenditure of resource and effort thus represented carries within it the seeds of a danger, recognised by many – for example, Richard Cobden in the nine-teenth century and President Dwight D. Eisenhower in the twentieth century – that such a degree of investment in the machinery of war itself makes war more likely. It is accordingly cited as one of the precipitating causes of war – and sometimes perhaps the chief cause, as suggested in the case of 1914.

Once war is in the offing, in the approach to it and in the course of it, the question of emotion enters in a different way, and focally involves management of psychological attitudes to war on the part of soldiers and civilians. This ranges from encouragement of patriotic sentiments, the idea of *dulce et decorum est pro patria mori* ('it is sweet and right to die for one's country'), the ceremonial honouring of the dead of past wars, the theatre of uniforms and parades, the importance of regimental histories and achievements in battle, to the encouragement of feelings of hostility and revulsion towards the enemy. War would not be possible without arousing and directing hostility against others to the point of willingness to kill them, not just on the part of the military personnel who carry out the killing, but on the part of enough of the population to support and applaud the military in its endeavours, while themselves being prepared to accept various kinds of sacrifices also – such as being bombed, giving up various civil liberties for the duration of the war, accepting privations such as rationing, and dealing with the deaths of family members in the armed forces.

In this latter case, the typical manoeuvre is to collectivise the enemy as 'Other' and to invoke not just a sometimes real and sometimes imagined threat to one's own security and values, but to exaggerate the enemy's atrocities, crimes and enormities. For example, in encouraging anti-German sentiment in the First World War much was made of the execution of Edith Cavell, an English nurse in Belgium accused by the Germans of spying. But this was the least of it: claims that German soldiers skewered babies on their bayonets during episodes in which civilians were rounded up and shot in Belgium and northern France in the early months of the war, received widespread currency after publication in 1915 of *False Witness*, an account of the German invasion of those countries by Danish writer Johannes Jørgensen.[2]

The aid given by the press to the British war effort in the First World War is indeed a paradigm of this. In addition to massacres and cruelty to children (it was alleged that German soldiers mutilated children before their parents' faces by amputating their hands and slicing their ears off), great outrage was caused by the claim that a Canadian soldier had been crucified on a barn door with German bayonets through his hands and feet. Prime Minister Asquith set up a commission of enquiry under Lord Bryce, the 'Committee of Alleged German Outrages', and it duly reported in 1915 that German troops had committed civilian massacres, rape, looting, and the aforementioned barbarisms against children. Along with enraged responses to Zeppelin air raids, the sinking of the *Lusitania*, and the use of poison gas in the trenches, these demonisations prompted outrage in the United States and other neutral states at the moral vileness of Kaiser Wilhelm's Germany.

Bad things were undoubtedly done, but the propaganda technique of encouraging pro-war sentiment in one's own country by claiming that the enemy commits atrocities is both too tempting to resist and too commonplace to ignore. Its effect is to make going to war against a supposed such enemy more acceptable, providing a moral justification and the requisite preparedness to make and accept sacrifices.

What of the suggestion that war is the outcome of a natural propensity in humans, or at least male humans? Humans are primates, indeed 'great apes', and as background it is of interest to note the nature of organised violence among fellow great apes. Note the expression 'organised violence'. Contrary to Mark Twain's assertion that *Homo sapiens* is the only species that kills its own kind, there are many animal species that do so. For example, males of various species might kill each other in rutting combat, though among ruminants it is more usual for one of the combatants to accept defeat, suffering a resultant drop in testosterone, while testosterone surges in the victor, who has a herd of females to impregnate. Male lions invariably kill the cubs in a pride when they assume control of it after ousting its previous leader; this is to bring the females into oestrus. Ant colonies fight great battles, and appear to control their own population by culling some of their own number. More robust chicks in the nest can kill other chicks to monopolise the food provided by parent birds. Rodents eat their own young when food is scarce.

Although in the case of ants there is concerted activity in fighting off invading ants, or in culling their own numbers, conspecific killing is in general individual-to-individual or parent-to-offspring. Reports of male chimpanzees forming groups to attack and kill other chimpanzees introduce a different set of questions, not least about the implications for understanding human aggression.

Anthropologists Cláudia Sousa and Catarina Casanova argue that the evidence of aggression and conflict among contemporary great apes, plus the evidence from fossil remains and ethnography, does not support the idea that early hominins were 'killer ape-like creatures'.[3] The implication is that humans are not genetically programmed to be killers either. Observation of primate communities both in captivity and the wild has led

Douglas Fry to the conclusion that co-operation, empathy, toler-
ance and impulses to reconciliation after conflict are fundamental characteristics of our closest genetic relatives, even if, as
in the case of humans too, these behaviours show an in-group
bias.[4] This conclusion emphasises features different from those
emphasised by a number of other palaeoanthropologists and
primatologists. Richard Wrangham and Dale Peterson, the latter
a colleague of Jane Goodall whose work they quote, show in
their studies of chimpanzees (*Pan troglodytes*) and bonobos
(*Pan paniscus*) that male chimpanzees murder, rape and form
gangs to commit acts of out-group aggression. Nevertheless
they temper their account of the 'demonic male' by showing
also that the social arrangements of the other *Pan* species,
bonobos, have eradicated almost all such behaviour.[5] What is at
stake in such contrasting views is the question of whether
biological theories, rooted in the concept of evolution, provide a
clue to the deepest underlying level of explanation as to why war
occurs. In the essays collected by Fry for *War, Peace and Human
Nature*, the idea that violence and war have roots in human
nature as such are questioned both by the ethological observations cited and by the paucity of palaeoanthropological and
archaeological evidence for war in pre-agricultural societies.[6]

The personal inclinations or wishes, the optimism or the
cynicism, of those examining the question undoubtedly have a
role in which features they select for emphasis. For most of the
history of thinking about war, from the Greeks to contemporary theorists, the dominant theme has been that human nature
is responsible for war. The misanthropic Hobbesian view has
prevailed because the impact of war in history makes war
salient; like mountain peaks in a landscape wars are more visible
than the years and decades of peace, in which far less of note

stands out. Religious conceptions of human nature, most notably those premised on doctrines of original sin and the fallen character of human nature, abet this view. Accordingly, one has to be alert to the fact that the culturally dominant view of human nature, in long having consisted in the pessimistic view that it contains all the darkness required to amplify greed, selfishness, cruelty and aggression into war as such, lies in the background of much of the debate.[7]

There is of course an important assumption buried in the idea that human nature is responsible for war, which is that there is such a thing as 'human nature'. Of course in one sense the characteristic features of human beings and their societies are readily enough contrasted with (say) zebras and their social arrangements, to give content to the idea that something answers to the concept of humanness. But the question is whether the putatively essential constituents of humanness are such that we can see among them the factors, if such there are, that are war-inclining ones. The problem is that theories of human nature are cultural ones, philosophical ones, and the sciences – for naturally one would look to anthropology and genetics for objective answers if they exist – do not settle the matter. The evidence pushes both ways.[8] Which way it pushes – to stress the point – might be heavily influenced by some very human prejudices and beliefs.[9]

It is, however, with the scientific debate that one does well to begin. Even those who are sceptical about direct inferences from primate studies and evolutionary theory agree that biology has something to offer the study of war and conflict in general. Two areas of debate, sociobiology and biopolitics, have been particularly active, made all the more urgent now that war, in the extreme – to which it could alas rapidly escalate in various plausible scenarios – threatens the human species itself. Sociobiology owes itself to E. O. Wilson in his influential 1975 book of that name; the idea of biopolitics has an even earlier origin in Thomas Landon Thorson's 1970 book, also titled for its concept.[10] But both strands of thought in turn have their roots in the application of Darwinian ideas to social and psychological explanation, put forward almost immediately after Darwin's own seminal publications in the second half of the nineteenth century, and thereafter developed and, notably, parlayed into unattractive and not infrequently dangerous theories about race and eugenics.

The first application – or misapplication, as it is widely recognised – of Darwin's views was to social and economic questions. The 'Social Darwinists' of the nineteenth century used the phrase coined by Herbert Spencer, 'survival of the fittest', to justify their claim that the capitalist class system of their own day was the best one because it was the adaptive outcome of a struggle that eliminated less fit social and economic orders.[11] It was inevitable that evolutionary ideas would very soon be used to justify ideas about the superiority of 'Caucasians' over the 'Mongoloid' and 'Negroid' races, and further still – and therefore – to justify ideas and even actual programmes (as in Nazi Germany) of eugenics to promote 'superior' human stock while eliminating 'inferior' stock.

A principal influence on theories of eugenics was the man who coined the word 'eugenics' itself, Francis Galton. He was Darwin's cousin, and was profoundly influenced by him, especially by his remarks early in *The Origin of Species* about 'variation under domestication', that is, selective breeding of dogs, horses and cattle. Galton instantly saw the application to human beings. He was a polymath, explorer, and innovator in mathematics as well as social anthropology. His studies of heredity and statistics together led him to formulate the concept of genetic 'regression to the mean'. He argued that high-born people should be incentivised to have many children early in adulthood, for they tended to marry late and have few children, which he regarded as dysgenic. Under his influence a Eugenics Education Society was founded to encourage eugenic breeding and to discourage 'inferior' people from having children. From 1909 onwards it published a journal, the *Eugenics Review*.[12]

The excesses of Nazi eugenics programmes, which involved sterilising or simply killing the 'unfit', so regarded either on racial or disability grounds, were the logical extension of such practices as the US restriction on immigration after the First World War of Slavs and Jews on the grounds of their supposed racial inferiority.[13]

Advances in genetics inspired a spate of popular books in the 1960s arguing that those aspects of human behaviour that so often led to war – competitiveness, aggression and territoriality – were biologically programmed. The most widely read of them were by Konrad Lorenz, Desmond Morris, Robert Ardrey and Lionel Tiger.[14] Collectively they asserted the view that humans, or at least human males, are innately programmed to use aggression and violence – and by extension therefore, war – in furtherance of the ends of territoriality and competition. The idea appears to be a completely natural inference from the fact, for fact it is, that in the animal world generally many, if not all, aspects of behaviour are genetically determined: mating displays and competition, female nurturing of newborns, guarding of territory, feeding patterns, and the rest. Sociobiology had begun as an extension of ethology – the study of animal behaviour – to incorporate insights from biology in the explanation of that behaviour; this was simply a matter of bringing humans into the same explanatory framework. The tendentious point is easy to identify. E. O. Wilson explicitly subordinated cultural factors to genetic ones; culture, he said, is 'held on a leash' by genes, and is in fact 'a circuitous technique by which human genetic material has been and will be kept intact'.[15] The similarity to Richard Dawkins' *Selfish Gene* thesis – though in other respects these two evolutionary biologists disagree about much – is closer than Wilson elsewhere allows.[16]

The first problem for views of this kind is how they can explain altruism. It is a datum that people sacrifice their own interests and even themselves for others; this is a commonplace of human experience. Darwin was conscious of the difficulty, and as a result of pondering the question why bees have evolved to die when they deliver a sting in defence of the hive, concluded that what mattered was the hive as a whole, which benefited from the individual's sacrifice. This later came to be understood in terms of the gene pool, and different terms were coined to capture the idea; 'kin selection' by John Maynard Smith and 'inclusive fitness' by W. D. Hamilton.[17] Wilson himself thought that there were several strata of levels at which selective pressures have their effect, from the gene up to populations and even ecosystems. He argued that altruism is mainly determined by cultural factors, which themselves have evolved as a result of kin selection, and that kin selection is the ultimate explanation for war: 'The force behind most warlike policies is ethnocentrism,' he wrote:

> warfare evolved by selective retention of traits that increase the inclusive genetic fitness of human beings . . . [who are] strongly predisposed to respond with unreasoning hatred to external threats and to escalate their hostility . . . We tend to fear deeply the actions of strangers and to solve conflict by aggression'.

Wilson also held that we have a genetic predisposition to learn communal forms of aggressive behaviour, which in its fullest form is war.[18]

Leaving aside the strenuous disagreement between biologists over the concept of 'group selection' now favoured by Wilson, is anything like the view just described right? On the face of it, it appears plausible to see humans as social animals wired to be co-operative with fellow in-group members and aggressive towards out-groups.[19] But for all the surface plausibility, the idea faces objections from a range of sources, in science, social science, ethics and politics. The most obvious is a rebuttal drawn from the very point just invoked, about humans as social animals. This implies that the genetic determination of human behaviour is towards co-operation, not aggression. In all societies and for the greatest part of the time, most people – including most males – do not engage in violent behaviour, still less in warfare; and even most of those who take part in warfare are more likely to be followers rather than fighters, 'sheep not wolves'.[20] Visible all around us are the evidences of co-operation and trust-keeping, in the cities and systems, cultures and institutions built by the social impulses of human beings. In comparison to the normal forms of interaction between people every minute of every day everywhere in the world, war and even lesser forms of violence constitute a minority occupation.[21]

Nevertheless, wars happen often enough, so if a propensity to war is not genetically determined, why does it happen? The answer offered by the non-determinists is: culture. In just the same way as cultural development has resulted in many co-operative behaviours of a positive kind – science, art, literature, music, education, noble aspirations and acts – so circumstances can prompt culture to negative outcomes – disagreement, hostility and conflict prompted by tribal, national, cultural and ideological differences, leading to the organisation of means to give effect to that hostility in war. No aspect of social behaviour has been reliably identified with any specific set of genes, so the inheritance of social structures and memes must occur through cultural transmission.[22] Campbell talks of 'sociocultural evolution', in which altruism and its extreme in self-sacrifice, 'including especially the willingness to risk death in warfare, are, in man, a product of social indoctrination counter to rather than supported by genetically transmitted behavioural dispositions'.[23] The genetically transmitted dispositions would predispose to self-preservation, a powerful instinct with an obvious adaptive utility in evolutionary terms, and might accordingly support the idea that because genetics would select for self-interested behaviour, the opposite – altruistic behaviour – must be culturally acquired.

The idea that culture can override genetic predispositions can be supported biologically, so its ability to do this – even indeed its existence – does not have to seek support from anything non-biological as its source. Large brains, high intelligence, long childhoods and language more than adequately explain both the fact of culture, the diversity within it, and the changes that culture and cultures historically undergo. No other species compares. And this includes maladaptive as well as positive aspects. Indeed the idea that humans can both value truth and tell lies suggests a single underlying basis for both: intelligence.

Further, it has been argued that there is no basis for treating the idea of kin selection as the explanation for in-group loyalty and out-group hostility. This would only be plausible if humans were fragmented into genetic subgroups within which there had evolved kin-preferring behaviours specific to that group; but there are no human genetic subgroups. 'Race' is a fiction, all human beings are closely related genetically, and superficial differences in skin tone, hair type and eye shape are of recent origin in the human story.[24] Ethnic differences exist, of course, given obvious cultural variations in language, religion, customs and food preferences. But ethnicity is not race.[25] On this view it is a function of ethnic identification to prefer and privilege one's own tribe or nation over others, not a matter of genetic propinquity.

Arguments for and against the idea that war is a product of kinship in fact predate genetic theory. The sociologist Ludwig Gumplowicz argued in his briefly influential 1885 work *Der Rassenkampf* (*The Struggle of the Races*) that there will always be contest and conflict between groups or races until one subjugates the other. A 'folk-state' or nation, once it has achieved internal homogeneity, will 'naturally' seek to conquer neighbouring nations, he claimed: 'Conquest and the satisfaction of needs through the labor of the conquered, essentially the same though differing in form, is the great theme of human history from prehistoric times . . . It cannot be otherwise, since man's material need is the prime motive of his conduct.' A follower of his, Gustav Ratzenhofer, summed up the most extreme form of the theory in two sentences: 'The contact of two hordes produces rage and terror. They throw themselves upon one another in a fight to exterminate, or else they avoid contact.'[26]

Racialist theory of this kind is polygenist, and it is the polygenism that is taken to explain the natural antipathy that occurs when different 'hordes' (races, thus putative separate genetic groups) meet. In their day these theories were novel and appeared to have the force of science behind them. But they were criticised by contemporaries nevertheless. I. A. Novikow wrote:

> It was [formerly] believed that men fought their fellows in order to obtain food, women, wealth, the profits derived from the possession of the government, or in order to impose a religion or a type of culture. In all these circumstances war is a means to an end. The new theorists proclaim that this is all wrong. Men must of necessity massacre one another because of polygeny. Savage carnage is a law of nature, operating through *fatality*.[27]

Here 'fatality' means (natural, genetic) determinism.

Novikow offered two counters to such a view. First, until his own recent times there had been no race wars because people did not have the concept of race and accordingly did not perceive themselves as racially different from others or as fighting against a different race. Second, people of the same race fight each other: Swedes, Danes and Germans are all Teutons but have battled each other fiercely at times, while some very different peoples, for example the Welsh and the Tehuelche of Patagonia, get along very well.[28] These observations refute the Gumplowicz theory at a blow.

Paradoxically, the idea of kinship actually contains the germ of a powerful argument *against* the idea that conflict and war have a genetic basis, namely, that the development of society has occurred because people have transcended ethnic boundaries to include others in the sphere of moral interest and concern. Moreover, most states that have gone to war with each other in the past two millennia have been highly genetically mixed; it would seem that loyalty to the community rather than actual genetic kinship is the chief factor in play. Once again, that makes genetic factors subordinate to cultural ones.[29]

A final thought is that if fighting and war are genetically determined, they would be adaptive evolutionarily. Another way of putting this is to say that they would be observably rational and productive from the point of view of the species and its members' reproductive chances. It is not clear that they are either of these things always or even most of the time.

Some critics of sociobiology see it as the political inheritor of the Social Darwinist mantle in at least the sense that it justifies the status quo in society, supports stereotypes of (for example) male and female behaviour, and provides grounds for differential value judgements about (for example) white and black people. One of the sharpest critics of genetic behavioural determinism is the evolutionary biologist Richard Lewontin, who sees the tendency of sociobiological theory as politically conservative.[30] Genetically underpinned conservativism is in essence pessimistic, implying that what happens is not within the control of human thought and choice, and that therefore it has to happen because we are programmed for it.

But manifestly, matters are otherwise. Take the case of ethical and political views: the treatment of animals, the social status of women, attitudes to people with sexualities that fall outside the narrow conventional heterosexual model, have all changed significantly as a result of ethical reflection; and the growth of more democratic forms of government in many polities, and with them respect for human rights and civil liberties, has largely displaced monarchy, aristocracy, feudal systems and forms of tyranny. If genetic determinism ruled human behaviour it is hard to see how cultural evolution could take place, but it obviously does. This would seem to imply that war is a cultural, not a genetic, phenomenon, and is or at least should be under the control of human choice. And this in turn would mean that there is a genuine possibility of removing war from human interaction.

If war is a cultural artefact, why and in what way is it? On the principle that 'if your tool is a hammer everything looks like a nail' we have just seen that psychologists and biologists seek the causes of war in psychology and biology; now we can expect that economists will see war's causes as economic, while political theorists will see them as political. And so indeed they do. But the 'hammer' observation does not entail that any of these approaches is wrong. The right immediate inference to draw is that the explanation is unlikely to lie wholly within just one of them. After all, the drivers of economic activity are psychological; psychology, in turn, is biologically based, and economic activity involves political debate and decision, so the picture is sure to be complex. Nevertheless, examining the question from the point of view of sociology and anthropology – from the point of view of culture – is a more inclusive vantage point, not least because it bears on the question of human nature more informatively.

One prompt for the idea that war is a product of culture is that the evidence suggests it entered human history only about 10,000 years ago, along with settlement and agriculture. If war were a genetically encoded behaviour, so the argument goes, there would be palaeoanthropological and archaeological evidence for it from long beforehand.[31] Moreover changes in social and political conditions have seen changes in the frequency and kinds of war, with smaller percentages of populations taking part in them and dying in them over time, which is another reason for thinking that culture determines whether and how war happens.

A point of contention arises here, between those who hold that war entered history with culture and those, such as Steven Pinker, who say that the numbers of those who have died violent premature deaths in war have declined over time as percentages of populations.[32] This is because the former resist the implications of the view that war was more frequent in earlier periods. In fact evidence of the historical decline in war deaths is more than consistent with the cultural hypothesis; cultural factors are here being seen to act as much against war as in other periods or circumstances it acts for it. Where the disagreement between R. Brian Ferguson and Pinker lies is in the matter of whether war as such predated the rise of culture.[33] On the evidence of the case assembled by Ferguson, war would indeed seem to be a feature of humanity's latest 10,000 years, and practically absent beforehand.

There is an added and even more compelling point in favour of this view in the argument that, for 99 per cent of the 2 million years that a 'recognisable human animal' has existed, that animal was a hunter-gatherer, and therefore anthropological data from hunter-gatherer societies is centrally relevant to the question.[34] And indeed the data are convincing: nearly a dozen forager societies studied variously in Malaysia, Tanzania, Australia and southern India are peaceable, anti-aggressive, compassionate, co-operative and generous, with very low rates of conflict and homicide. When problems occur, typically caused by sexual jealousy or theft, they are mediated and resolved by discussion.[35] These data relate to intragroup relations; much the same appears to be the case with intergroup relations among foraging peoples.[36]

Another consideration to bear in mind in preferring a cultural approach, when remembering the 'everything is a nail to a hammer' point, is that if we were to take just one field of enquiry as constituting the *main* explanatory resource, we must be careful not to miss anything of importance that the radar of that theory is not calibrated to register. For example, until recently, political theorists tended to focus on interstate conflict when debating the causes of war, but it has been argued that civil war is more common than interstate war in history, and that civil wars, as is also the case for tribal, ethnic and colonial wars, have causes different from interstate wars, even if there are some commonalities too.

Moreover, some civil wars have become 'internationalised' by the intervention of other, and sometimes major, parties; and regional wars have sometimes been proxy wars for larger powers; and both these phenomena are characteristic of most conflicts in south and west Asia and the Middle East since the Second World War. So it is no longer possible even to see civil and inter-state wars separately in unmixed fashion. The international and the internecine scenes are both messy, and too often merge into just one even messier scene, as in the case of Syria following the 'Arab Spring' of 2010–11. The danger is that a local, perhaps internal, conflict might become internationalised in its locality, only to then explode into a major international conflict well beyond that locality, even at worst into another world war. One thinks of the Balkans in the period 1912–14. Given the state of the world's arsenals and what they contain, such developments threaten disaster on an unprecedented and perhaps terminal scale.

The moral when thinking about what causes war is that one has to be alert to the types of conflict under discussion, and their interactions, and that the likelihood is that this will change the nature of the question from 'What is the cause of war?' to 'What are the causes of war?', where this latter still treats 'war' as a sufficiently unitary phenomenon in human affairs to require a general explanation, but which recognises that the causes of any given war are a permutation of a number of factors out of a larger number of war-causing factors. This also accordingly means that the question is still not the same as 'What are the causes of this and that particular war?', for that question has to be asked about each war on its own merits, whether or not there is an answer to the general question 'What are the causes of war?'

If this general question has no general answer of the form 'The causes of war are . . .' then there are two possibilities. Either each war will be *sui generis*, with its own unique causes that are different from all other wars. Or it might turn out that one can only venture answers to the question why *types* of war happen, where the causes are specific to the types. And now one can see why the general question still presses: in either case men (almost always men) will equip themselves with instruments capable of causing death, and will go out to slay men on the other side, and to impose themselves on the survivors in one or another way. The question really is, why is *war* the resource fallen back upon when other means of adjusting differences or conflicts have failed? And maybe the real question then is: why do those other means fail? It is easy to see, from this point in the process of getting the question right, why even on a cultural approach considerations from psychological and biological theories might come back into focus.

In the Introduction to this book, war was defined as 'a state of armed conflict between states or nations, or between identified and organised groups of significant size and character'. The second half of the definition is designed to take account of the fact that non-state actors can be parties to war, and that war predates the existence of states as such – indeed, by a long way. It might be better to expand the definition to substitute 'political entity' for 'state', if 'political' is understood in the broadest sense to embrace almost any organised grouping of people. The parties to a war are always groups, not individuals, and moreover groups with cohesion, a common purpose, leadership, division of responsibilities, and a sharing of hardships and, if they come, benefits. One might not think of the Huns as a state, but they were a political entity in the foregoing sense, and the sustained periods of fighting between them and those they attacked, not least the Romans, cannot be described other than as war.

Clausewitz took the paradigm of war to be interstate war because that is where the political nature of what is at stake is clearest. In such wars there is a measure of symmetry, in that contending states have similar forces with similar weapons, and the state itself monopolises in its own interests the sanctioned use of force that can be applied internally and externally. The wars in the two centuries preceding Clausewitz's writing of *On War* (1832) fitted this model. The point of the (over-quoted) definition of war that he premised on this model, that war is 'an extension of politics by other means', is well illustrated by an exchange between an American colonel and a Vietcong colonel after the Vietnam War, in which the United States was defeated. The former said to the latter, 'Your side never beat us on the battlefield,' to which the latter replied, 'True but irrelevant.' It was the political result alone that counted.[37]

In the last chapter it was noted that major wars have become less frequent over the last five centuries, though their lethality has increased dramatically. In the last five centuries almost all the major wars were fought in Europe, then the dominant quarter of the world whose states were expanding their reach both locally and globally, and therefore contesting one another. Since 1945 the former Yugoslavia, Georgia and the eastern Ukraine have seen hostilities, but Europe has been free of war until this time of writing, in major part because of the European Union, whereas elsewhere in the world civil wars have proliferated in the aftermath of decolonisation, and a combination of great power intervention and sectarian strife has precipitated the Middle East and west Asia (Afghanistan and parts of Pakistan) into what seems like perpetual conflict.[38]

Moreover, the form of war has changed: insurgency, civil war, asymmetric war, trans-state war, have mainly replaced the clash of states since 1945, though that trend could reverse quickly enough – the irredentism of Russia in Eastern Europe, or of China in the South and East China Seas, or further heightening of tensions on the India–Pakistan border, are all plausible scenarios for major interstate wars to break out. Some of the practices involved in asymmetric warfare, where insurgents use terror and cruelty to coerce local populations (Daesh in Syria, Iraq and elsewhere provides an example), and where powerful missile and drone armaments fail to control 'collateral damage' in efforts to deal with fighters who are often indistinguishable from, and anyway supported by, local populations, raise human rights concerns as serious as conventional war, and sometimes more so. But in any case, methods of coercive terrorisation are as old as war itself – Waffen SS troops massacring villagers in retaliation for resistance activity, Soviet troops raping their way towards Berlin, Daesh publicly beheading 'infidels', are no different from the Mongol strategy of unnerving enemies by acts of vast cruelty as happened at Samarkand in 1220 CE and elsewhere; and the practice was an ancient one even then.

Since the seminal work of Kenneth Waltz in the late 1950s, students of war and international relations have used a conceptual approach known as the 'levels of analysis framework' to think about the causes of war. In the basic form of this framework three levels are identified: the individual level, the state level, and the international level.[39]

The individual level is the level of political leaders and the outlook and interests of individual members of society, as well as of appeals to facts or supposed facts about human nature, as discussed above.

The second level is the level of the state. The nature of political and economic institutions and practices are the focus here. Political systems and ideologies, decision-making processes, the relation of leaderships to populaces, the degree of economic equality or otherwise in the system, the role of bureaucracies and lobbies, all require inspection. A government might make external war to distract the populace from internal failure. Arms manufacturers might be a powerful lobby, urging state leaderships to increase and perhaps even use their stocks of weapons. Popular sentiment might motivate a government to take aggressive foreign policy stances even to the point of war, over perceived or claimed ideological, territorial or historical grievances. On the other hand, the nature of social, economic and political organisation in a state might dispose it more to peace than belligerence.

The third level is the international order. As the failures of the League of Nations and the United Nations demonstrate, the international system is practically anarchic. In a situation where each of the players has very little external constraint on its behaviour apart from war being made upon it by another player whom it has sufficiently provoked, the factors that invite consideration include how many significant parties there are in the system, the degree of capacity they each have to make war, and the networks of relationships among them: alliances among some, and the existence and persistence of grievances and disagreements among others. And then there are the opportunities and the threats that relations between states pose to individual states and groups of states, which would naturally count among the triggers of armed conflict when other factors accumulate to the appropriate level.

What the basic model says of the third level is varied by different international relations theorists in various ways, one obvious variant being to account for subsystems at the international level, given that the dynamics, history and pressures of relations within a set of, say, South American countries differ from those within a set of, say, Far Eastern ones. But the assumption is the same both regionally and globally: that an account of the causes of war must address questions about the system of interstate relations, for it may be the system itself that is to blame.

Let us look at these levels of explanation.

Much has already been said in this chapter about the first level of explanation, the individual level, in considering psychological and biological ideas. Waltz was sceptical about the value of any explanation that locates the causes of war in human nature. As we see above, he is far from alone in this. His main reason was that human nature is a constant, whereas the causes and nature of war vary. It might be replied that individuals vary enough for those who are aggressive and violently disposed to be instrumental in making actual conflict arise out of competition and disagreement, the circumstances of the latter making for the differences in the wars thus started. But the rejoinder to this, in turn, is that peace is a fact of history also – and a more common fact than war – and this too would be explicable on the basis of facts about human nature. So if human nature is invoked to explain both peace and war, it cannot be (so this argument goes) the principal explanation for war.

These thoughts certainly suggest that human nature cannot be the whole story, even if psychological and biological explanations are part of it. To say this is not to deny that individual personalities – individual psychologies – are significant. Consider the impact in history of the ambition and character of such leaders as, say, Genghis Khan and Adolf Hitler. It is clear that leaders can at the very least be catalysts in harnessing and directing war-making energies among their followers. In the case of Ghengis and Hitler themselves it underplays their role to see them *merely* as catalysts, however; who and what they were as individuals must definitely be counted as part of the cause of the war-making associated with their names. Churchill might be an example of a catalyst, an inspiring war leader who nevertheless was unlikely to have encouraged a people to undertake a war in the first place, in the circumstances in which he found himself. And we can play with counterfactual hypotheses about how different history might be if, say, Al Gore had become US President in 2001 instead of George W. Bush, or if Churchill had not become Britain's war prime minister in 1940 but the appeasement wing of government had signed a treaty with Hitler's Germany in 1939, leaving the latter free to subjugate continental Europe and defeat the Soviet Union. The mere possibility that history might have been different is enough to show that the individual level of explanation matters.

There is also the consideration that a people – remember the Huns and Mongols – might have developed a culture of war-making as their way of life, and actively enjoy it and seek it; that the construction of masculinity in that society might largely be predicated on the activities of war-making; that its war leaders are *ipso facto* its cultural and political leaders too. These are first-level considerations of a different kind. A more diffuse form of them relates to the pride that a nation might take in that section of itself dedicated to the profession of arms. Contemporary US society accords great respect and consideration to its armed forces, whose size, power and technological sophistication figure positively in the nation's self-image.

It is even more obvious that the second and third levels of explanation provide resources for investigating the causes of war. They lie on the cultural plane of analysis. As one would expect, the twentieth-century explosion of academia has produced a babel of theories about the causes of war at these levels, at just the time that war reached the point at which, in the extreme, it could extinguish humanity itself. This latter fact in part explains the babel, though it is a well-motivated one: the quest to understand why war happens is at the same time a quest for mechanisms of promoting peace. Of course the latter would benefit from there being fewer explanations, and more that were obviously correct. Nevertheless there is much of interest in many of the theories, as the following indicates.[40]

The dominant theory since 1945 about the causes of war is 'realism'.[41] At base realism sees individual states as interacting with each other in an anarchic international arena – 'anarchic' because it is without a controlling and adjudicating authority over it – in ways designed to protect or enhance their self-interest. Not only is the international arena anarchic, but no state has full information about the desires and intentions of other states; together these two facts produce insecurity. Planning to protect or enhance one's own state's interests in a situation of uncertainty requires taking worst-case scenarios into account, and being prepared for them. That, among other things, means arming, and being prepared to use one's arms. Being armed offers the chance of imposing one's will, or deterring someone else from trying to do so, in situations where other means of sustaining one's interests are unavailable.

Robert Keohane summarises realism as holding that: (1) 'States are the most important actors in world politics'; (2) states are 'unitary rational actors, carefully calculating costs of alternative courses of action and seeking to maximise their expected utility, although doing so under conditions of uncertainty'; and (3) 'States seek power . . . and they calculate their interests in terms of power.'[42]

Realism is a pessimistic view, which is never fully persuaded that peacemaking processes will succeed. It does not think that in situations of unequal distributions of power internationally, the stronger will invariably show self-restraint towards the weaker – remember Thucydides' account of what the Athenians said to the Melians. It recognises that wars can start for accidental as well as deliberate reasons, and that when two or more parties fall out with each other forces can get to work that exacerbate matters, creating an uncontrollable spiral leading to war.

Classical realists are those who emphasise (3) in Keohane's definition, that is, they are those who think that states, and the individuals who lead them, have as their primary interest the acquisition and maintenance of power. This might be for its own sake, but more likely because it provides security and the means to maintain it. In his version of realism, Waltz argued that the desire for power is instrumental in this way, and not an end in itself; for him the chief end of a state's activities is security, given the context of insecurity in which states relate to each other; and power is the means to that end.[43] This is plausible given that an overriding interest of states is preservation of their territorial integrity and their freedom from outside imposition or coercion. Relative peace in the international order is achieved when states have a measure of security in relation to one another – when, in short, there is a balance of power between them. In Waltz's view, balances of power have been achieved between most states throughout most of history.

The idea of a balance of power was the driving idea behind much of the international diplomacy of the great European powers of the eighteenth and nineteenth centuries, and it was expressly aimed at maintaining peace. It explains the shifting alliances forged to counteract other alliances or to constrain aggressors, as with the coalitions formed variously by Britain, Russia, Prussia and Austria against Napoleon's France, and the opposing alliances in 1914 of the 'Triple Entente' of France, Russia and Britain on the one side, and the 'Central Powers' of Germany and Austria (originally with Italy also) on the other.[44] But in theorising about the causes of war the phrase has a wider meaning, to denote the imbalances of power that could and too often did have destabilising effects on international relations. In the years leading to 1914, Germany perceived the Triple Entente as encirclement, and on one view of Germany's role in the outbreak of hostilities in August of that year, it can be explained in part as a preventive or even defensive measure against the tightening of a noose.

As this suggests, a threatened disturbance to the balance of power can be an impulse to war. Long before Polybius asserted that 'we should never consent to one state attaining power so great that none dare oppose it', the growth towards dominance by a state had been seen as a *casus belli* by other states. That was what led to the Peloponnesian War, for example, in which Sparta and its allies refused to countenance the burgeoning power of Athens's empire after the Greeks' defeat of Persia.

Churchill was iterating an ancient view when he said in 1948, with reference to the Soviet Union, 'For four hundred years the foreign policy of England has been to oppose the strongest, the most aggressive, the most dominating Power on the Continent.'[45]

Implicit in the balance-of-power model is the assumption that the system which is being balanced or unbalanced by shifting alliances and changing power relations is a polyadic one, that is, with a number of states in play. But the same problems can arise when there is rivalry between just two states, usually geographical neighbours, in competition or disagreement with one another. War is unlikely if the disparity between the two is very great – in the event of force being used to resolve a problem, it is unlikely to result in a prolonged conflict in that case – so a dyadic balance-of-power relationship requires more rather than less equal parties to it. History is full of examples; the long-standing rivalry and many wars between England and France provide an example.

In more recent times the dyadism has obtained not between two states but between two blocs – NATO and the Warsaw Pact is the principal example, but even this confrontation had a geographical border along the 'Iron Curtain' in Europe. Any actual shooting was done by proxies in what were then called 'Third World' countries, in wars between states or groups armed and financed by the opposing blocs. Depending upon how they are counted, there were close to a hundred such proxy wars during the Cold War between 1945 and 1989.[46]

If the assumption is made that a decision to go to war is a rational one, then given the fact that war is a very costly and generally unpredictable enterprise, the motivations have to be powerful ones, so powerful that they outweigh the costs and risks. Non-rational (purely emotional or even downright irrational) decisions to go to war are presumably those where the costs and the dangers, however great, do not weigh. It is hard to bring non-rational motives for war under a general theory; the madness of a ruler, the degree of ambition which is prepared to risk everything, a red mist of anger or a thirst for revenge, a profound sense of honour or preparedness to die even for a hopeless cause rather than live under someone else's rule – all and any of these can prompt to war. In these cases it is at level one alone – the individual level – where explanations are to be sought.

But when rational calculation is in the picture it invites a different perspective. The question can be asked, 'under what conditions is peace promoted and maintained between states who see the destructiveness of war as against their longer term interests?' A compelling answer is offered by liberal arguments to the effect that economic relationships, principally trade, are prompts to peace. A litany of names subscribes this view, among them Adam Smith, Montesquieu and Thomas Paine. The latter wrote, 'If commerce were permitted to act to the extent it is capable, it would extirpate the system of war.'[47]

The background to the liberal view was provided by the mercantilist system of closed trading, in which war was used as a means of securing markets while simultaneously excluding others from them. That policy was predicated on the belief that trade is a zero-sum game, the advantage of one state entailing the disadvantage of another. The liberal thinkers disagreed; free trade would be to everyone's advantage, and increase would feed on increase. By the middle of the nineteenth century, Richard Cobden and like-minded colleagues were vehement in their opposition to war as a destroyer of trade and wealth. Cobden further argued that it was not just war but the standing preparation for war which militated against economic benefit.[48]

Views of this kind had become the orthodoxy among many by 1914. The Labour MP and Nobel laureate for peace, Sir Ralph Norman Angell, argued in his 1910 book *The Great Illusion* that the great illusion in Europe was that war, conquest, or even just armed defiance, was a means to enhance the power and wealth of a nation, whereas in fact the mutual economic entanglement of states through trade and finance meant that war could only be harmful to them.[49]

Some took Angell to have argued that economic relationships had already made war impossible, and that therefore his thesis and that of his liberal forerunners was disproved by the 1914–18 war. In fact he had not said this; his point was the different one, which was indeed proved true by the war, that war in those circumstances is futile and harmful. The proof provided by the events of 1914–18 accordingly were only a temporary setback to the liberal theory, and the belief that economic interdependence secures peace revived in the aftermath of the Cold War, only to be met with the objection that considerations of trade pale into insignificance when diplomatic and military crises occur. The question is pointedly asked, 'Were the Western liberal democracies seriously concerned about the short-term loss of trade when they made decisions to go to war against the hegemonic threats posed by Germany in 1914 and again in 1939?'[50]

And perhaps interdependence – so another objection goes – if unequal and if it prompts suspicion or resentment, might even be or at least become a cause of war; that was a view held in the eighteenth century by Rousseau. Defenders of the liberal view can answer that interdependencies offer a plurality of channels through which differences and disagreements can be addressed and resolved. They also offer ways of applying pressure far short of war, such as withdrawal from agreements or the imposition of sanctions. The latter has become an increasingly common instrument in the international sphere since 1945.

Critics of the liberal view have history on their side in pointing out that war has often been a more efficient instrument, when successful, for gaining markets and increasing a state's wealth. The liberal rejoinder is to say that this was only true when territory and maritime trade were the bases of wealth, but in the contemporary international economy, where knowledge and services are key, and where war is potentially far more destructive, such considerations no longer apply.

The period between the Second World War and the end of the Cold War saw no wars between capitalist states. Some put the point differently, and say that there have been no wars between democracies. The classes of capitalist and democratic states are not coterminous, though there is a large overlap; which gives rise to the question whether it is capitalism or democracy which is the peace-sustaining condition. There is something of an orthodoxy to the effect that it is the latter, so much so that the absence of direct conflict among advanced liberal polities since 1945 is described as the 'democratic peace'. But as Gartzke argues – and a number of independent studies appear to support his view – it is not democracy but capitalism which is doing the trick. Gartzke writes:

> Economic development, capital market integration, and the compatibility of foreign policy preferences supplant the effect of democracy in standard statistical tests of the democratic peace. In fact, after controlling for regional heterogeneity, any one of these three variables is sufficient to account for effects previously attributed to regime type in standard

samples of wars, militarized interstate disputes (MIDs), and fatal disputes.[51]

This is at least consistent with the facts upon which Cobden and earlier theorists relied in urging the peace-productive benefits of economic relationships, for they did not live in an era of democracy, though they were able to claim that there was a greater benefit to the general population from peace-promoting trade, than the benefit of war to that restricted portion of the population constituting the aristocracy, as had been the case in history.[52]

A major argument in favour of the European Union has been the promotion and preservation of peace in what had been one of the most war-torn quarters of the world for many centuries beforehand. Many internal critics of the EU complain about the 'democratic deficit' it appears to suffer from – although the rejoinder is that this is more the fault of electorates' lack of engagement than the structures of the EU itself, together with the fact that the EU parliament is constrained by the prerogatives of the Council of Ministers (though the latter's members are themselves democratically elected in their home countries). If the argument of Gartzke and others is right, the economic integration of the EU is the chief factor in the peace that obtains between its members. In the light of history, peace among the EU states is a magnificent success story, and it is hard not to see economic integration as a prime factor.

But have claims on behalf of democracy as a peacemaker among democracies been rebutted? Both Kant and Thomas Paine believed that popular sentiment would almost always be for peace because it is the populace that bears most of the burdens of war, whether in fighting it or suffering its privations, or both. Theorists looking at the relations between states, however, see matters through the lens of foreign policy imperatives, where popular sentiment is an irrelevance at best and an obstacle at worst. They share the view of Alexis de Tocqueville that 'Foreign policies demand scarcely any of those qualities which are peculiar to a democracy. They require, on the contrary, the perfect use of almost all those in which it is deficient.'[53] This is because 'a democracy can only with great difficulty regulate the details of an important undertaking, persevere in a fixed design, and work out its execution in spite of serious obstacles. It cannot combine its measures with secrecy or await their consequences with patience . . . [they] obey impulse rather than prudence [and] abandon a mature design for the gratification of a momentary passion.'[54]

This line of thinking suggests to some theorists that democracy is more rather than less likely to prompt war, therefore, because popular sentiment might encourage ideological crusades, for example to impose democracy where it is lacking. Woodrow Wilson justified US entry into the First World War by saying it was to 'make the world safe for democracy', and the extension of democracy to the Middle East was George W. Bush's professed aim in invading Iraq in 2003.

Opposing this scepticism about democracy as a peace-ensurer, however, is the empirical claim that, as a matter of historical and current fact, democracies do not go to war with each other.[55] Both 'democracy' and 'war' require precise enough definition for a count of democracies and wars to substantiate this claim. This matters, given that the American Civil War and the First World War could be regarded as counters to it, as could the tensions and occasional actual warfare between Pakistan and India. A more circumscribed claim would be sustained by the idea that there have been no wars between states that are *unambiguously* democracies.[56]

The reasons given as to why democracies do not fight wars with each other, although they fight imperialistic wars and wars against autocracies, are various. One is that the interests of democratic states tend to be aligned with each other in economic and foreign policy matters. A second is that grounds of dispute between democracies have already been removed, so there is little if any friction left between them. Another is that a constraint on war-making exercised by the populace of one democracy is greater because there is natural sympathy for the populace of another democracy, a sympathy lacking when a putative opponent is not a democratic state. This might be because democracies are more transparent to one another, and communicate with one another more, resulting in greater mutual understanding.

However, most of the arguments reported by Levy and Thomson in their survey do not appear to explain why democracies do not go to war *with each other*, but – less persuasively – why democracies are less inclined to war, a claim far harder to substantiate given the empirical evidence to the contrary. Such putative reasons are variants of the ones offered by Kant and Paine, but the numbers of wars fought by democracies do not support even their hypothesis. Those who remain sceptical about the claim that it is something in the nature of democracy itself which preserves inter-democratic peace point out that democracies are a recent phenomenon, emerging fitfully and in many cases incompletely in the nineteenth century, and the data on interdemocracy relations is only good for the post-1945 world. The lack of conflict between democracies could therefore be an artefact of the circumstances of the Cold War, or even just a coincidence.

For anyone keen on extirpating war from human affairs, the concept of democratic peace implies that states should be encouraged and helped to become democratic; for cynics, the only assurance of peace will always be the maintenance of greater strength than possible enemies. Because the latter is costly and dangerous, hopes are better attached to the former. Or perhaps, if it is not the politics of democracy but the economics of capitalism that promotes peace, even those who find capitalism unpalatable might be persuaded to seek a form of it which, while promoting international peace, is less abrasive and inequitable for populaces at home. This last thought matters, because economic inequality within a society is a major source of unrest and, in the extreme, civil war, and capitalism has a propensity to create inequality if left unchecked. What might preserve interstate peace could therefore cause intrastate conflict. As in so many things else, balance would be the key, and the inward- and outward-facing tasks of politics would meet at the striking of that balance.

The second level of analysis, the societal level, attracted the attention of Enlightenment thinkers and of Karl Marx. The former blamed the personal ambitions of ruling elites for the wars that wracked Europe's history, and as noted they argued that if political power were diffused among the many they would be less likely to desire war because they were the ones most likely to suffer its effects. Marx focused on the economic rather than the political conditions in a society, arguing to the contrary of the theory just sketched that the exigencies and inequalities of capitalism were prompts to war. At this level too one finds the various suggestions that cultural, institutional and ideological factors play their part in disposing a people to war.

The Enlightenment view was able to invoke history in support. Almost all the wars of preceding centuries had been top-down wars, wars made by and for monarchs and ruling classes in which populations were subject to drag-along necessities. It provided Kant with his motivation for the peace-securing principles set out in his essay 'Perpetual Peace' (1795), and the necessary conditions for the application of those principles, namely that states should have 'republican constitutions' (that is, have responsible and representative government), that there should be a law of nations based on 'a federation of free states', and that people should be 'world citizens' in conditions of 'universal hospitality' (among other things implying free movement of people and mutual recognition of rights). Bentham's proposal for perpetual peace focused on the idea of international law (he coined the word 'international' in putting forward this idea). His view was that disarmament, the abolition of colonies, and above all an effective system of international arbitration, would result in the abolition of war.[57]

Marx was not a pacifist, and he was greatly influenced by Clausewitz. His collaborator Engels wrote more on war than on any other subject, though to find a 'Marxist theory of war' as twentieth-century Marxism understood it one has to turn mainly to the writings of Lenin.[58] Engels was a close student of Clausewitz, and made a thorough examination of the American Civil War, writing about it in weekly columns in the press (over Marx's name) as it happened. But the thinking of Marx and Engels on the subject of war took place in a period of prolonged European peace, whereas Lenin's development of their ideas took place against the background of war.

The Marx–Engels view was that wars occur for reasons specific to the cultural and economic circumstances of their time, sometimes with positive and sometimes with negative effects. For this reason they were not opposed to war as something inherently bad, because it might sometimes result in the liberation of classes or the demolition of an oppressive order. Nor did they value peace merely for its own sake; Marx was critical of what he saw as the stagnation of China because of its long centuries of peace. In sum, they saw war as acceptable if it was a catalyst for progress, which for them meant movement towards the eventual passing away of class and state, when they believed peace would prevail because conflict-engendering inequality and exploitative relations of production would no longer exist.[59]

As developed by Lenin, the view is that capitalist regimes require the stimulus of aggressive foreign policies because without it they become stagnant and feeble. Over-production and lack of home consumption (because of the poverty of the proletariat) requires expansion into new markets. Surplus capital that the home economy cannot absorb likewise requires new arenas for investment. Both exert pressure for expansionist foreign policy; and as competing capitalist states vie for these domains, so conflicts arise. A variant is to say that capitalist production requires ever-new sources of raw materials and cheaper labour, again creating outward pressure.[60] Other Marxist theorists and some Keynesian theorists have added new sources of that pressure, for a chief example high levels of defence spending designed to stimulate the economy internally, but therefore spurring arms races with competitors, and the creation of conditions in which continued or increased such expenditure might actually need war to help sustain it.[61]

The Marxist–Leninist characterisation of imperialism and its wars as a necessary adjunct of capitalism is opposed by the claim, already noted, that war is harmful to capitalism, and that the economic relations between capitalist states ensure peace, not conflict. To accept that imperialism and warmongering are in the interests of capitalism requires accepting either that capitalists control the military, or that the military controls foreign policy. Although Dwight D. Eisenhower warned against the lobby power of the 'military-industrial' complex, plausibly suggesting a cartel arrangement between the military and the arms industry, it is less plausible to think that such a lobby could capture the state apparatus and apply it to its special ends. That would mean the Pentagon and its friends in the arms industry dictating the making of war and peace to president and Congress. Matters might rather be, as Waltz suggested, the other way round: economic flourishing gives rise to power, and it is the possession of power that prompts imperialist activity.[62]

The large and growing literature on the subject of the causes of war is such almost as to defy summary, and makes drawing conclusions difficult.[63] Sometimes the subject is discussed in ways that confuse the question of proximate and generic causes of war, even if making useful contributions to our understanding of each. Stephen van Evera in his *Causes of War*, for example, gives an interesting account of *when* wars tend to occur – at moments when offence–defence balances between hostile parties shift, and perceived opportunities are ripe, principally – which is of significance in evaluating the risk of war breaking out. But as one can see, this is a debate different from the general one about what causes war.[64] Culture and personality figure as key determinants in the generic causes of war according to Jeremy Black; here is an example of a choice of the level at which the impulses to war chiefly arise.[65]

If anything is clear – and most of the literature acknowledges this – it is that the recurrent human phenomenon of war is the product of a logical sum of the family of typical causes of individual wars, and that the these causes operate at one or all levels of motivating forces – the individual, organisational and (for interstate wars) international levels. To say this is not, however, to capture the essence of the cause of war. That still evades analyses such as these.

What might a more promising route to an answer be? Perhaps an indirect approach would be better: to discern the sources of war by asking after the causes of peace. What might we learn from imperial *paces* – the *pax Romana* and *pax Britannica* for example, so far as the internal *pax* of each empire was mainly concerned? Cynics, not far from the mark at least in the latter case, might say: suppression of opposition, and they would note that the borders of these empires were anything but peaceful.

A yet more optimistic answer might be inferred from the great European peace of the post-1945 world, made possible by the growing interdependence and interconnection of the European nations. Operative factors in this case, and indeed in all these cases of peace, seem to be: interdependence and mutuality. The other side of this coin is, familiarly, the potentially inflammatory presence, and often mixture, of nationalism, ideological differences, economic and territorial competition, and suspicion. By an adapted Mill's Methods one might begin to specify these latter as 'the causes of war' and not be surprised to find them so.[66]

But the really interesting outcome of this reflection, if correct – and equally unsurprisingly – would be that deliberate creation of interdependencies in economic respects and interconnections in political respects is a strong specific against war. This in turn suggests that the causes of war lie in structures of political relationships – a social matter, arising from the organisation of societies and polities, and the creation of interests self-identified with a given group and challenged by the interests similarly self-identified by another group. One can see how the emergence of states would make conflicts of interests a generator of war when discussion and diplomacy fail and the difficulties become intractable. The solution to war as a human problem is therefore integration, mutual linkages of a practical and beneficial kind, and the elimination of boundaries between interests.

In my view this would be facilitated by the end of the nation state and associated nationalism as a sentiment. At the time these words were written I had just returned from a visit to Zagreb, there to be told by my host, a lawyer, that Croatians had resisted their inclusion in the Austro-Hungarian empire, then deeply regretted no longer being part of it when it collapsed in 1919. There is a familiar ring to this sentiment, and all that it suggests in historical terms.

From the foregoing discussion the answer I infer to the question, 'What are the causes of war?' is this: the causes of war are the divisions and differences between self-identified groups with interests opposed to, or by, other such groups. War is therefore a product of a sufficient degree of organisation and structure to make such divisions and differences material. This implies that war is an artefact of the political, economic and cultural arrangements that evolved when settled societies emerged into history about 10,000 years ago.

Of course people fought each other before then, singly and in groups: skulls with holes in them suggest as much. But fighting is not war. War is organisation of and preparation for fighting in ways that lie above the military horizon, and that horizon is set in turn by the cultural horizon.

On this view, all the aspects and practices of civilisation that produced its great advances – involving as they do bureaucracy, engineering, literacy, education and training, social structure, law, hierarchy, centralisation, technology and more – also produced war. Among the more important lessons to be drawn is that civilisation has the capability of getting rid of war as it has got rid of poliomyelitis, if it would apply the will and means to do so. It would take co-operation, it would be difficult, it has been tried and it has at least twice in the last century failed badly (in the case of the League of Nations and so far of the United Nations), but it is necessary. 'Necessary' hardly captures the urgency. In a world armed with the means to destroy the very civilisation that brought war into being, it is absolutely and existentially necessary.[67]

CHAPTER 5

The Effects of War

The question of what causes war, like the question of what caused this or that particular war, has consumed mountains of paper and oceans of ink, and the answers are still disputed. There is a much clearer understanding of the effects of war. The most obvious and dramatic effect is the destruction of people and their homes, their factories and offices, their schools and museums. Pictures of blasted buildings, rubble-strewn streets, corpses of humans and animals, such poignant icons of lives ended or ruined as a broken doll lying among shell craters – all this provides a familiar point of reference concerning the hideousness of war. There is a near-consensus that war is evil; and yet, driven by the inexorabilities of how our world is constituted, billions of dollars are spent annually all round the world on guns, missiles, submarines, soldiers and all the other preparations for conflict, as if conflict were as inevitable as death itself.

Employment of the phrase 'near-consensus' implies that not everyone thinks war is bad – indeed, there are some who think it is a positive good. One can dismiss the posturing of the poet

Filippo Tommaso Marinetti, the ninth paragraph of whose 'Manifesto of Futurism' (1908) says 'We will glorify war – the world's only hygiene – militarism, patriotism, the destructive gesture of freedom-bringers, beautiful ideas worth dying for.' This feverish document, written after Marinetti and his equally young friends had stayed up all night becoming hysterically pleased with themselves, then racing off in Marinetti's car and overturning it in a ditch, is really a paean to that new thing, the car, and its speed, which Marinetti loved; completed by a hefty dash of misogyny ('scorn of women' is oddly tacked to the end of the 'we will glorify war' paragraph) and complete rejection of the past ('museums are cemeteries' – 'We will destroy the museums, libraries, academies of every kind'). As an intoxicated *jeu d'esprit* it would overstate its importance as symptomising weariness with peace in the years before the catastrophe of 1914. But it is oddly prophetic. In the Second World War, museums, libraries and academies lay beneath the onslaught of 'carpet bombing,' in which there might have been a deliberate effort at 'culturecide' involved.[1]

Marinetti was neither alone nor the first in describing war as a form of hygiene. Few could think that it is the kind of hygiene that cleanses a society of its dregs, for it is the brave and the fit who go to perish in wars, not the skulkers and dodgers and black marketeers, who survive and reproduce. Instead it is extolled as the kind that summons humanity's highest virtues and best creative powers. Thus Ruskin:

> When I tell you that war is the foundation of all the arts, I mean also that it is the foundation of all the high virtues and faculties of men. It is very strange to me to discover this, and very dreadful – but I saw it to be quite an undeniable fact . . . I

found, in brief, that all great nations learnt their truth of word and strength of thought in war, that they were nourished in war and wasted by peace; taught by war, and deceived by peace; trained by war, and betrayed by peace; in a word, that they were born in war, and expired in peace.[2]

One does not have to claim that war is good to say that there can sometimes be good reasons for going to war. This point is made by John Stuart Mill:

> War is an ugly thing, but not the ugliest of things: the decayed and degraded state of moral and patriotic feeling which thinks that nothing is worth a war, is much worse. When a people are used as mere human instruments for firing cannon or thrusting bayonets, in the service and for the selfish purposes of a master, such war degrades a people. A war to protect other human beings against tyrannical injustice; a war to give victory to their own ideas of right and good, and which is their own war, carried on for an honest purpose by their free choice, – is often the means of their regeneration. A man who has nothing which he is willing to fight for, nothing which he cares more about than he does about his personal safety, is a miserable creature who has no chance of being free, unless made and kept so by the exertions of better men than himself. As long as justice and injustice have not terminated their ever-renewing fight for ascendancy in the affairs of mankind, human beings must be willing, when need is, to do battle for the one against the other.[3]

A cautionary note sounds when one reads that 'a war to give victory to their own ideas of right and good' is counted as one for which there are good reasons, because of course one person's idea of what is right and good might not be another's. Suppose the then US President George W. Bush was sincere in having this as his reason for launching the Second Gulf War of 2003; even when sincerely believed, it rings hollow. But the general tenor of Mill's view is understandable. Basil Liddell-Hart made the same point seventy-odd years later when he said, 'War is always a matter of doing evil in the hope that good may come of it.'[4]

Apart from those who extol war because they think it romantic and dramatic – Erasmus long ago drily remarked that 'war is delightful to those who have no experience of it' – there are more who point out that war is not always unmitigatedly bad in its effects. There have been occasions when military expenditure by a government has boosted the national economy and increased employment. It can bring positive social change, sometimes very significant, as witness the position of women in society after the First World War – many tens of thousands of them had worked in munitions factories, on farms and as nurses, experiencing life in ways quite different from their sheltered versions of it beforehand. Witness likewise the major social adjustments following the Second World War almost everywhere.[5] In this latter war the armed forces of the United States unconsciously laid the foundations for Native Americans and African Americans to begin their painfully difficult assault on racial divisions in society.

Technology advances by giant leaps in the emergency of war; in 1939 biplanes were still in active service in Britain's Royal Air Force, but by 1945 jet fighters, missiles and atom bombs were already in use. More acceptable technological advances than these, such as radar, computing and aircraft design, proved of lasting value. The science behind these developments advanced because it was given the amount of resources in funding and personnel that in peacetime would have been difficult to obtain.

Other benefits of war sometimes cited are that they result in alliances, they bring otherwise intractable conflicts to an end, and they stop the spread of malevolent ideologies such as Nazism. Some even add it as a plus – though this is a rather disagreeable claim – that they keep populations down. Conquerors in war have sometimes brought benefits to the conquered; consider Napoleon and the liberation of Jews in the parts of Europe that succumbed to him. Other warmakers have alleged less convincing benefits, usually to themselves: strengthening the nation, inculcating patriotism, gaining *Lebensraum*, averting the danger posed by an enemy growing in power. Another doubtful advantage of war is said to be that it helps one be better practised and prepared for the next war.

Perhaps the most considered defence of the positive aspects of war is offered by Ian Morris in *War: What Is It Good For?*[6] His view is summarised in one of his section headings: 'War makes the State, and the State makes peace'. The argument is that 'by fighting wars, people have created larger, more organised societies that have reduced the risk that their members will die violently'. This works by more powerful societies conquering and absorbing less powerful ones, then imposing peace upon them. In less organised states of human affairs conflict, strife and homicide were far more prevalent, Morris says; so it is by grasping the nettle of violence that violence has been controlled, and with the peace thus won has come the preconditions for prosperity. 'War, I will suggest, has not been a friend to the undertaker', Morris begins; 'War is mass murder, and yet, in perhaps the greatest paradox in history, war has nevertheless been the undertaker's worst enemy.'[7]

There are several challengeable assumptions underlying Morris's thesis. One is that war created the 'bigger societies with stronger governments' that he says impose peace. Another is that such societies are indeed imposers of peace rather than – in their tensions and conflicts of interest *vis-à-vis* other such societies – the chief cause of major war. A third is that life was less peaceful and safe for people before the big societies came into being. Let us consider these points in reverse order.

Morris adduces the view that violent death was more common in the Stone Age – taking this term to denote the period of 2 to 3 million years before the rise of settled cultures and metalworking about 8,000 years ago – with as many as 10–20 per cent of Stone Age people dying as a result of murder or fighting.[8] This view, inferred by Lawrence Keeley from examination of conflict-related death rates in contemporary hunter-gatherer societies, is contested by Douglas Fry and his colleagues as discussed in the previous chapter.[9] Suppose, however, that it is true that Stone Agers were violent. It could plausibly be argued that this could be a barrier to social aggregation into larger units with stronger forms of government, so the question of how these arose and succeeded in diminishing the violence – given that violence presupposes division – becomes acute. It could more plausibly be argued that as social groups grew larger and more organised, so their ability to assert their interests over other such groups likewise grew; and that this gave rise to war.

These thoughts in fact address both the third and second of Morris's claims, because – in relation to the second – the argument that war needs organisation, planning, mustering of resources, direction of the energies of the group to the prosecution of hostilities, suggests that it is organisation that is a precursor of war and not its inhibitor.

The first point about violence in prehistoric human life either implies that war or the preconditions for war lie in human nature, or that the social arrangements of prehistoric societies were such as to goad otherwise co-operative human beings into smashing one another's heads with stone axes. In the previous chapter we saw some reason for thinking that it is the social arrangements rather than human nature which merit the blame. If this is right – and it remains in dispute – it challenges Morris's case.

It is indisputable that the number of people who have died violently and prematurely, as a percentage of overall population, has decreased throughout recorded history, with an even steeper drop since the seventeenth and eighteenth centuries – the centuries of the Enlightenment. This is a case made powerfully by Pinker and others.[10] Figures are variously cited to illustrate the claim; an order of magnitude according to some estimates is that in the year 1250, 1 in 100 people were victims of murder, but by the year 1600 that had dropped to 1 in 300, and by 1950 to 1 in 3,000.[11] Note that these are homicide figures, not figures for war deaths; and they could more plausibly be attributable to better policing or more education or increasing prosperity than a change in human nature. But war deaths *as a percentage of population* have also declined dramatically, not just since medieval times but, as noted, throughout known history. Is this a beneficial effect of war, as Morris argues?

It is not as simple a matter to answer this as Morris claims. The number of wars has also been in decline since medieval times, but their lethality has dramatically increased; so even though smaller percentages of the rapidly growing world population are killed in them, the absolute numbers have grown vastly larger. A count over the last 400 years tells us that there were twenty-two wars between major powers in the sixteenth century, eleven in the seventeenth century, eight in the eighteenth, five in the nineteenth and six in the twentieth. The standard, and convincing, reason given for the decline in the number of wars is their increasing cost and destructive capability; firepower and the cost of increasingly necessary standing militaries from the sixteenth century onwards are a disincentive to war-making.[12]

It is therefore no surprise that the figures for the twentieth century's wars, and especially for the First and Second World Wars, should be horrifying, and eradicate any sense of satisfaction one might feel that population percentages of violent deaths have fallen. The numbers for these wars include, as they must, civilian deaths, and deaths from all causes incident on the prevailing state of war; recent and contemporary warfare puts everyone on the front line. The death toll in the First World War is estimated at 20 million, in the Second World War between 40 million and 85 million with a geometric mean at 58 million. Add in the other wars and civil wars of a violent century – another 20 million at least – and the total conservatively hovers around 100 million. The number of deaths in war since the beginning of recorded history is put at about 500 million. This makes the combined death tolls of the wars of the twentieth century nearly 20 per cent of recorded history's entire war mortality.[13] This is a shocking figure. It makes the Morris thesis, and indeed the optimistic view of human progress implicit in Pinker and elsewhere, less plausible.

We talk of deaths here, but must not forget that the greater firepower of modern war means that the destruction of things that matter to lives – homes, workplaces, cultural artefacts, infrastructure, fields and crops – is also involved. The rampaging of medieval crusaders might be destructive of towns and farms in their path, but the range of their annoyance was far more limited than that of a single squadron of missile-armed fighter-bombers today. This effect of war, therefore – the demolition of lives and things that matter to lives – not only has not changed but has worsened by far.

War's effects do not stop when the shooting stops. At the end of the Second World War 40 million Europeans were refugees. Even as the Syrian civil war that began in 2012 was continuing, 12 million Syrians had become refugees. Every war has driven people from their homes and homelands, and although most return when peace supervenes, many cannot. At time of writing the UN refugee agency (UNHCR) was still dealing with more than half a million refugees from the Balkans conflict of the 1990s. In Colombia, in the half century of conflict with FARC which started in the 1960s, 4 million people were displaced from their homes – 10 per cent of the population. War's consequences in these respects are fruitful in prolonging problems and laying the foundations for recurrent conflicts; the Israel–Palestine situation is a paradigm case.[14]

And then there is trauma. The impact of war on combatants and non-combatants alike is one of the effects of war which has come to be more studied and understood in the course of the last hundred years than ever beforehand, doubtless because the nature of weaponry has produced more pronounced and observable effects. The closer one gets to the present day, the more frequent and pronounced is the war trauma experienced by soldiers in the armies of advanced countries, because more of them survive as a result of improvements in body armour and medical care on the battlefield. Mental illness and impaired cognition are the two principal 'invisible wounds' noted in studies of post-traumatic stress disorder (PTSD), major depressive disorder and traumatic brain injury (TBI). The first is typically a reaction to trauma; the second to loss, as in the death of comrades; and the third to the effects of blast exposure or concussive impacts to the helmet or head.

Boxing, American football, soccer, rugby, even cricket and baseball, can all cause TBI, though a bullet or shrapnel hitting one's helmet, and proximity to an explosion, doubtless have greater effects. Depression arising from grief at the death a friend, a loved one or a family member, is a familiar and widespread phenomenon, though its being so does not make it easier to bear. So the war-induced version of both these categories is readily understandable in comparison to the non-war-induced instances of them.

With PTSD one can speculate that matters are the other way round. The condition was formally recognised and labelled in 1980 and is defined in the American Psychological Association's *Diagnostic and Statistical Manual of Mental Disorders* as 'a reaction to a psychologically traumatic event outside the range of normal experience'. There are of course plenty of cases of non-war-induced PTSD; people involved in, or who are witnesses of, a murder, train wreck, earthquake or any highly shocking and disturbing event that is out of the ordinary, might suffer PTSD as a result. But a combat zone is where traumatising events occur repeatedly and on large scales, and where anticipation of their occurrence is a constant. Fear, extremely loud sudden noises, uncertainty, confusion, hyperventilation and high levels of adrenaline, with death a real prospect and not untypically the witnessing of others' deaths, mutilations or agonies, can readily be imagined as an experience apt to leave a profound mark. Military psychiatry accordingly has much to offer the general understanding of PTSD. It is likely that studies of 'shell shock' in the First World War gave the first major impetus to better understanding of this and related mental health phenomena.[15]

One of the reasons for war-induced PTSD among soldiers in combat units is a factor central to their role: the question of killing. David Grossman, a psychologist and career soldier, stresses this point in *On Killing* – the first full study of the psychological experience of killing based on examination of soldiers' experiences. He observes that there is a 'powerful, innate human resistance toward killing one's own species' which armies have had to work hard to develop 'psychological mechanisms . . . to overcome'; and that acts of overcoming this resistance is one primary source of the trauma soldiers feel.[16]

This is so even with the training and conditioning that front-line troops are given. Grossman writes, 'Just as I do not wish to condemn those who have killed in lawful combat, nor do I wish to judge the many soldiers who chose *not* to kill. There are many such soldiers; indeed I will provide evidence that in many historical circumstances these non-firers represented the majority of those on the firing line.'[17] He cites examples:

R. C. Anderson, a World War II Canadian artillery forward observer, wrote to say the following:

I can confirm many infantrymen never fired their weapons. I used to kid them that we fired a hell of a lot more 25-pounder [artillery] shells than they did rifle bullets. In one position . . . we came under fire from an olive grove to our flank. Everyone dived for cover. I was not occupied, at that moment, on my radio, so, seeing a Bren [light machine gun], I grabbed it and fired off a couple of magazines. The Bren gun's owner crawled over to me, swearing, 'It's OK for you, you don't have to clean the son of a bitch.' He was really mad.

Another example:

> Colonel Albert J. Brown, in Reading, Pennsylvania, exemplifies
> the kind of response I have consistently received while speaking
> to veterans' groups. As an infantry platoon leader and company
> commander in World War II, he observed that 'Squad leaders
> and platoon sergeants had to move up and down the firing line
> kicking men to get them to fire. We felt like we were doing
> good to get two or three men out of a squad to fire.'[18]

By the time of the Vietnam War this picture had changed.
Training had made combat units achieve a much higher firing
rate than the 15–20 per cent in the First and Second World Wars.
As a psychologist, Grossman was especially sensitive to the
complex set of stresses Vietnam veterans had been subjected to in
a losing war condemned rather than supported by people at
home in the USA. He comments critically on 'How the American
soldier in Vietnam was first psychologically enabled to kill to a
far greater degree than any other soldier in history, then denied
the psychologically essential purification ritual that exists in
every warrior society, and finally condemned and accused by his
own society to a degree that is unprecedented in Western history.'[19]

There are other sources of PTSD of course. Survivor guilt is
one. Loud explosions and gunfire in conditions of great danger
would be enough by themselves to unnerve anyone. From the
perspective of considering the effects of war, it is the sequelae
of traumatic combat experiences that matter; the operative part
of the label 'PTSD' is the 'post' part.

Manifestations of PTSD include recurrent and intrusive
dreams and recollections of the experience, emotional

blunting, social withdrawal, exceptional difficulty or reluctance in initiating or maintaining intimate relationships, and sleep disturbances. These symptoms can in turn lead to serious difficulties in readjusting to civilian life, resulting in alcoholism, divorce, and unemployment. The symptoms persist for months or years after the trauma, often emerging after a long delay.[20]

The manifestations are not only psychological. There is also a 'far higher incidence of divorce, marital problems, tranquilizer use, alcoholism, joblessness, heart disease, high blood pressure, and ulcers'.[21] During the First World War, when proper psychiatric study of 'shell shock' began, some of the more extreme immediate manifestations included uncontrollable shaking, paralysis, spasms, deafness, blackouts, aphasia and exhaustion. These symptoms of shock might well be expected to leave persistent effects, and indeed were seen in the days and weeks following first hospitalisation of the victims. It is the yet longer-term effects that manifest as PTSD. But the troubling fact is that PTSD can emerge in individuals who did not display any of the immediate symptoms of shock. Soldiers who survived their tours of duty, even in some cases returning to duty after physical wounds had healed, and who showed every sign of tolerating the stresses and challenges of war, might nevertheless turn out to be victims of PTSD later, as veterans. In studies of Vietnam veterans it was found that PTSD symptoms were almost exclusively experienced by soldiers who had been in 'high-intensity combat situations'; other military personnel in Vietnam who had served in non-combat roles were psychologically indistinguishable from those who had served in posts at home in the USA.[22]

The incidence of PTSD among veterans is large both in percentage and absolute terms. Some 3 million US soldiers served in Vietnam, of whom anything between 18 and 54 per cent were estimated by the Disabled American Veterans Association to be suffering from some degree of PTSD – that is, between half a million and one and a half million people. Figures for US veterans of the conflicts in Afghanistan and Iraq between 2002 and 2008 were given as 14 per cent or 300,000 individuals by the Center for Military Health Policy Research report *Invisible Wounds of War*.[23] That figure could be viewed as conservative; psychiatric disorders were cited as the reason for 30–40 per cent of soldiers discharged on medical grounds from the British Army during the Second World War.

Understanding the traumatic effects of combat began in the First World War when it dawned on the medical profession that the concept of 'shell shock' – a term coined by psychiatrist Charles Myers in a *Lancet* article in 1915 – was misleading. It had been thought that proximity to an explosion caused actual physical trauma to the brains of afflicted individuals. But it then became clear that this organic explanation was unsatisfactory, because the same symptoms were apparent in men who had not been close to a shell blast. Physicians accordingly realised that they were witnessing a functional disorder caused by the stress of actual or even anticipated vulnerability to danger in the trenches. They further began to see that supplementary factors such as fatigue, poor diet, long periods of exposure to the elements, and pre-existing factors such as psychological problems present before enlistment, were involved. Myers himself accordingly argued that the term 'shell shock' should be abandoned, though it remained lodged in common parlance throughout most of the twentieth century.[24]

It is painful to think how often soldiers suffering the trauma of war were described as 'lacking moral fibre', and treated as cowards or deserters. Three hundred and six British and Commonwealth soldiers were shot for cowardice or desertion in the First World War; most were probably suffering from trauma.[25] Doctors were sympathetic enough to trauma victims to see, in the military's keenness to return physically fit men to the front, and in its aversion to malingerers, a chance not just to help the victims overcome their trauma, but to protect them from court martial for cowardice. They did this by dealing with the trauma as quickly and as close to the front lines as possible. This technique came to be known as 'forward psychiatry', and Myers was one of its pioneers along with his French medical colleagues. The idea was to prevent victims getting used to their state of anxiety, which would ingrain it and make it more difficult to treat later. The further soldiers got from the front the more reluctant they were to return to it, so speed was of the essence. However Myers also recognised that hypnosis, a calm environment, and a chance to talk to the victim about his experiences and to make him aware of what had caused the trauma, were all helpful. These techniques were applied close to the trenches whenever possible.

Another pioneer of this approach was William Rivers, who treated Siegfried Sassoon and Wilfred Owen at Craiglockhart Hospital, a psychiatric unit for officers in Edinburgh. Some of Owen's and Sassoon's poems first appeared in the hospital's magazine *The Hydra* (so called because before the war Craiglockhart had been a hydrotherapy institute), which Owen edited for six issues in 1917. But different approaches were tried at other hospitals. The London neurologist Lewis Yelland Andrews used electrical stimulation, applying electrodes to parts of the body afflicted by trauma-induced paralysis, thus treating the symptom but not the underlying cause. He was sometimes successful, thereby engendering unclarity about which kind of therapeutic approach was best – an unclarity that might have been resolved earlier if military psychiatry had not suffered the same fate as everything else as soon as the war was over, namely to be dismantled and forgotten. In the interwar years the British armed forces did not have a dedicated psychiatric service, which meant that veterans of the war received no long-term help. It was not until the third year of the Second World War that military psychiatry was again put on an organised footing.

This did not mean a complete absence of thought about the matter. The military decided to try screening psychologically vulnerable individuals at the point of recruitment in order to limit the potential for breakdowns and incapacity in the field. At the Sutton Emergency Hospital in Surrey psychiatrist William Sargant dealt with traumatised soldiers evacuated from Dunkirk in the summer of 1940, using hypnosis to achieve cathartic discharge of horrifying memories. But as the war went on, so the need for psychiatric services in the field again became pressing. The main theatre of British army operations in the years between 1941 and 1944 was the Western Desert and Italy, and it was here that an updated version of 'forward psychiatry' was implemented, known as 'PIE' for 'Proximity, Immediacy, Expectation of Recovery'. Considerable claims were made for the success of the technique; after the D-Day landings, in the fighting through north-western Europe, it was claimed that two-thirds of psychologically traumatised men were returned to combat duty after PIE treatment close to the front. After the war the figure was revised down to near 10 per cent, a truer indication, borne out by experience in conflicts after the Second World War also.

A number of pointers appeared to emerge from the renewed endeavour of military psychiatry. Soldiers were seen to be more likely to suffer psychological trauma when retreating than when advancing, in circumstances of defeat rather than victory. They were more vulnerable to breakdown if there were prior indicators of low intelligence, lack of education or pre-existing mental conditions. It helped stiffen resolve if duty and loyalty to comrades was strongly and repeatedly emphasised. More significantly still, it had become evident that even first-rate and highly courageous fighting men, with outstanding service records, were susceptible to breakdown if over-exposed to intense combat. This taught the lesson that exposure to front-line conditions should be reduced, with correlatively increased opportunities for rest and recuperation.

In the overwhelming number of all medical cases being treated by army doctors it was not always possible to apply the kinds of therapies pioneered by Myers and Rivers in the First World War, so there was much resort to sedation, even to the use of induced coma – a treatment employed by William Sargant who, highly sceptical of 'talk' therapies, saw it as a way of preventing bad memories and anxiety states from taking a permanent grip on the victim's psyche. In Egypt one of the army psychiatrists, Dugmore Hunter, applied a highly robust approach, separating trauma victims into those who were unlikely to be much use on further deployment, and those who could be encouraged to stiffen their upper lips and return to duty. His method was one of selection rather than treatment, relying in effect on self-cure of those he deemed capable of it. He wrote:

In psychiatry, almost everything depends on the basic personality of the patient. Thus, one can afford to evacuate a good man early, knowing that he will return to the unit with high morale, having clearly benefited from rest and treatment. The poorest human material is like a cheap car, which must be run to the limit and then discarded. The psychiatrist cannot make good fighting men out of inadequate individuals.[26]

He dealt with 'screaming and jabbering' patients by slapping them or pouring cold water over them. Some he gave a humiliating dressing-down in front of comrades, others he publicly praised for their courage and determination to return to the fray. His no-nonsense approach was similar to the approach bordering on cruelty practised by French doctors during the First World War, who treated military 'war hysterics' with electric shocks or sent them to fester, abandoned, in public lunatic asylums.[27]

A very different approach was tried at Hollymoor Hospital in Birmingham for repatriated psychiatric cases: group therapy. In fact part of the motive for treating victims in groups was a logistical rather than a theoretical one, because there were not enough staff to deal with them one-to-one, but making a virtue of necessity proved interesting. Wards were organised on community lines, with patients taking part in discussions about how treatment and rehabilitation might work. Bonds between patients were forged, mutual help encouraged. Patients mentored newcomer patients. There were activities such as art classes, swimming and drama. Many of these ideas were preserved into peacetime psychotherapy in Britain's National Health Service.

The effectiveness of these different approaches was always a matter of dispute and scepticism. But as more recent advances in dealing with PTSD evolved, especially as survival rates have risen because of effective body-armour, rapid helicopter evacuation of wounded men and expert front-line surgery, a significant shift has taken place: an understanding of the longer term effects, and the need for longer term help. In their carefully documented analysis of both the need for and the provision of such help in the United States, Tanielian and Jaycox describe new thinking about the kinds of facilities required and the barriers that stand in the way of traumatised veterans receiving help – not least among them individual veterans' own reluctance to seek it.

On the principle that prevention is always better than cure, the US military introduced the 'Battlemind' system into its training regimes. The programme is:

> designed to help soldiers cope with the stressors of the deployment cycle. Specially tailored pre- and post-deployment briefs inform soldiers on what they are likely to see and experience, describe common and normative [*sic*] mental health reactions, and give guidance for seeking mental health support. The briefings convey a key message: that soldiers are responsible for each other's emotional well-being. This responsibility includes speaking to each other about troublesome experiences and being on the look out for budding mental health problems.[28]

NCOs are trained to encourage the sense of cohesion and mutual loyalty in a unit as a means of supporting its members in stressful conditions. This last, though, is an old idea – perhaps as old as military history itself.

War does not only affect soldiers. As we have seen, civilian victims of bombing, sieges, mistreatment at the hands of invading forces including rape and rapine, refugee crises, starvation, arbitrary arrest and execution, anxiety and grief for loved ones because of any of these afflictions, and anxiety and grief for sons and husbands – and increasingly now, daughters and wives – on dangerous postings in the armed forces, adds up to a mountain of misery for non-combatants. Stress disorders are accordingly found among them too. But both during and after conflicts, civilian sufferers have received much less attention than military sufferers, partly of course because the more urgent matter has always been the welfare of the latter, especially when the need was great to return physically fit personnel to duty. But the distinction between chronic and acute conditions, and the fact that medical professionals are the ones who define which conditions are worth dealing with, means that civilians in war take a back seat in discussions such as this.

Indeed some of the information relevant to understanding civilian wartime trauma is distorted by the very conditions of war itself. For example, it was noted in France during the First World War that admissions to lunatic asylums dropped considerably. A natural explanation might seem to be that when there are real external concerns and threats to worry about, the incidence of neurosis falls: outer realities swamp inner imaginings. Closer examination reveals a more accurate story: many people left the towns for the countryside, where facilities for psychiatric care were sparser. Asylums closed or purposely reduced admission because many of the staff were called to support military medical services. A significant number of asylums changed function, being requisitioned by the military as hospitals for wounded and recovering personnel.[29] A side-effect of the reduction in facilities for civilian mental health sufferers during the war meant that comparisons between them and soldier sufferers were ignored; on the face of it, a more synoptic view of the effects of stressful times and experiences on all who were mentally damaged by them might have been valuable to research.

In his account of the effects of war on the minds of those caught up in it, focusing principally on the First and Second World Wars and the Vietnam War, Ben Shephard makes two striking points, among others: that there is a cycle in the degree of attention given to the matter, in that the problem is first denied, then exaggerated, then understood, then forgotten, the forgetting taking place between wars; and that there are two contrasting approaches to the problem which he characterises as the 'realistic' and the 'dramatic', the former being the one dedicated to getting physically fit service personnel back into action as quickly as possible, while the latter is focused on the complex manifestations and symptoms of the disorders caused by trauma.[30] He argues that the realist approach was discredited in the USA by the experience of Vietnam, and that the relative success of Second World War handling of the phenomenon variously called 'shell shock', 'battle fatigue' and PTSD, as efforts to understand it unfolded through the twentieth century's wars, is under-appreciated. This last point is a valuable one to take away; perhaps the techniques developed at Hollymoor Hospital, reprising in a therapeutic setting the comradeship on the front line that to some degree works preventatively in supporting military personnel through stress, continued to be used after the war because, among all the alternatives tried, it best offered something of hope.

There is another intriguing point to be considered. Jones and Wessely raise the question in their history of military psychiatry whether each war produces its own distinctive kind of war trauma, related to the technology and military practices current in that war, and the attitudes and state of theory of medical practitioners also then current. Or are the traumas the same in all wars?

> Supporters of the latter case will argue that differences are superficial related to cultural developments and reporting biases of patients and doctors. New diagnoses were coined for what many regarded as established syndromes. For example, Smith and Pear argued [in 1917] that 'shell shock involves no *new* symptoms or disorders. Every one was known beforehand in civil life.' By contrast, many believe that so-called Gulf War syndrome is a unique and novel illness related to modern toxic exposures and therefore quite unrelated to any previous phenomenon.[31]

The question that has to be asked about the effects of war is whether those regarded as positive – technological and social advances, the liberation of suppressed populations, the defeat of nasty regimes – compensate for negative effects such as destruction of homes, cities and cultural artefacts, and more especially still, the human suffering that occurs. Do the positive effects sometimes do even more than that – do they sometimes justify war? This question can be asked either specifically or generally. It can be asked of particular wars, either retrospectively, in the passing of historical judgement, or in anticipation, by national leaders calculating whether to go to war. And it can be asked of war as such, in the form: is war ever justified, given what and how it is? This topic is discussed in the next chapter, on just war theory.

One answer long since given, however, by someone who had witnessed the effects of the First World War with the keen eye of a great writer and the keen mind of a sensitive thinker, is this:

How senseless is everything that can ever be written, done, or thought, when such things are possible. It must be all lies and of no account when the culture of a thousand years could not prevent this stream of blood being poured out, these torture-chambers in their hundreds of thousands. A hospital alone shows what war is.

The writer was Erich Maria Remarque, in *All Quiet on the Western Front*.

PART III

Ethics, Law and War

CHAPTER 6

Ethics, Law and War

Few rational individuals would include war in their idea of a
perfect world. Fighting, killing, horror and destruction are not
among the appurtenances of any imagined paradise. The effort
to constrain war – to impose conditions on its beginning and
limits on its conduct – is among the chief marks of civilisation.
'Just war' theory, and the more recent development of international humanitarian law, are central to that effort.

Discussions of just war theory typically begin by sketching
the history of thinking about justifications for going to war
and the constraints on behaviour in the course of war. There
is a sound motive for this, because the very idea of 'just war'
seems paradoxical. How can killing and maiming people and
destroying their homes and economic resources ever be just?
How can the idea that there are moral restraints in the waging
of war make sense in the light of what war is and does? Yet on
the other hand acceptance of the reality that war happens and,
in the present state of the world, is likely to keep happening for
a while yet, obliges us to think of ways of trying to prevent war,

or at very least to limit its harms. There has long been serious reflection on the question.

Thucydides' concern about the morally corrupting effect of war was cited in the Introduction to this book, showing that questions about what made war necessary and right were already present to the mind of classical antiquity. Herodotus stated that the Greeks' primary motivation in resisting the Persian invasions was the preservation of their freedom; that too tells us that questions of value entered the calculation of accepting the costly and dangerous burden of war. In the *Republic* Plato says that neither fellow-Greeks nor their homes should be treated as targets for destruction, and when beaten in war fellow-Greeks should not be enslaved. That left non-Greeks vulnerable to enslavement and abuses; but it does not wholly undermine the prospects for humanity to find charity beginning somewhere, if only at home. More promisingly, Euripides enjoins good treatment of enemy prisoners in the *Heracleidae*, and in the fifth book of his *Histories* Polybius comments on the 'laws of war' in ways that markedly prefigure Augustine's ideas.

One can also cite ideas about restraint and acceptable conduct in war from ancient sources in other civilisations. Laozi urged that war should be embarked upon with the greatest reluctance, and minimalistically limited to the achievement of its aims. The seventh chapter of the Hindu *Book of Manu* (*Manusmitri*) says that war should be avoided if at all possible, with negotiation and arbitration as the preferable alternatives, and that if war occurs non-combatants must be protected, weapons must not be poisoned or so fashioned as to cause gross injury, and the use of force must be proportionate.

In the third part of the *Mahabharata*, just as the forces of the Kauravas and Pandavas are about to engage in combat, they agree on certain rules: celestial weapons are not to be used, fighting must occur in daylight only, no-one retreating or unarmed is to be attacked, no-one is to be struck on the back or the legs. Although all of these rules are broken in the fighting that follows (though not by the good king Yudhishthira), at least they were suggested. And in the celebrated passage known as the *Baghavad Gita* between this section and the description of the fighting, Arjuna and Krishna discuss the former's agony of conscience over warfare and its consequences, an agony experienced also by Yudhishthira after the fighting is over, when he reports that 6 million have died in the fighting, and declares that he no longer wishes to rule because it would condemn him to involvement in more violence and harm.

The foregoing shows that moral thinking about war is indeed practically coterminous with civilisation. Many writers, however, follow each other in asserting that just war theory as such is the product of Christian thought, citing Augustine and Aquinas – and mainly the former – as principal sources. Because of the prevalence of this view, it is important to note the following.

Christian thought about just war was not only a product of charitable efforts to mitigate the horrors of war, but was just as much a casuistical endeavour to justify war despite the fact that Christianity is manifestly a non-violent and pacifist religion. It was, indeed, a search for wriggle room, made necessary by the fact that the documents selected by the Church as its scriptural canon had inconveniently made appeal to Old Testament justifications for war difficult, if not in logic impossible, by asserting that the old law had been replaced by a new law in which, among other things, enemies are to be loved and the other cheek is to be turned – 'love your enemies', Luke 6:27 and Matthew 5:44; 'turn the other cheek', Luke 6:29, Matthew 5:39; 'blessed are the peacemakers', Matthew 5:9 – indeed the whole Sermon on the Mount in Matthew chapter 5 is a hymn to pacificism. Such sentiments scarcely license war or encourage the degree of belligerence required for war. In fact all fighting, and any kind of violence, not only war itself, seems to be forbidden to Christians, for even self-defence is prohibited: Romans 12:19 says 'Dearly beloved, avenge not yourselves, but give place unto wrath' ('wrath' being the vengeance that will be taken by God), and Matthew 26:52 says, 'All they that take the sword shall perish by the sword.' Martin Luther quite justifiably took these passages to entail strict pacificism and non-resistance.

In the Old Testament the deity repeatedly and bloodthirstily delivered the enemies of Israel into its hands to be 'devoted to destruction' – as (for just one of many examples) in Joshua 6:21; when the city of Jericho fell to Joshua, he and the Israelites killed every living thing in it, 'both men and women, young and old, oxen, sheep and donkeys, with the edge of the sword' – except for Rahab the prostitute who had helped Joshua's spies escape from the city earlier in the story. When Christians were moved to punish their faith's enemies, as in the Inquisition and crusades, they cited Old Testament sources in justification, precisely because New Testament sources were insufficiently galvanising: Deuteronomy 13:6–9 and Exodus 22:18 are examples.

Because the pacifist principles of the New Testament were an inconvenience both to temporal rulers who adhered to the Christian religion – Christianity had become the official religion of the Roman empire by the Edict of Thessalonica in 380 CE, and the Roman empire was a major military power being harassed by enemies on all its borders – and to the Church itself when intent on suppressing heresy by force and, later, encouraging Crusades, a defence of war was needed. It is in the light of this that we are to understand the efforts of Augustine, Aquinas and their successors in the Christian just war tradition, to state – in contrast to the pacific sentiments of their religion's founder – when and to what degree there could be organised and sanctioned murder of fellow human beings. The resulting rationalisation that became just war theory is a curious hybrid of legal, moral and prudential notions, as we shall see, in a way that undermines its usefulness in thinking about justifications for going to war and constraints on behaviour in war.

It is in fact possible to see an impetus to the idea of just war in the call of Pope Urban II to the first crusade. His call was in part a response to the dilemma of a situation in which 'half of the upper society that did not labour wore godly cloth while the other half wore armour and kept warhorses' – and these latter spent a good deal of time feuding with each other.[1] At the Council of Clermont in 1095 Urban invoked the idea of the 'Truce of God' which placed limits on feuding, with armistices on holy days and protection from violence against clergymen, women, children and peasants; and he urged instead that Christians should 'leave off slaying each other and fight instead a righteous war' against the Islamic invaders of the Holy Land.[2] His idea evidently was that if the upper classes could not be dissuaded from fighting each other, their bellicosity might be redirected in ways more useful to him and the Church. The idea of a 'righteous war' left behind the notions of turning the other cheek and being a blessed peacemaker, and required only a formal ethical justification to solve the problem bequeathed by scripture.

Augustine is the dominating influence in the Christian development of such a justification. He originated the phrase 'just war' itself in *The City of God*, where he remarks that 'the wise man might lament the necessity of just wars', but he would anyway fight on the grounds that, because they were just, they were permissible.[3] And their being so, in turn, was to be understood in light of the fact that God had given authority to governments (Romans 13:4) and therefore no-one need be ashamed to take arms on behalf of peace or against the wicked if required to do so by government. Indeed, it would be a sin not to kill in the service of justice and at the behest of wise government; doing so is therefore not, he said, a violation of the commandment against killing.

Later writers, especially Aquinas, quoted him extensively on the subject, not least his assertion in the *Epistle to Marcellus* that:

> If the Christian religion forbade war altogether, those who sought salutary advice in the Gospel would rather have been counselled to cast aside their arms, and to give up soldiering altogether. On the contrary, they were told: 'Do violence to no man . . . and be content with your pay' [Luke 3:14]. If he commanded them to be content with their pay, he did not forbid soldiering.

This nice piece of casuistry scarcely stands up against the adjurations in Matthew and Luke quoted above, but it was good enough for Aquinas.

Encouraged and armed by Augustine's views on the subject, therefore, Aquinas sought to formulate the principles of just war more precisely in *Summa Theologica*, as follows:

> In order for a war to be just, three things are necessary. First, the authority of the sovereign by whose command the war is to be waged. For . . . as the care of the common weal is

committed to those who are in authority, it is their business to watch over the common weal of the city, kingdom or province subject to them. And just as it is lawful for them to have recourse to the sword in defending that common weal against internal disturbances, when they punish evil-doers, according to the words of the Apostle (Romans 13:4): 'He beareth not the sword in vain: for he is God's minister, an avenger to execute wrath upon him that doth evil'; so too, it is their business to have recourse to the sword of war in defending the common weal against external enemies. Hence it is said to those who are in authority (Psalms 81:4): 'Rescue the poor: and deliver the needy out of the hand of the sinner'; and for this reason Augustine says: 'The natural order conducive to peace among mortals demands that the power to declare and counsel war should be in the hands of those who hold the supreme authority.'

Secondly, a just cause is required, namely that those who are attacked, should be attacked because they deserve it on account of some fault. Wherefore Augustine says: 'A just war is wont to be described as one that avenges wrongs, when a nation or state has to be punished, for refusing to make amends for the wrongs inflicted by its subjects, or to restore what it has seized unjustly.'

Thirdly, it is necessary that the belligerents should have a rightful intention, so that they intend the advancement of good, or the avoidance of evil. Hence Augustine says: 'True religion looks upon as peaceful those wars that are waged not for motives of aggrandisement, or cruelty, but with the object of securing peace, of punishing evil-doers, and of uplifting the good.' For it may happen that the war is declared by the legitimate authority, and for a just cause, and yet be rendered unlawful through a wicked intention. Hence

Augustine says: 'The passion for inflicting harm, the cruel thirst for vengeance, an unpacific and relentless spirit, the fever of revolt, the lust of power, and such like things, all these are rightly condemned in war.'[4]

In sum and in brief, the Aquinas doctrine is: war is just if it is instigated by a legitimate authority, is waged for a good purpose, and is aimed at achieving peace. His doctrine is squarely based on Augustine and what can be cited from scripture for its support. His successor in the tradition, Francisco de Vitoria, founder of the School of Salamanca in the sixteenth century, had both a more extensive and a more practically minded view. He was prompted to formulate it by the pacificism of Martin Luther, who had said that even if the Turks should attack Christendom it would be the will of God that they did so, and in obedience to the above-quoted scriptures one should not resist.

Given that the principle that war was not forbidden to Christians had already been established, Vitoria focused on the grounds that one would have for legitimately going to war (and incidentally, he took it that anyone possessed of these grounds, not just a government, could make war). His argument in *De Jure Belli* (1532) was that there was only one such ground, namely, that a wrong had been done. He did not regard religious differences as a ground, nor the desire to extend an empire, nor the gaining or enhancement of a prince's personal glory. Moreover, not every kind of wrong is a ground, he said, nor is the mere belief or opinion that a wrong has been done. But once a state of war exists, everything is permitted which conduces to the defence of the common good. It is lawful to take back what the enemy carried away, and to exact restitution out of the enemy's property for damages, losses and expenses.

And victory, said Vitoria, entitles a prince to punish an enemy for the wrong they have done.

A point on which Vitoria insisted was that if there is any doubt about whether a war is just, a subject may refuse to fight even if his prince commands him to do it. Therefore the question whether a war is just has to be carefully examined. So must questions about the treatment of innocents, children and captives. Anyone on a battlefield can be killed, but it is not justified to kill boys captured in a besieged city, even though they might grow up to become warriors. If an innocent is killed in the course of a greater harm being prevented, Vitoria said, the doctrine of double effect provides an exoneration. And he acknowledged that both sides in a conflict might regard themselves as fighting a just war, and in good faith; that is because of the fallibility of human reason, and the difficulty of judging aright. This is an interestingly grown-up admission, though it led Vitoria to insist that because the prince or ruler is in possession of most of the facts, people less close to the centre of power must generally take on trust his judgement as to the justice of the cause. This qualification is not fully consistent with the requirement that one can refuse to fight if there is serious doubt on that head.[5]

A fourth figure of importance in the theory's development is another Spanish Thomist, the Jesuit priest Francisco Suárez, whose life spanned the turn of the seventeenth century. To him is owed the clearest early distinction among the three arenas in which questions of the justification of war arise: just cause for going to war, just behaviour in war, and just settlement when hostilities are over: respectively, *jus ad bellum, jus in bello, jus post bellum.*[6]

Like Vitoria, Suárez regarded the commission of wrong as the sole just cause for war. He was careful to specify 'grave wrong', which only a war can put right because no other remedy is sufficient or available. Three examples are seizure of territory, violations of rights and (less convincingly) insult to the honour of the prince or people. He was careful to distinguish between defensive and offensive war, and to insist as Vitoria had done that the question whether a war is just needs to be debated beforehand so that all can be assured of the cause. This applies especially to offensive war, because whereas the justification for defensive war is usually obvious, greater justification is needed for starting a war. His view is that meting out justice for an international wrong is the same as justice meted out internally by a sovereign for a subject's wrongdoing, and that analogy is what provides the required ground.

Suárez agreed with Aquinas that it must be a sovereign or other legitimate authority who is alone entitled to make war, and with Vitoria in requiring all advisors and assistants to counsel the sovereign well on both the justice and wisdom of going to war, for he must take into consideration whether there is a rational expectation of success, how much of a burden on the national coffers the endeavour will be, and how his forces must behave during the conflict and while in enemy territory. The latter – the *jus in bello* considerations – involve thinking about innocents, what we now call 'collateral damage', and the employment of deceit and subterfuge, which as forms of lying threaten to plunge the sovereign and his generals into sin.[7]

The fifth in the founding just war tradition is a younger contemporary of Suárez, the Dutch jurist Hugo Grotius. In his view there is not only a case for regarding war as justified in appropriate circumstances, but on occasion as positively necessitated by all three types of law – natural law, divine law, and the law of nations. On the principle that to will a given end is to will the means to attaining that end, and given that the deity

wills us to preserve ourselves, to protect our means of liveli-
hood, to punish the wicked, and to defend the state, it follows
that it is justified to wage war for these ends. The principal
grounds for war are therefore self-defence, avenging wrongs and
the recovery of property. Hence Grotius's famous remark that if
'negotiation and judicial processes fail, war begins'.[8]

Grotius also addressed the *jus in bello* point. In light of the
means–end principle stated above, it follows that all necessary
actions to achieve the desired ends of war are permissible, which
scarcely sounds like a doctrine of the required kind; but Grotius
lists a number of constraints on what is permissible.[9] The general
rule is humane and self-controlled behaviour, in which conscience
and a sense of shame govern one's actions. The law of nations
might permit vengeance upon the enemy and looting of his
goods, but observance of the requirements of justice, together
with the moral inhibitions outlined, prescribe what Grotius
called *temperamenta*, which means 'moderation' or 'restraint'.
Acting temperately will motivate respect for innocents, mercy to
foes, remission of punishments, forgiveness of war debts, resto-
ration of a conquered enemy to self-rule and the keeping of
one's agreements and promises.[10]

Grotius's version of the idea of just behaviour in war was
influential in the wider debate in moral philosophy in the seventeenth and eighteenth centuries. One reason was the horrors
of the Thirty Years' War, 1618–48, the most vicious and destructive war in Europe's history to that point. Among many atrocities and much destruction was the Sack of Magdeburg in 1631,
when all 30,000 inhabitants of the city were massacred.

Even more important was Grotius's influence on the
development of theories of international law and international
relations, offering in the latter respect a third position alongside

the sharply contrasting views of Hobbes, who saw the international domain as a wilderness, and Kant, who dreamed of a comity of nations. Grotius thought that although there was not enough in the way of common interests between states to allow for a cosmopolitan world settlement, as Kant wished, there was yet enough for consensus to be reached on a degree of order in international affairs that would limit the harm done by conflict – for example, by agreement between states on observation of treaties, diplomatic arrangements and respect for mutual independence. In this way his views tread a middle way between Hobbesian international anarchy and the rather hard-to-achieve Kantian vision of closer international amity.

From the views variously evolved by these thinkers, a body of principles described as 'just war theory' emerged. A standard formulation is as follows. A war can be accounted just if:

1. It is a last resort after the failure of all other means to solve the conflict in question.
2. It is initiated and prosecuted by a legitimate authority.
3. There is a just cause for it.
4. It has a reasonable chance of being successful.
5. The intention has to be right, namely, to re-establish peace and justice.
6. The use of force must be proportional, that is, just enough to achieve the end in view.
7. Civilians and the innocent must not be targets; 'collateral damage' is acceptable only if genuinely unavoidable.

Thus tabulated, the principles are a somewhat curious mixture. Consider 4; it is a prudential requirement the moral force of which presumably relates to the harm that going to war might do to oneself or one's own people. The idea is that it would be more than merely unwise but actually unethical to take one's own side into a war either unwinnable or likely to result in defeat – rather as King Croesus of Lydia did, so Herodotus tells us, having been told by an oracle that if he went to war he would destroy a great kingdom; the oracle was right, but the kingdom was his own. However, if the Polish army had thought in these terms in 1939 when their country was invaded by Hitler's forces, they would not have set the moral example of resistance and defiance which in the end proved of value in the struggle mounted by Russia and Britain against those same forces. On this view, it could be right – heroic, justified, because better than submission and enslavement – to fight even in a hopeless cause.

Principle 2 is a legal, even a legalistic, principle, which as we saw was not accepted by Vitoria. If a war is just on other grounds, it would seem to be irrelevant who wages it, or on whose authority. The principle reads like an attempt either to protect the authority of princes, or to prevent *condottieri*-style activity which, as history amply testifies, was too often mere brigandage on a large scale; or both.

Principle 1 assumes that one can know that all resources short of war have been tried and cannot possibly succeed. Impatience and frustration might make one think that this is so, and one can be wrong. A realist might also say that it would be reasonable to impose limits on such efforts, given that some parties to them might be using delay and prevarication for ill purposes. Either way the principle, although desirable, is difficult to apply in practice.

Principle 3 also stands out as problematic, because it is the only one that actually addresses the heart of the matter – the *reason* for going to war – and yet at the same time it is hope-lessly vague. If there were a just reason for going to war it would weaken or negate the force of the other principles, as for example the case of Polish defiance illustrates. In the founding tradition we see 'wrongs' cited as just cause, and some examples given. But examples are not enough, for their degree of persuasiveness is relative to circumstance: insult to our current ruler, for example, would no longer be a persuasive reason for starting a war. Accordingly, what is to be understood as a 'wrong' of the required kind and a sufficient degree, given that it must justify death and destruction, needs a more precise specification. Some wrongs might seem obvious: being invaded, say; but even here pacifists, though recognising it as a wrong, would not agree that it justifies going to war, for on their view there is never justifica-tion for war. Just war theory has to counter that strong claim.

There are two kinds of questions that can be raised about just war theory. One concerns the merits of the principles them-selves, individually and together, as just shown. The other concerns whether and in what way they apply in the circum-stances of a world that has changed greatly since just war theory was first developed. During the Cold War, for example, Michael Walzer stated that 'nuclear weapons explode the theory of just war', arguing that they justify a 'supreme emergency exception' to the principles, such that if one's own country is threatened with annihilation by another country, it would be legitimate to strike at that country first even though doing so would annihi-late *its* population, thus violating principles 6 and 7 in the above list.[11] Walzer cited as a precedent the use by Britain of 'area bombing' of German civilian populations in the Second World War. This is not a good example, and I have rebutted its validity in my examination of the ethics of Allied bombing campaigns in that war.[12] But the inefficacy of the example does not undermine Walzer's case for such an exception; that needs further argument. In application to terrorism or the threat of terrorist attack, and in response to acts of genocide, the idea that there can be exceptions to the principles also carries weight.

That said, it is also the case that the idea that there are indeed principles of justice at stake is one that almost all advanced countries have accepted since the mid-twentieth century. Walzer himself remarked that 'justice has become, in all Western countries, one of the tests that any proposed military strategy or tactic has to meet – only one of the tests and not the most important one, but this still gives Just War theory a place and standing it never had before'.[13] But in the new environment of different – and far worse – threats than were anticipated by the early just war theorists, revisiting them seems desirable. One such effort was made in a United Nations report in 2004 after a re-examination of what is needed to further the aim of collective security laid out in the UN Charter. The question asked by the report's authors was 'What should the Security Council consider as sufficient to persuade it to endorse the use of military force?' They framed their answer as five 'basic criteria', these being: the seriousness of the threat, the purpose of the military action, whether there is no other remedy for or means to resolve the problem, whether the force to be used is proportional, and whether the likely consequences are acceptable.[14]

The first criterion embodies the standard thought that a clear and present danger to a state or the security of its peoples is a justification for war, but adds the second thought that such justification would also be present if genocide, ethnic cleansing and major violations of humanitarian law were occurring or imminent. This is an example of how recent history has enriched the notion of just cause, by extending the specification of wrongs that would license military action if other remedies failed. The remaining four criteria are iterations of the traditional view, though the last, specifying 'consequences' as a more general criterion than 'likely success', clarifies that condition by asking if the consequences are likely to be better, in at least the sense of 'less bad', than the consequence of not going to war, all round (and not just for 'us')?

As one would expect, this restatement brings fresh questions into view. If preventing genocide is a just cause for war, is punishing genocide after the fact also a just cause? Is imposing regime change, either as prevention or punishment for actual or threatened genocide, a just cause – this, for example, being the stated intention of the United States in invading Iraq in 2003? Terrorism and insurgency raise a host of new questions. If terrorists and insurgents conceal themselves among civilians, under what conditions can they be targeted? If collateral damage is caused in such targeting, or indeed in the course of more conventional action, should those harmed be compensated? Are there constraints on interrogation techniques even in the direst of emergencies – of the kind that Walzer might regard as permitting exceptions to humanitarian criteria? For example, you have captured someone who has hidden a dirty nuclear device in the centre of a large city; is it justifiable to torture his wife and children before his eyes to get him to reveal its whereabouts in time? Protection of civilian populations, not least one's own, has always been a priority of a state's security arrangements, so in a time when both the fact and the instruments of terrorism have greatly increased, Winston Churchill's blunt observation – that one cannot fight wars with one hand tied behind one's back – returns ominously into view.

Indeed, in the light of new kinds of dangers and the new kinds of agents who or which pose them, the very framing of these matters in terms of just war theory might now be insufficient and even misleading. The security threats that face the world come not only from interstate conflict, terrorism, humanitarian crises, and transnational organised crime, but also from environmental threats, infectious disease pandemics, mass refugee migrations, and misuses of technology. Some of these might sometimes require the use of military and militarised police forces to exert control, to combat armed activity by large-scale criminal forces, to protect some populations against others, or to otherwise intervene when serious difficulties occur. Ethical questions about when, how, to what degree, and with what objectives, arise here too, and they are not obviously comprised within the purview of just war doctrine.

Take a particular example: at the time of writing drones are being used in Afghanistan to 'find, fix and finish' (as drone-speak has it) Taliban fighters, with 'collateral damage' as a frequent risk. The Taliban are insurgents from the perspective of the entity recognised as the legitimate government of Afghanistan and its supporters, but they do not constitute an army in the conventional sense, and they are not fighting a declared war, which means that the action being taken against them is technically closer to a police operation than a war, though doubtless it feels very much like a war to those on the ground. Definitions matter; if it is not a war, does it follow that the 'laws of war' do not apply? A soldier can kill an enemy soldier in combat, and be rewarded for it, but cannot kill somebody in a saloon bar brawl without being indicted for murder. The action in the first instance is legitimised by the laws of war. If action against the Taliban is not war, what legitimises it?

Such questions abound in the grey area of asymmetrical, insurgent and terrorist conflict now commonly requiring organised military response.

As these thoughts show, just war theory appears to raise more questions than it answers, though at the same time it offers a framework in which these very necessary questions demand to be asked. Because of the insufficiency of the traditional terms of reference of the theory, which are primarily moral, a different and more formalised approach capturing the moral considerations is on offer, in the form of international humanitarian law.

International humanitarian law is about *jus in bello*, leaving questions about *jus ad bellum* to the discussion noted above in connection with provisions in the United Nations Charter about when the Security Council can justify endorsing military action. Drawing on just war theory and the first attempts at codification of humanitarian constraints in the nineteenth century, the bulk of international humanitarian law is contained in the four Geneva Conventions of 1949, supplemented by the two Additional Protocols of 1977 extending protection to civilians, and a set of separate agreements and conventions aimed at restraining the use of particular types of weapons and tactics. As the date of the Conventions signifies, the experience of the Second World War and the formal institution of the United Nations immediately afterwards provided the opportunity to make a more concerted effort on *jus in bello* matters, giving them the status of law with enforcement and sanctions attached. As regards enforcement and sanctions, success has been very limited and patchy; but as regards clarification and codification, international humanitarian law is a major advance on the *jus in bello* considerations implied in just war theory. Nearly every state in the world is a signatory to the Geneva Conventions, and although they apply primarily to interstate war, some of its provisions apply to non-international conflicts also.

The rapid evolution of military technology and the nature of conflict has meant that humanitarian law has had to work hard to keep pace. In 1954 a Convention was adopted for protecting cultural property – 'culturecide' might have been part of the aim of 'carpet bombing' in the Second World War, but deliberate targeting of cultural treasures, such as the destruction of the Bamiyan Buddha statues by the Taliban in Afghanistan, of parts of Palmyra by Daesh in Syria, and damage to the Golden Temple in Amritsar in the troubles of 1984, are examples. In some cases only luck – or a miracle, depending on your point of view – has saved a priceless cultural artefact, as with Leonardo da Vinci's 'Last Supper' mural, left unscathed after the church of Santa Maria della Grazie in Milan was bombed on 15 August 1943.[15]

Conventions on biological and chemical weapons were adopted in 1972 and 1980 respectively, the Ottawa Convention on anti-personnel mines followed in 1997, and in 2000 an 'Optional Protocol' was added to the Convention of the Rights of the Child to address the question of child soldiers. Many of these provisions, though not all, are now accepted as customary law binding all states in the international community.

International humanitarian law has two principal aims. One is to protect non-combatants, whether they are civilians caught up in the fighting, medical teams working in conflict zones, wounded or sick military personnel no longer taking part in the fighting, and prisoners of war. The other aim is to constrain the weapons and methods used in warfare.

The first aim specifies what counts as 'protection'. Not merely is it forbidden to kill wounded or sick enemy soldiers, but they must be afforded medical help and humane shelter as prisoners. They must be allowed to communicate with their families while detained. Medical centres and prison camps must be identifiable (for example, by prominently displaying the Red Cross or Red Crescent symbols) to ensure that they are not attacked. Non-combatants must be distinguished from combatants and must not be targeted; this applies to persons and their property alike.

It is one thing to have a set of desiderata, of course, and quite another to see them obeyed. International humanitarian law is far more often breached – and often enough flouted – than observed. Violations of them are war crimes. The reason they are breached is the simple one captured in Churchill's remark about having one hand tied behind one's back in war: how can one fight with one hand in the emergency, danger and confusion of conflict, when the lives of oneself and one's own are at risk, and decisions have to be made extremely quickly? Principle and reality clash all the time. And yet the matter of applying principle is every bit as urgent as the urgency of war itself, given that the danger war poses is not just to combatants, and the potential harms done by war are great.

And indeed efforts are made to achieve adherence to humanitarian law. States which are signatories to the Conventions are obligated by them to enact laws in their own countries for prosecution of war crimes committed by their militaries. Special tribunals to try war crimes charges have been empanelled, such as those for Rwanda and the former Yugoslavia, following a pattern set by the ad hoc Nuremberg trials at the close of the Second World War. One of the responsibilities of the International Criminal Court (ICC) set up by the 1998 Rome Statute is to handle war crime cases.

The fate of the ICC is illustrative of the difficulty that enforcement faces. Not only is it hard to bring individuals and states to trial, but the perceived lack of even-handedness in the administration of international justice weakens the instruments – both the ICC and ad hoc tribunals – used to administer it. For example, some African states (South Africa is a salient example) feel that they are singled out whereas major world players such as the USA or Russia – the latter widely accused of deliberately bombing hospitals in Syria, a very serious violation – are not prosecuted.

As one of the key aims of humanitarian law is to protect non-combatants in war, it is of interest to see how the principles involved are stated, because these are most directly descended from just war theory. Five are of particular note. One is the principle of distinction, requiring that military targets be distinguished from non-military targets at all times. A second is the principle of humane treatment, which is comprehensive: respect for the physical and psychological integrity of non-combatants, whether civilians or *hors de combat* military personnel, includes immunity from cruel, humiliating and degrading treatment, summary execution, and use as hostages or human shields.

The principles of necessity and proportionality are indispensable to a regime of constraint; the intention is to limit the amount of 'collateral damage' that fighting inevitably involves, by requiring that the amount of force used, and indeed whether it is used at all in a given circumstance, should be carefully calibrated to the unintended and unwanted side-effects of its use.

There is, finally, a qualified application of a general consideration of human rights: the principle of not discriminating against anyone on the grounds of race, nationality, religion or political opinion. The qualification is that preferential treatment is to be accorded women and children, protecting women from sexual violence, and children under the age of eighteen from being obliged to take part in military activities.

Women are disproportionately affected by war. Rape is a weapon of war by which countless numbers of women have been harmed over history, though documented instances in the Second World War, the Balkans conflict of the 1990s, and in post-colonial Africa – notably Uganda, South Sudan, the Central African Republic and the Congo – bring these horrific facts sharply into focus. In addition to the psychological and physical trauma of sexual violence there is the burden of disease and pregnancy that can follow; in the case of women who carry their rapist's (or too often, one of their rapists') baby to term, there is the social difficulty, and not infrequently opprobrium, attached to the child's parentage. There might also be rejection by society of the rape victim as soiled or polluted, a profoundly unjust compounding of victimhood. The Harvard Humanitarian Initiative studies into the effects of war on women, to give just one example, found that up to a quarter of survivors of sexual violence in the Congo suffer rejection by their communities.[16]

An *Economist* report in 2008 on atrocities against women and girls in the Democratic Republic of the Congo read as follows:

> All sides – government troops, says the United Nations, as well as the militias – use rape as a weapon of war on a barbarous scale. Most victims, as ever, are women and girls, some no more than toddlers, though men and boys have sometimes been targeted too. Local aid workers and UN reports tell of gang rapes, leaving victims with appalling physical and

psychological injuries; rapes committed in front of families or whole communities; male relatives forced at gunpoint to rape their own daughters, mothers or sisters; women used as sex slaves forced to eat excrement or the flesh of murdered relatives. Some women victims have themselves been murdered by bullets fired from a gun barrel shoved into their vagina.[17]

Ann Jones, an aid worker in Liberia, Sierra Leone and Ivory Coast, wrote an article in the *Los Angeles Times* entitled 'A War on Women':

Of all the civilians who suffered, none suffered as disproportionately as women. Today, millions of women in these three West African countries are still struggling to recover; for them, the wars aren't really over at all. To understand why, consider this description from Amnesty International last March of the least of the West African wars, the relatively short civil war in Ivory Coast: 'The scale of rape and sexual violence . . . in the course of the armed conflict has been largely underestimated. Many women have been gang-raped or have been abducted and reduced to sexual slavery by fighters. Rape has often been accompanied by the beating or torture (including torture of a sexual nature) of the victim. . . . All armed factions have perpetrated and continue to perpetrate sexual violence with impunity.' The Amnesty International report documents case after case of girls and women, ages 'under 12' to 63, assaulted by armed men. A more recent and thoroughgoing report by Human Rights Watch records the rape of children as young as 3. During the civil war, women and girls were seized in their village homes or at military roadblocks, or were discovered hiding in the bush.[18]

In another article in the *Los Angeles Times*, United Nations official John Holmes reported:

> From the start, sexual violence has been a particularly awful – and shockingly common – feature of the conflict in Congo. Women and girls are particularly vulnerable in this predatory environment, with rape and other forms of sexual abuse committed by all sides on an astonishing scale. Since 2005, more than 32,000 cases of rape and sexual violence have been registered in South Kivu alone. But that's only a fraction of the total; many – perhaps most – attacks go unreported. Victims of rape are held in shame by Congolese society and frequently are ostracized by their families and communities. The ripple effect of these attacks goes far beyond the individual victim, destroying family and community bonds and leaving children orphaned and/or HIV positive.[19]

In a *New York Times* report on the work of a doctor in eastern Congo's Kivu Province the same dreadful story is told:

> Every day, 10 new women and girls who have been raped show up at [Dr Denis Mukwege's] hospital. Many have been so sadistically attacked from the inside out, butchered by bayonets and assaulted with chunks of wood, that their reproductive and digestive systems are beyond repair. Eastern Congo is going through another one of its convulsions of violence, and this time it seems that women are being systematically attacked on a scale never before seen here. According to the United Nations, 27,000 sexual assaults were reported in 2006 in South Kivu Province alone, and that may be just a fraction of the total number across the country. Dr. Mukwege

performs as many as six rape-related surgeries a day. In one town, Shabunda, 70 percent of the women reported being sexually brutalised. Honorata Barinjibanwa, 18, said she was kidnapped from a village during a raid in April and kept as a sex slave until August. Most of that time she was tied to a tree, and she still has rope marks ringing her neck. Her kidnappers would untie her for a few hours each day to gang-rape her, she said.[20]

These appalling reports could alas be reprised, with different names for the places and the wars, many times over. For just one more example: Antony Beevor's book *The Fall of Berlin* describes the rape of hundreds of thousands of German women by Russian troops in their advance on Berlin in 1944–45 – Russia banned his book as a result – and photographic evidence of murdered women who had been subjected to sexual assault before death has survived from the atrocities.[21]

On a far less ghastly note, but pertinent to the disproportionate effects of war on women, one recalls that in most societies women have traditionally been the principal carers of children and elderly relatives, responsible for keeping them safe, well and fed, and that therefore the stresses of wartime are magnified for them in a different way. Such conventional duties can be onerous enough in peacetime without bombs, invaders and starvation making life vastly more difficult. As a result of major wars, early widowhood, perhaps with a young family, was the lot of many tens of thousands of women whose husbands or partners were killed in battle. Others, whose menfolk did not die but returned with psychological scars, personality changes, perhaps physically disabled and unable to work, had yet further burdens to bear.

The last hundred years have seen women cease to be merely passive bystanders in wartime. Mobilisation of women on a large scale into work in factories, hospitals, farms, administration and the armed services themselves – until recent years, exclusively in auxiliary roles – brought with it major social changes in the aftermath of war. The point is now a familiar one: the First World War in particular was a significant catalyst for bringing women out of the restricted domains of the preceding Victorian ethos into wider domains of possibility. With the achievement of increased gender equality in Western societies women have begun to seek and gain a greater role, and at higher levels of seniority, in militaries.

Reservations about admitting women to ground combat roles has been a factor in all Western militaries, though in insurgencies and revolutions, as throughout history, women have often fought alongside men, giving the lie to the idea that fighting and war-making are exclusively masculine proclivities – still less, capabilities. When critics produce the standard arguments about women's lesser physical strength, vulnerability to hormone-influenced mood swings in the menstrual cycle, alleged different priorities in relationships with others, alleged greater timidity, and the like, one is hearing equally standard sexist tropes: these arguments should by now have gone into the bin.[22] To prove the point, women soldiers now have combat roles in many armies, from Finland to Australia; one of the most resistant to change in this respect, the US Army, changed its policy in 2013, although Ranger and SEAL units remained restricted to men for two or three years afterwards.

There are harms that might be done to women combatants in case of capture that are less likely to happen to male captives – sexual assault being the principal one – but which naturally fall under the protective requirement for 'humane treatment'. It is unlikely that when the principles were first drafted, the kinds of maltreatment envisaged included possible harms to women soldiers. But the discourse of humanitarian law is easily capable of alerting the few who might not see this point for themselves.

In just war theory and international humanitarian law we see one side of human reality, the aspiring, benevolent moral aspiration that rises from the deepest wells of human compassion and community. In war itself we see the other side of human reality, the tough, contentious, pugnacious ambition either to defend or to conquer, for any of the reasons canvassed in Chapter 4. In the first there are proofs of amazing sacrifice and tenderness; in the second there is frightening evidence of cruelty and barbarism. Both sides are represented in human affairs, and even quite often in human individuals: many SS officers on duty at Second World War death camps had their families with them, and at least many must have been affectionate husbands and fathers. It is taken to be a chilling reflection that some of them listened to Beethoven and read Goethe in their off-duty hours, a comment on the failure of culture to prevent barbarism, all the more troubling because the barbarians are meant to be outside the gates, not within them.

Humanitarian law as *law* marks an implicit admission that moral adjuration by itself will always be insufficient to stay the slayer's hand. As law it attempts to impose a stronger limit, a more definite disincentive than moral persuasion alone, because as law it carries with it the idea that it can be enforced, and that breaches of it can be punished; that there are sanctions more formidable than a troubled conscience. It goes without saying that the relative failure so far of international humanitarian law to be properly enforced by a system of courts carrying international respect and weight, is profoundly regrettable. But it does not negate an important effect of its existence. This is that it acts somewhat in the following way: if you aim at fifty, you might hit less. But if you aim at a hundred, even if you are unlikely to hit it, you might do much better than fifty. By increasing the stakes, sharpening definitions and drawing on the actualities of recent experience, international humanitarian law does a better job of making people mindful of *jus in bello* considerations than do the scholars picking over Aquinas and Grotius.

Its provisions bring to life the meaning of such words as these:

> But now, for the first time, I see you are a man like me. I thought of your hand-grenades, of your bayonet, of your rifle; now I see your wife and your face and our fellowship. Forgive me, comrade. We always see it too late. Why do they never tell us that you are poor devils like us, that your mothers are just as anxious as ours, and that we have the same fear of death, and the same dying and the same agony – Forgive me, comrade; how could you be my enemy?[23]

Curse war; but acknowledging that it happens, and that expunging it from human affairs is going to require a great improvement in human intelligence first, forces us to the difficult task of trying to mitigate it. That is what just war theory and conceptions of humanitarian law seek to do. In practice their effect is limited. But in refining our vision of what is desirable in this most undesirable of arenas they are a significant help. One thing we note is that the key motivation is the moral one of respecting the humanity of all those caught up in war, on the unstated but profound assumption that something is owed to

214

human beings just in virtue of their being such – and owed by each human being to all others. This assumption is susceptible of independent debate, though it would be easy enough to justify it. As the key motivation, moral concern trumps the prudential and legalistic principles, respectively 'do not go to war unless you can win it' and 'war can only be started by a duly constituted authority'. These are subordinate to the moral imperatives of not making war unless it is genuinely unavoidable, and of treating all caught up in it with as much humanity as is consistent with the circumstances. Thus summarised, one sees that the intention is simple, clear and unarguable. Underlying it is unbearable pity for the suffering that war causes, and the rich common sense that sees meliorism as the only viable alternative to perfectibilism in human affairs.

CHAPTER 7

The Future of War

On Wednesday 25 October 1854 the 13th Light Dragoons, 17th Lancers and 8th and 10th Hussars, combined into a cavalry unit known as the Light Brigade led by the seventh Earl of Cardigan, undertook an action so disastrous that it entered the annals of heroism and – courtesy of Lord Tennyson – poetry. A series of mistakes made the Light Brigade, with Cardigan galloping at its head, charge down the length of a valley directly into the mouths of more than fifty cannon supported by twenty battalions of Russian infantry. It is as memorable a fact of the Crimean War that the Charge of the Light Brigade happened in it, as that Florence Nightingale walked the wards of Scutari Hospital, shedding the beams of her lamp into the painful nights.

The Light Brigade was shot to pieces; there were 275 casualties dead, missing and wounded; 335 horses were killed; only 195 men survived with their mounts, less than half the force. Cardigan, who also survived, having galloped the length of the 'Valley of Death' in both directions and hacking at Russians troops in between, took himself aboard his personal yacht in

Balaclava harbour afterwards and had a champagne dinner. A French commander who witnessed the action, Marshal Pierre Bosquet, famously remarked, 'C'est magnifique, mais ce n'est pas la guerre.'

Various accounts were given as to what had gone wrong. There was mutual detestation between Lord Cardigan and his brother-in-law, Lord Lucan, who was in command of the Heavy Brigade of cavalry which was meant to support the Light Brigade's attack, had it gone in the right direction. In the event Lucan did not commit his men to the cannon's mouths, though this gave rise to rumours that he was hoping they would dispose of his brother-in-law. The overall commander, Lord Raglan, had wished Cardigan to attack an artillery unit on the other side of a nearby hill, but because Cardigan could not see over the hill, and because the officer who brought him his orders pointed ambiguously in the general direction of the Russian army when Cardigan asked which bit of it he was to attack, misunderstanding was inevitable.

I mention this famous or infamous incident because it offers a number of startling contrasts to the subsequent 150 years of war. There, in the mid-nineteenth century, a group of lords, pursuing the traditional aristocratic occupation of war-making, were leading men born to the plough, the sheepfold and the forge – or, increasingly, the factory – into the mouths of cannon. Social class and military tradition were hard to shake off; in 1914 the British Army was still divided on class grounds between officers and men, but the First World War was not a galloping war, because weapons had changed, and machine guns and cavalry did not mix. The introduction of the tank late in the First World War gave cavalry units a new kind of horse, an iron one; and in the Second World War the mobility and firepower of tanks played a significant role in battles in the Western Desert, on the Eastern Front, and during the highly mobile *Blitzkrieg* conducted by the Wehrmacht early in the war.

In the Vietnam War, the successor of the horse was the helicopter; it remains so, now bristling with even more armament, along with the 'Humvee' (High Mobility Multipurpose Wheeled Vehicle). Technology in the service of anti-insurgent war fought in Vietnam's and Cambodia's jungles in the 1960s took a more than usually sinister turn when those jungles were dusted with Agent Orange to strip their foliage, in the hope of revealing Vietcong troop movements and supply lines.

The television-reported wars in the Gulf in 1990–91 and 2003–11 showed a new–old kind of soldier, a man wearing armour once more, under his camouflage battledress, but highly technologised, wired up, in full communication with comrades and commanders, supplied with night-vision goggles, and carrying in his hands weapons of vastly greater power than his predecessors in earlier wars.[1]

What all this shows is how war has changed in a number of dramatic respects, technologically and therefore in character, though in other respects it is as it ever was, with people killing other people at the bottom of it all, though in ever more sophisticated ways. Could it be, however, that further changes already in progress will make war a new kind of phenomenon, prompting new and urgent ethical questions? The answer seems to be 'Yes'.

The reason is the advent of remote unmanned military machines, and the prospect that such machines will not merely be unmanned but autonomous. The world is already familiar with military hunter-killer drones such as the Predator and the Reaper, used in Afghanistan, the border territories of Pakistan and Iraq to 'find, fix and finish' human targets. These devices suggest – perhaps indeed presage – a future of war in which the fighting is done by machines increasingly free of direct human control, which is a nightmare prospect.

Almost every technological advance in the means of warfare brings new ethical problems. In 1868 the Declaration of St Petersburg outlawed newly invented bullets that split apart inside a victim's body to increase their incapacitating effect; this was endorsed by the 1899 Hague Conference, which also outlawed aerial bombardment, before heavier-than-air flight had become possible (it had in mind the throwing of grenades from balloons). After the 1914–18 war chemical weapons were outlawed. After the 1939–45 war energy was devoted to attempts at banning or at least limiting the spread of nuclear weapons.

These are all examples of how futile has been the attempt to limit the extent of harm threatened by technologies of war. Throughout history it has been technology that has made the chief difference in warfare – the spear, the metallurgy of swords and shields, armour, the crossbow, the arquebus, artillery, rapid-fire small arms, aircraft, missiles, the logistical equipment used in moving forces and supplies, all represent the deadly inventive-ness prompted by times of emergency and danger. Whoever has had the superior technology in a war has always had the better chance of winning it.

Asymmetric warfare, in which small groups of insurgents can encumber huge military resources of an orthodox kind, directly challenge this trend. But the technologists are not wholly without answers. Unmanned drone aircraft, used for surveillance and offensive engagement in circumstances and terrains where conventional forces are at a huge disadvantage, are a leading example. The badlands of the Afghanistan–Pakistan border provide a classic example of where drones best do their work. Able to stay aloft for long periods, hard to detect and defend against, formidably armed, they are chillingly effective weapons and they put no operating personnel at risk. This is a very desirable consideration for the home team using them.

The fact that drones are unmanned, controlled from thousands of miles away by operators sitting safely before a screen, and that these operators are chosen for their video gaming skills, somehow seems to make them more sinister, somehow less 'fair' and right. In particular, the move from violent video games to the dreadful reality of killing actual human beings seems to cast a deeper moral shadow over their use, trivialising the deaths caused, and making cold and unfeeling the acts and actors that cause them.

One is reminded of the world press's reaction in 1911 when the very first aerial bombing took place. An Italian airman threw grenades out of his monoplane onto Ottoman troops in North Africa. The world's press were outraged at the 'unsporting' nature of the venture, on the grounds that the victims suffering on the ground were unable to retaliate. This quickly proved wrong: Ottoman troops shot down an Italian airplane the following week, with rifle fire. Less than forty years later the British and Americans were dropping millions of tons of high explosives on German and later Japanese civilian populations nightly.

Paradoxically, drone activity is at the less bad end, if there can be such a thing, of causing death from the air. It is more selective, more precisely targeted, and therefore marginally less likely to cause collateral damage, than conventional bombing, and it does not put one's own side in harm's way: this latter, to repeat, is a very great attraction for the home side. The seemingly inhuman nature of their operation – the deadly machine without a person in it, faceless, remote, weighed down with missiles, remorselessly homing in on its target – is a prompt for extra dislike of it; yet it reprises a form of killing that anciently recommended itself: like long-range missiles, or high-level carpet bombing, it embodies the same principle as stoning to death, distancing the killer from the victim at a sanitary remove.

Only consider: no RAF bomber pilot in the Second World War would have liked to shoot a woman and her child in the head with a pistol, but on repeated occasions he released huge tonnages of bombs on many faceless women and children in the dark cities below him. Not touching the victim, not being in the same corner of space, is a sop to the conscience. Screen-gazers in an American desert who steer their drones to targets in Afghanistan have the advantage over bomber pilots of guaranteed safety as well as the stone-thrower's remove.

The history of drones is surprisingly long, as a special form of 'unmanned aerial vehicle' (UAV) long since developed to undertake tasks considered 'too dull, dirty or dangerous' for human beings. UAVs were in rudimentary use before the First World War for target practice, they served as flying bombs in the First and Second World Wars, they were used as decoys and surveillance devices in the Arab–Israeli Yom Kippur war of 1973, and in Vietnam they undertook more than 3,000 reconnaissance missions. But after 2001 military UAVs increasingly became central to US operations in the Middle East and Afghanistan, and in hunter-killer roles. The Predator drone became operational in 2005, the Reaper in 2007; since then they have grown in number to constitute almost a third of US aircraft strength, and have been used in many thousands of missions against targets across those regions.

Hunter-killer drones over Afghanistan are remotely operated from air force bases in the United States, such as Creech

AFB near Las Vegas. The personnel selected to operate them are generally the kind of young men who are good at such video war games as *Call of Duty* and *Combat Mission*. In the terminology of remote warfare, drones are described as 'human-in-the-loop' weapons, that is, devices controlled by humans who select targets and decide whether to attack them. Another development is the field of 'human-on-the-loop' systems, which are capable of selecting and attacking targets autonomously, though with human oversight and ability to override them. The technology causing most concern is 'human-*out-of*-the-loop' systems, which are completely autonomous devices on land, under the sea or in the air, programmed to seek, identify and attack targets without any human oversight after the initial programming.

The more general term used to designate all such systems is 'robotic weapons', and for the third kind 'lethal autonomous robots', 'lethal autonomous weapons' (LAWs) or – colloquially and generally – 'killer robots'. The acronym 'LAWs' is chillingly ironic. Expert opinion has it that they could be in operational service before the middle of the twenty-first century. It is obvious what kind of concerns they raise. The idea of delegating life-and-death decisions to unsupervised armed machines is inconsistent with humanitarian law, given the danger that they would put everyone and everything at risk in their field of operation, including non-combatants. Anticipating the dangers and seeking to pre-empt them by banning LAWs in advance is the urgently preferred option of human rights activists.

It was noted in the last chapter that international humanitarian law already has provisions that outlaw the deployment of weapons and tactics that could be particularly injurious, especially to non-combatants. LAWs are not mentioned in the founding documents, of course, but the implication of the appended agreements and supplementary conventions is clear enough. They provide that novel weapons systems, or modifications of existing ones, should be examined for their consistency with the tenor of humanitarian law. One of the immediate problems with LAWs is whether they could be programmed to conform to the principle of discrimination, that is, to be able to distinguish between justified military targets and everything else. Could they be programmed to make a fine judgement about whether it is necessary for them to deploy their weapons? If so, could they be programmed to adjust their activity so that it is proportional to the circumstances they find themselves in? Distinction, necessity and proportionality are key principles in the humanitarian law of conflict, and in each case flexible, nuanced, experienced judgement is at a premium. Could a computer programme instantiate the capacity for such judgement?

An affirmative answer to these 'could' questions requires artificial intelligence to be developed to a point where analysis of battlefield situations and decisions about how to respond to them is not merely algorithmic but has the quality of evaluation that, in human beings, turns on affective considerations. What this means is best explained by considering neurologist Antonio Damasio's argument that if a purely logical individual such as Star Trek's Mr Spock really existed, he would be a poor reasoner, because to be a good reasoner one needs an emotional dimension to thought.[2] A machine would need extremely subtle programming to make decisions in the way human beings do, and humanitarian considerations are premised on the best possibilities of the way human beings make decisions about how to act. In particular, creating a machine analogue of compassion would be a remarkable achievement; but a capacity for compassion is one of the features that intelligent application of humanitarian principles requires.

An answer to this is that the human emotional dimensions invoked are just what should *not* be required on the battlefield. Machines, says this answer, would be less erratic because never emotionally conflicted, and swifter and more decisive in action, than most if not all humans.

This is true. But the question is whether we wish the decision-maker in a battle zone to be this way, given that among the necessary conditions for conforming to humanitarian law is the capacity to read intentions, disambiguate and interpret odd behaviour, read body language and the like. These are psychological skills that humans usually develop early in life, and which they apply in mainly unconscious ways. Would a killer robot be able to tell the difference between a terrified individual trying to surrender and an aggressive individual about to attack? Grasping what a person intends or desires by interpreting their actions is a distinctive human skill. To programme killer robots with such capacities would be yet another remarkable achievement.

And who would be held accountable if a LAW went haywire and slaughtered children in an orphanage, demolished hospitals full of sick and wounded, killed everyone it encountered irrespective of who or what they were and what they were doing? Would it be the military's most senior commanders? The programmers? The manufacturers? The government of the state using them? Identifiable accountability is an important feature of humanitarian protection in times of conflict, because the fact of it imposes some restraint on what is done by militaries, and unclarity about it or the absence of it affords too much licence.

Agencies such as Human Rights Watch have called for prohibition of the development, manufacture and use of LAWs internationally and by individual states, and adoption by technology firms and laboratories of codes of conduct against research leading to them.[3] But there is little chance of the call being heeded. The usual calculation is: if a thing can be done it will be done, because everyone will be thinking that 'the other side' is probably doing it and might get there first, so one had better get on with doing it oneself. These game-theoretic thoughts guarantee that everyone will indeed do it. It is too late for this genie to be replaced in the bottle. The task therefore is to try to get agreements governing their use and management – specifically, to try to keep 'human-out-of-the-loop' weapon systems out of the picture altogether.

Does talk of LAWs sound like science fiction? In 2004 the US Navy produced a planning paper on 'UUVs' (unmanned undersea vehicles) – saying of them that although 'admittedly futuristic in vision, one can conceive of scenarios where UUVs sense, track, identify, target, and destroy an enemy – all autonomously'.[4] If underwater, then on land or from the air. Human Rights Watch quotes a US Air Force document predicting that 'by 2030 machine capabilities will have increased to the point that humans will have become the weakest component in a wide array of systems and processes'.[5] The UK Ministry of Defence estimated in 2011 that artificial intelligence 'as opposed to complex and clever automated systems' could be achieved in five to fifteen years and that fully autonomous synchronised aircraft could be available in 2025.[6]

While attention is fixed on the idea of killer robots roaming enemy territory and perhaps, as a result of being damaged, going haywire – or even just obeying their instructions but inflexibly and indiscriminately – it is easy to forget that there already exist weapons systems, which are already in service, that are fully automatic. These are defence systems, triggered by incoming missiles or aircraft. One such is the US Navy's Phalanx system, which in the Navy's words is 'capable of autonomously performing its own search, detect, evaluation, track, engage and kill assessment functions'.[7] Israel's Iron Dome system regularly and automatically intercepts incoming rockets and shells fired from Palestinian territory. Both Israel and South Korea have automated sentry systems whose heat and motion sensors inform human monitors back at base if they have detected people in their vicinity.

In short, no-one doubts the feasibility of automated systems, even if it is not yet clear how human-like decision-making can be programmed into them, if such were thought necessary – and not everyone will agree that it is. At present the governments of countries developing unmanned weapons and robotic systems say that they have no intention of allowing their use without human supervision. But one knows what can happen to the best intentions.

In the tradition of Mr Donald Rumsfeld one can add that whereas we know that there are live prospects of LAWs and other automated systems entering the domain of war, we cannot at this juncture know what we do not know. What might the future possibilities be for ethically complicated and anxiety-provoking developments? War in space, war using technologies not yet developed, biological weapons, weapons that target minds – the science-fiction imagination, so often anticipating science fact, might be called in aid here.

Or it could be that systems will be developed that render weapons ineffective – the ultimate stop to war, if the instruments of war were spiked, given that most people would rather make peace than try to kill one another. Is that a pipe dream? In every house connected to an electricity supply there is a trip switch which, when the system overloads or there is a short, turns the power supply off. A trip switch for weapons of every kind would be wonderful. To some extent – so far – the mutual risks of nuclear warfare have constituted, as deterrence, a trip switch against that kind of war; other kinds of trip switches against other kinds of war might be yet possible.

One futuristic form of conflict which is already entrenched in the present is 'cyberwar'. A preliminary definition, much in need of refinement, was given by Richard Clarke as 'actions by a nation-state to penetrate another nation's computers or networks for the purposes of causing damage or disruption'.[8] In line with the definition of war given in the Introduction to this book, the phrase 'nation-state' would need to be supplemented or replaced by a term that would include non-state actors, and indeed it would be necessary to include not just non-state actors whose level of organisation and activity puts them above the military horizon, but those below that horizon, whose actions are more accurately described as terrorism. Thus extended, the term 'cyberwar' encompasses any endeavour to disrupt the computer systems on which practically all organisation, military and civil, now depends.

In his submissions to the US Senate Arms Services Committee in 2010, General Keith Alexander described cyberwar as the effort to target, and to defend, computer-based military command-and-control systems, communications, weapons systems and air defence networks.[9] He could have added that civil networks operating a wide range of facilities, from power supply to security and policing arrangements, are also obvious targets, as are the operations of many hospitals, research institutions, industries and commercial businesses.

One complaint about the term 'cyberwar' is that it fails to capture the many different ways in which penetration of the security of computer systems occurs, and the purposes that attacks on computer security serve. Spying is not the same as sabotage; in the case of efforts to learn the military secrets of a hostile party, sabotaging that party's systems would be self-defeating. Crime and spying between them constitute a massive problem, obliging much effort and expense to keep computer systems secure. When it is a case of militaries and their intelligence services trying to penetrate another's systems while keeping their own safe, we are close to war as such. And certainly, if missiles are being fired and counter-efforts are made to disrupt the systems launching and guiding them, we have genuine war by other means.

Because of hacking, private sector commercial spying, identity theft and other such activities, the security of cyberspace is a major issue well beyond the military sphere. But because of the ubiquitous reliance on computing in managing almost every aspect of military activity, cyberwarfare is an inevitable feature of present and future war. And as an alternative to bombing industrial centres, or attacking civilian populations to undermine morale, attacks on the civil systems of modern life to interdict electricity, water supply, transport, communications and more, is an obvious and almost certainly far more effective choice.

Even as these words are written there are doubtless researchers developing devices whose role in the future of war we do not yet know or cannot even anticipate. So long as war continues, there will be a race to gain technological advantages over real and putative enemies. One of the lessons history emphatically teaches is that although technological superiority in the means of making war is not an absolute necessity – Vietnam shows this – nevertheless such superiority is close to being so. LAWS, murderous drones the size of mosquitoes, sonic and laser weapons, cyberspace marauders, infiltrators and saboteurs, violence in space, interdictions of the means of economic and personal life, refined techniques of psychological warfare, indeed approximations of almost anything that science fiction writers and film makers can offer, could be in development at this moment. One cannot speak of the unknown, except in this case and in this connection to say that it is assuredly there.

Concluding Remarks

Everything one says about war from a liberal and humane point of view – that it is an evil, that it should be stopped, and that while it still happens we should do everything in our power to lessen the harms it causes – is obvious to the point of banality. But this is all nevertheless true, and however banal and clichéd it is to repeat it, I repeat it.

There are some things one can add, however. A survey of the history and causes of war, and reflection on the ethical concerns war raises, suggests a number of points about how the task of lessening the evil of war, and eventually bringing it to an end, might be furthered.

One is that war seems to be far more a matter of how we arrange ourselves politically than it is an outcome of human nature. If most people are traumatised by war, and if almost every idea of human good and flourishing is negated by violence and destruction, loss, grief, and premature death, then war is not an expression of human nature. Anger, aggression and a desire or willingness to fight an opponent on occasion are human characteristics, but the overwhelming evidence of co-operation and mutual interest among members of our essentially social species (think cities, bridges, schools, hospitals, airports, civilisation itself) puts this feature of human psychology in its place, along with other and perhaps allied features such as greed and selfishness. We can all be selfish, we can all be generous; we can all be kind and sometimes unkind; but look around at the streets and buildings of any city, and one sees the marks of mutuality and co-operation more largely and enduringly displayed, even if the marks of humanity's less appetising sides are visible too.

But the nation state, the tribe, the organised groupings of people between whom conflicts of interest can arise over resources, territory, ideology, religion – in short, the political structures, taken in the broadest sense of 'political' – are the units on which war as such is predicated. And war as such is not a saloon bar brawl started and conducted in a flash of aggression. It is a calculated matter organised on a large scale over periods of time in which feelings of anger could not sustain themselves. War is not anger, except at the sharp point of soldier-to-soldier contact; and then only maybe. Aggression is a *feeling* in an individual, but it is a *choice* in a state.

If this is right, then one major step to the control of war is adjustment of how international relations are conducted. Long before Richard Cobden in the nineteenth century and Thomas Paine in the late eighteenth century, it was recognised that ties of trade and co-operation are sovereign prophylactics for war. The European Union, a form of co-operation among nations which had been horrendously at each others' throats for centuries beforehand, is an outstandingly promising example.

Of course, efforts at making international relations work better are indeed made. And they still fail, too often and in too many places. Therefore more has to be done. One step is to deinstitutionalise war. The raising, training and supplying of military forces is a given in almost all states, as if it were as natural as breathing. Government defence contracts play an important part in economies. Military personnel are respected, honoured, applauded: quite rightly, in cases where the defence of the nation or its interests was achieved by their courage and commitment. But one sees how, therefore, the whole matter of military forces, the money for them, the relationship between the arms industry and the economy at large, the encouragement of positive social attitudes to those whose business is war, result in an institutionalisation of the idea of war: it is built into the DNA of the society and the economy. Eisenhower famously warned against the 'military-industrial complex' when he left the White House at the end of his presidency in 1961, handing over to John F. Kennedy at a time of high tension between NATO and the Warsaw Pact – yet even then, in the midst of those tensions, the former general could warn against the militarisation of society's economy and culture.

Eisenhower's warning came too late and in the wrong circumstances, perhaps, but it still stands as valid in connection with the thought that war should be deinstitutionalised. The idea of war is a too accepted – too thoughtlessly accepted – feature of the very idea of the state and its behaviour. Instead of war being seen as an occasional bitter necessity, its mere possibility is a permanent presence in the budgets, decisions and attitudes of states. Deinstitutionalising the idea of war means changing this assumption.

This task, in turn, requires another. War is romanticised in novels, films and television programmes. War is cosmeticised; television news broadcasts do not show the blood and guts. The millions watching their television screens do not see the full ghastly reality of what is happening – what their own governments might actively be encouraging, for example. Little boys run about the garden making gun noises and being soldiers. Even those films that aim to portray the horror of war are avidly watched and enjoyed because there is romance even in the horror and danger, and both are vicariously enjoyed. Vicariously because they would not be enjoyed in reality.

How about stopping the romanticisation of war, then, by not censoring the news reports on television? How about the aversion therapy of truth – mangled bodies, blown apart children, blood running into gutters, people screaming in pain or terror? How about truth as an antidote to war? This would be really to educate people about war and the realities of war. Words are one thing: one can write about it, and describe horrors – but seeing is really believing. Stop censoring television news. Show the reality.

And then again: the energy, determination, inventiveness and cohesive effort of a people at war – the camaraderie, the solidarity, the sacrifices made and shared – why not transfer this to much better causes, such as the problem of climate change, reducing world poverty, overcoming disease, providing education to all the world's children, rectifying the unjust situation of women everywhere, fighting human rights abuses, solving the impending water crisis facing the world, resisting conflict rather than engaging in it? There are many better things to which money and energy can be applied, and yet far more of both go into the preparations for war and the conduct of war than to any of these other things. This is madness.

So: deinstitutionalise war. Stop romanticising it. Stop censoring the truth about it. Redirect the energies and solidarities that go into the making of war far more than they go into the making of things of peace. Let us educate ourselves about the realities and costs of war, without pussy-footing about. Let us wean our economies and societies off the addiction to the idea that things military are a commonplace necessity. Let us be hard-nosed about it: that it is only the presence of bad people elsewhere that requires us to be ready for our defence, but that war as an instrument of anything but defence is totally, completely, humanly, morally unacceptable: a crime of the blackest kind on the part of those who cause it.

The obverse of this claim is that there are therefore only two justifications for making war. They are self-defence against aggression, and defence of those who cannot defend themselves against aggression.

If there is one key to the entire question of war, it is *justice*. A fair world would be a far less conflicted one. Inequality and injustice are ripe causes of social unrest within a society; they have analogues in the international sphere which are heady prompts for conflict.

Organisations like the UN and many others are indeed engaged in trying to make the world a fairer and more co-operative place, thereby promoting peace and the conditions for peace. So this is already being tried. But cynics observe that the efforts do not seem very successful. One can say two things in response. One is: 'yet'. They might not yet seem to be successful. Give it more time: do not give up. The other is: maybe the cynics are too hasty; perhaps these organisations and their work have indeed limited the amount of conflict that might otherwise have occurred had they and their efforts not existed. Indeed it is a certainty that this is so. Cynicism is therefore misplaced. The human story is a work in progress.

Concluding Remarks

The marks of progress in human affairs are many and varied. Undoubtedly, however, the consignment of war to history will be one of the greatest and most laudable such marks. The work of ending war is in hand; it is long, and arduous – a 'work of long breath' as the French say (*un ouvrage de longue haleine*). It takes, and will continue to demand, even more resolution, courage and determination than going to war takes. That is a fact. It is where the real heroism of the human species will be displayed.

Meanwhile we are still having to live with war, and therefore have a battle to fight: to prevent it whenever possible, to limit it if not, to press for humanitarian restraint when it happens, to hold warmakers to account, to argue and educate against it always. As the technologies of war grow ever more sophisticated and destructive so the truth enunciated by John F. Kennedy comes ominously closer: that if we do not end war, it will end us. Perhaps one day it will. Or perhaps one day everything recounted in the pages of this book will be the stuff of old and outdated things, as a book about witchcraft or astrology might now be – past nonsense, from irrational times, when folly too often reigned.

I hope so.

Notes

1 Ancient War

1. J. Keegan, *A History of Warfare*, London: Hutchinson, 1993, p. 173.
2. H. H. Turney-High, *Primitive War: Its Practice and Concepts*, 2nd edn, Columbia, SC: University of South Carolina Press, 1971.
3. Ibid.
4. Ibid.
5. Julius Caesar, *Gallic Wars*, see for example Book 4, Chs 14–15.
6. 'Hominin' refers to humans and their ancestors and ancestral relatives on the evolutionary tree following the split from chimpanzees; 'hominid' refers to *all* modern and extinct great apes including all hominins – and therefore contemporary humans – gorillas, the two chimpanzee species *Pan troglodytes* and *Pan paniscus* (bonobos), and orang-utans (but excluding gibbons, which are classified as lesser apes).
7. M. Meyer et al., 'Nuclear DNA Sequences from the Middle Pleistocene Sima de los Huesos Hominins', *Nature* 531 (24 March 2016), pp. 504–7.
8. Keegan, 1993, p. 118.
9. K. M. Kenyon and T. A. Holland, *Excavations at Jericho*, Vol. 3, London: British School of Archaeology at Jerusalem, 1981.
10. J. Keegan in *War and Civilization* television documentary, dir. Stephen Trombley and Tony Bulley, Learning Channel, 2016.

11. L. H. Keeley, *War Before Civilisation: The Myth of the Peaceful Savage*, Oxford: Oxford University Press, 1996; A. Gat, *War in Human Civilization*, Oxford: Oxford University Press, 2008.

12. See Gat, 2008.

13. Turney-High, 1971.

14. Ibid., p. 23.

15. Ibid.

16. Ibid.

17. Ibid., pp. 26–7.

18. Ibid.

19. The wall, known as 'The Repeller of the Amorites' (a pastoral people) was built by King Shu-Sin, ruler of Sumer and Akkad in the Ur III period.

20. Keegan, 1993, p. 155.

21. Ibid., p. 158.

22. Ibid., p. 161.

23. Ibid., p. 174.

24. A nice philological point arises here: almost everyone, it seems, remembers the *Iliad* as saying that Achilles tied Hector's corpse to his chariot and dragged it at a gallop round the walls of Troy. In fact, Achilles chased Hector three times round the walls of Troy – on foot – Athene intervening on the fourth circuit to stop Hector so that Achilles could catch and slay him. Achilles then roped the body to his chariot and dragged it to his camp, Hector's wife Andromache and the rest of the Trojans watching in grief as their greatest warrior was thus dishonourably treated.

25. Keegan, 1993, p. 177.

26. Ibid., pp. 171–4.

27. Ibid., p. 182.

28. Ibid., p. 187.

29. See H. J. Kim, *The Huns, Rome and the Birth of Europe*, Cambridge: Cambridge University Press, 2013.

30. Keegan, 1993, p. 188.

31. Ibid., pp. 190–1.

32. Herodotus, *The Histories*, Bk VI.

33. A good account is given in E. Creasy's 1851 work, *The Fifteen Decisive Battles of the World*.

34. Plutarch, 'Alexander' in *Lives of the Greeks and Romans*.

35. There is a superb biography of Alexander by P. Cartledge, *Alexander the Great: The Truth Behind the Myth*, Macmillan: London, 2004.

36. The term denoted a war leader with plenipotentiary powers for the time of emergency, and did not have the connotations it now bears.

37. M. Beard, *SPQR: A History of Ancient Rome*, London: Profile Books, 2015, pp. 174 ff.

38. Accounts of Archimedes' siege defences occur in Polybius, Livy, Plutarch and Dio Cassus, the later sources relying on the earlier. Some of the ingenious methods he devised have been questioned, but experiments (including the use of mirror-reflected sun rays to set fire to a wooden ship) have shown that they worked.

2 Medieval to Modern War

1. For this period see M. Bennett et al., *Fighting Techniques of the Medieval World*, New York: Thomas Dunne Books, 2005.

2. The Battle of Poitiers is alternatively known as the Battle of Tours; it was fought between these two cities near a village called Moussais, which was therefore renamed 'Moussais-la-Bataille'.

3. *Mozarabic Chronicle of 754*, trans. K. B. Wolf, in *Conquerors and Chroniclers of Early Medieval Spain*, Liverpool: Liverpool University Press, 2000, p. 145.

4. Henry Wadsworth Longfellow: 'And the night shall be filled with music/ And the cares, that infest the day/ Shall fold their tents like the Arabs/ And as silently steal away.'

5. See J. Riley-Smith, *The Feudal Nobility and the Kingdom of Jerusalem, 1174–1277*, London: Macmillan, 1973; H. Nicholson, *The Crusades*, Westport, CT: Greenwood Press, 2004; and especially S. Runciman's three-volume *A History of the Crusades*, Cambridge: Cambridge University Press, 1951–54.

6. Matthew Paris, *Chronica Majora*, 1240–53.

7. See P. Brent, *The Mongol Empire: Genghis Khan: His Triumph and His Legacy*, London: Weidenfeld & Nicolson, 1976.

8. See J. Man, *Kublai Khan: From Xanadu to Superpower*, London: Bantam Press, 2006.

9. Keegan, 1993, p. 207.

10. Quoted in D. W. Tschanz, *History's Hinge: 'Ain Jalut*, available at http://archive.aramcoworld.com/issue/200704/history.s.hinge.ain.jalut.htm.

11. Keegan, 1993, p. 211.

12. J. Saunders, *The History of the Mongol Conquests*, London: Routledge & Kegan Paul, 1971, p. 174.

13. V. D. Hanson, *The Western Way of War*, Berkeley, CA: University of California Press, 2009.
14. Keegan, 1993, pp. 332–3.
15. Ibid.
16. A superb account of this is given in J. H. Parry, *Europe and the Wider World 1415–1715*, London: Hutchinson, 1949.
17. A. C. Grayling, *The Age of Genius*, London: Bloomsbury, 2016, pp. 107–16.
18. It has been argued that if the RAF had concentrated its resources on Coastal Command rather than Bomber Command in the Second World War, to combat the U-boats holding a knife to Britain's jugular in the North Atlantic, the war would have been won sooner. See A. C. Grayling, *Among the Dead Cities*, London: Bloomsbury, 2006, Ch. 6 *passim*.
19. N. Machiavelli, *Discourses*, 1517, Book II.
20. Machiavelli was especially impressed by the account given by Polybius in *Histories* XVIII, 28–32 of Rome's successes against the Macedonians and Seleucids, and by the example of infantry effectiveness against cavalry as demonstrated by Swiss troops in conflicts in Italy and Burgundy.
21. Keegan, 1993, p. 342.
22. Grayling, 2016, Part II *passim*.
23. Keegan, 1993, pp. 344–5.
24. Ibid.
25. Ibid.
26. I make no mention of Israel and its neighbours because, again at the time of writing, internal troubles in the Arab states traditionally hostile to Israel render them incapable of concerted effort against it. That could change back to the open hostilities of the earlier Arab–Israeli wars, unless another peace process at last works.

3 Theories of War and War's More Recent History

1. See A. C. Grayling, *The Age of Genius*, London: Bloomsbury, 2016, *passim*.
2. A. Gat, *The Origins of Military Thought from the Enlightenment to Clausewitz*, Oxford: Oxford University Press, 1989, p. 15. Among those he cites are Mario Savorgnano's *Arte militare terrestre e maritima* (1599), Giorgio Basta's *Il maestro di campo generale* (1606), Johan Jacob von Wallhausen's *Corpus militare* (1617) and Henri de Rohan's *Le Parfait Capitaine* (1631).

3. Gat, 1989, p. 23.
4. Ibid.
5. Ibid., p. 21.
6. Diderot and d'Alembert, *Encyclopédie, ou dictionnaire raisonné des sciences, des arts et des métiers* (*Encyclopaedia, or a Systematic Dictionary of the Sciences, Arts, and Crafts*). The quotation is from Diderot's 'Preliminary Discourse' to Volume I.
7. The consequences of this way of thinking have been exceedingly far-reaching. See A. C. Grayling, *Towards the Light*, London: Bloomsbury, 2007.
8. Gat, 1989, p. 28.
9. Ibid., p. 41.
10. Ibid. p. 45.
11. Ibid., p. 80.
12. Ibid., p. 82.
13. Ibid., p. 87.
14. Ibid., pp. 115–16.
15. Ibid., pp. 119, 122.
16. Ibid., p. 154.
17. Ibid.
18. Ibid., p. 182.
19. It is an admirable feature of Gat's study that it situates Clausewitz so illuminatingly in the Counter-Enlightenment tradition, and brings out the connections between Clausewitz's thinking about art and the 'art' of war.
20. Carl von Clausewitz, *On War* (1832).
21. Ibid., Bk I, Ch. I, §24.
22. Ibid., Bk I, Ch. I. §28.
23. Quoted in R. T. Foley, *German Strategy and the Path to Verdun*, Cambridge: Cambridge University Press, 2007, pp. 16, 18.
24. B. Liddell Hart, *Paris, or the Future of War*, London: Dutton, 1925.
25. The following account of thinking about the bombing weapon is reprised from my *Among the Dead Cities*, London: Bloomsbury, 2006, Ch. 4 *passim*.
26. Caparetto is now Kobarid in Slovenia. Its battle is the setting for Hemingway's *A Farewell to Arms*.
27. G. Douhet, *The Command of the Air*, trans. D. Ferrari, New York: Coward-McCann, 1942, pp. 28, 47–8, 57–8, 309.
28. Quoted in R. A. Pape, *Bombing to Win: Air Power and Coercion in War*, Ithaca, NY: Cornell University Press, 1996, p. 61.

29. Ibid.
30. Ibid.
31. Ibid., pp. 61–2.
32. Liddell Hart, 1925, p. 50.
33. Ibid., p. 45.
34. Quoted in B. Bond, *Liddell Hart: A Study of His Military Thought*, London: Cassell, 1977, p. 145.
35. Memo of May 1928 to fellow service chiefs, quoted in C. Webster and N. Frankland, *The Strategic Air Offensive Against Germany 1939–1945*, London: HMSO, 1961, Vol. IV, p. 74.
36. A. D. Harvey, *Collision of Empires: Britain in Three World Wars, 1793–1945*, London: Hambledon Press, 1992, p. 665.
37. Webster and Frankland, 1961, Vol. I, p. 99.
38. Pape, 1996, p. 50.
39. Ibid., pp. 63–4.
40. Ibid., p. 64.
41. Ibid., p. 63. The lecturer quoted by Pape was M. S. Fairchild, an instructor at the Air Corps Tactical School. These lectures were delivered in 1939, and are to be found in the archives of the US Air Force Historical Research agency at Maxwell Air Force Base in Alabama.
42. Like Douhet, Mitchell's passionate enthusiasm for air power got him into trouble. He had shown brilliant imagination in using massed air power in support of ground operations in the reduction of the St Mihiel salient in 1918 as commander of US combat aircraft in France. His outspoken criticism of US Army and Navy foot-dragging over air power matters resulted in 1925 in court martial and dismissal. He held the rank of Brigadier General at the time. He wrote several books on air strategy, and enjoyed posthumous rehabilitation; a bomber aircraft type was named after him.
43. Pape, 1996, p. 65.
44. Quoted in ibid.
45. Ibid., Ch. 5 *passim*.
46. Presciently, Grey said when hostilities began, 'The lamps are going out all over Europe; we shall not see them lit again in our lifetime.' Given that the events of 1914 ushered in seventy-five years of hot and cold war, until the fall of the Berlin Wall in 1989, he was right.
47. The relatively successful naval conferences were held in 1921, 1927 and 1930.

48. P. S. Meilinger, *Airwar: Theory and Practice*, London: Cass, 2003, p. 112.

49. Ibid., p. 113.

50. Quoted in E. M. Emme (ed.), *The Impact of Air Power*, Princeton, NJ: Van Nostrand, 1959, pp. 51–2.

51. For jet aircraft: the Messerschmitt 262 and the Whittle jet, both in service by 1945; for missiles, the VI and V2 rockets fired at Britain by Germany from the summer of 1944; for atom bombs, the Hiroshima and Nagasaki attacks in August 1945.

52. B. Liddell Hart, *The Current of War*, London: Hutchinson, 1941, p. 93.

53. Ibid., p. 94.

54. Ibid., pp. 94–5.

55. Ibid., p. 98.

56. Ibid.

57. Ibid., p. 102.

58. Liddell Hart controversially claimed to have been the inspiration for *Blitzkrieg* by his championing of mobile battlefield armour. Given that he did so in the columns of *The Times* newspaper in the late 1920s it is not impossible that this was so.

59. It has been suggested that the grandfather of the former US president Barack Obama suffered abuse and torture at the hands of British military personnel while imprisoned during the Mau Mau uprising.

60. J. S. Levy and W. R. Thomson, *The Arc of War*, Chicago: University of Chicago Press, 2011, p. 5.

61. S. Pinker, *The Better Angels of Our Nature*, New York: Viking, 2011.

4 The Causes of War

1. R. Wrangham and D. Peterson, *Demonic Males: Apes and the Origins of Human Violence*, New York: Houghton Mifflin, 1996.

2. A recruitment poster for the British Army carried a portrait photograph of Edith Cavell and the words 'Murdered by the Huns: Enlist in the 99th and help stop such atrocities'.

3. C. Sousa and C. Casanova, 'Are Great Apes Aggressive? A Cross-species Comparison', *Antropologia Portuguesa*, 22/23 (2005–06), pp. 71–118.

4. D. Fry (ed.), *War, Peace and Human Nature*, Oxford: Oxford University Press, 2013, p. xiv.

5. Wrangham and Peterson, 1996.
6. Fry, 2013, Parts 2 and 3 *passim*.
7. M. Sahlins, *The Western Illusion of Human Nature*, Chicago: Prickly Paradigm Press, 2008.
8. Fry, 2013, Part 1 explores the ecological and evolutionary models that bear on the issue.
9. This is the view taken by Fry, 2013, p. 2.
10. E. O. Wilson, *Sociobiology: The New Synthesis*, Cambridge, MA: Harvard University Press, 1975; T. L. Thorson, *Biopolitics*, New York: Holt, Rinehart & Winston, 1970.
11. Because Spencer is not much read, it is erroneously believed that he derived his ideas from Darwin. In fact his own views about the evolution of society predate Darwin; see his 'Progress: Its Law and Cause', *Westminster Review* (1857), published two years before Darwin's *Origin of Species* (1859). After reading Darwin he coined the 'survival of the fittest' phrase which is, as one might say, inaccurately retrofitted as a description of Darwin's insight.
12. See F. Galton, *Hereditary Genius*, London: Macmillan, 1869, and *Natural Inheritance*, London: Macmillan, 1889. In his anthropological travels in Namibia he used methods of land surveying to estimate the size of Khoikhoi women's buttocks from a distance, they being celebrated for the degree of steatopygia they displayed: see F. Spencer (ed.), *History of Physical Anthropology*, Vol. I, New York: Garland, p. 567.
13. Southern Mediterranean peoples, especially Italians, were put into this category also by the US immigration authorities. This was the work of the US 'Eugenics Records Office' and the Public Health Service whose officials examined immigrants at Ellis Island and which recommended excluding people of 'inferior stock'. In 1924 the Immigration Restriction Act was passed, 'designed consciously to halt the immigration of supposedly "dysgenic" Italians and eastern European Jews, whose numbers had mushroomed during the period from 1900 to 1920', P. Lombardo, 'Eugenics Laws Restricting Immigration', Image Archive on the American Eugenics Movement, Cold Harbor Spring Laboratory, available at http://www.eugenicsarchive.org/html/eugenics/essay-9text.html.
14. K. Lorenz, *On Aggression*, London: Methuen, 1966; D. Morris, *The Naked Ape*, London: Jonathan Cape, 1967; R. Ardrey, *The Territorial Imperative*, New York: Atheneum, 1966; L. Tiger, *Men in Groups*, New York: Random House, 1969.

15. E. O. Wilson, *On Human Nature*, Cambridge, MA: Harvard University Press, 1978, p. 78.

16. R. Dawkins, *The Selfish Gene*, London: Oxford University Press, 1976.

17. J. Maynard Smith, 'Group Selection and Kin Selection: A Rejoinder', *Nature*, 201 (1964), pp. 1145–7; W. D. Hamilton, 'The Genetic Theory of Social Behaviour', *Journal of Theoretical Biology*, 7 (1964), pp. 1–52.

18. Wilson, 1978, p. 117. Wilson's criticisms of 'inclusive fitness' and his views in support of sociobiology are iterated in his *The Meaning of Human Existence*, New York: Liveright, 2014; see especially the Appendix. This book explains and defends his theory of 'eusociality', which he sees as an advance on the concept of the 'selfish gene'. The principal point of dispute between Wilson and Dawkins concerns 'group selection', in which Wilson believes and Dawkins (along with most other evolutionary theorists) does not.

19. See A. Montagu, *The Nature of Human Aggression*, New York: Oxford University Press, 1976, p. 184.

20. See T. Dobzhansky, 'the fittest may also be the gentlest', in *Mankind Evolving*, New Haven, CT: Yale University Press, 1962, p. 134.

21. Marshall Sahlins makes clear in a lecture on his theme of the 'Western illusion' about human nature as inherently prone to war that kinship is not only and always a genetic or genealogical matter; in a number of societies kin are those who take the same names as a bond or eat food produced on land shared by their ancestors – and so for other practices of social bonding, which predate all the other ties and divisions that social practices might further result in: see his lecture at the Fishbein Conference 2014, available at https://vimeo.com/87106630.

22. R. Lewontin et al., *Not in Our Genes*, New York: Random House, 1984; D. T. Campbell 'On the Genetics of Altruism and the Counterhedonic Components in Human Culture', in L. Wispe (ed.), *Altruism, Sympathy and Helping*, New York: Academic Press, 1978, pp. 39–57.

23. Campbell, 1978, p. 41.

24. As the standard view now, this contrasts sharply with the 'polygenism' of Louis Agassiz and other racialist (and racist) theories of the nineteenth century in general, and which Darwinian arguments showed are unsustainable.

25. T. E. Ore, *The Social Construction of Difference and Inequality: Race, Class, Gender and Sexuality*, Mountain View, CA: Mayfield, 2000.
26. L. Gumplowicz, *Outlines of Sociology*, ed. I. L. Horowitz, trans. F. W. Moore, New York: Paine-Whitman, 1963, pp. 203–5; G. Ratzenhofer, quoted in W. M. Johnson, *The Austrian Mind 1848–1938*, Berkeley, CA: University of California Press, 1983, p. 347.
27. I. A. Novikow, *War and its Alleged Benefits*, New York: Holt, 1912.
28. Ibid., Ch. 1.
29. P. A. Corning, *The Synergism Hypothesis*, New York: McGraw Hill, 1983.
30. Lewontin et al., 1984.
31. See R. B. Ferguson, 'Pinker's List', in Fry, 2013, Ch. 7 *passim*. The evidence mentioned in Chapter 1 above for pre-cultural warfare must be put in the context of these points.
32. Steven Pinker in *The Better Angels of Our Nature*, New York: Viking, 2011.
33. See Ferguson in Fry, 2013.
34. M. G. Bicchieri (ed.), *Hunters and Gatherers Today*, New York: Holt, Rinehart & Winston, 1972, quoted in Fry, 2013, p. 6.
35. These data are presented in Part III of Fry, 2013, Chs 12–15 inclusive.
36. C. Boehm, 'The Biological Evolution of Conflict Resolution Between Groups', in Fry, 2013, Ch. 16 *passim*.
37. Quote paraphrased from H. G. Summers, *On Strategy: A Critical Analysis of the Vietnam War*, New York: Presidio Press, 1982, p. 1.
38. See J. S. Levy and W. R. Thomson, *Causes of War*, Oxford: Wiley-Blackwell, 2010; M. E. Brown, *Theories of War and Peace*, Cambridge, MA: MIT Press, 1998.
39. K. Waltz, *Man, the State, and War*, New York: Columbia University Press, 1959; J. D. Singer, 'The Level-of-analysis Problem in International Relations', *World Politics*, 14(1) (1961), pp. 77–92.
40. Levy and Thomson, 2010.
41. See R. Keohane in R. Keohane (ed.), *Neorealism and Its Critics*, New York: Columbia University Press, 1986, pp. 163–5 for a definition of realism in this context. An application of realist ideas to the explanation of recent major wars is given by S. van Evera, *Causes of War*, Ithaca, NY: Cornell University Press, 1998.
42. Keohane, 1986, pp. 163–5.
43. Waltz, 1959.

44. M. Sheehan, *The Balance of Power*, London: Routledge, 1995.

45. Quoted in Levy and Thomson, 2010, p. 39.

46. There is a list on Wikipedia under 'List of proxy wars'.

47. Quoted in Levy and Thomson, 2010, p. 70. See M. Howard, *War and the Liberal Conscience*, Oxford: Oxford University Press, 1981.

48. W. Hinde, *Richard Cobden: A Victorian Outsider*, New Haven, CT: Yale University Press, 1987.

49. Norman Angell, *The Great Illusion*, New York: G. P. Putnam's Sons, 1910.

50. Levy and Thomson, 2010, p. 73.

51. E. Gartzke, 'The Capitalist Peace', *American Journal of Political Science*, 51(1) (January 2007), pp. 166–91, available at http://pages.ucsd.edu/~egartzke/publications/gartzke_ajps_07.pdf.

52. See also M. Mousseau et al., 'How the Wealth of Nations Conditions the Liberal Peace', *European Journal of International Relations*, 9(2) (2003), pp. 277–314; M. Mousseau, 'The Social Market Roots of Democratic Peace', *International Security*, 33(44) (Spring 2009), pp. 52–86. One can sympathise with those who would wish that matters were the other way round.

53. A. de Tocqueville, *Democracy in America*, 1835, Part I, Ch. 8.

54. Ibid.

55. Levy and Thomson, 2010, pp. 106 ff. canvass the literature on this topic; their main points are summarised here.

56. Ibid., p. 107.

57. E. Kant, 'Perpetual Peace' 1975, available at https://www.mtholyoke.edu/acad/intrel/kant/kant1.htm; J. Bentham, 'A Plan for an Universal and Perpetual Peace', *Principles of International Law* §IV, 1786–9, available at https://www.laits.utexas.edu/poltheory/bentham/pil/pil.e04.html.

58. W. B. Gallie, *Philosophers of Peace and War*, Cambridge: Cambridge University Press, 1978, p. 68 draws attention to the copious nature of Engels' writings on war.

59. Ibid., pp. 73–4.

60. Levy and Thomson, 2010, pp. 87–8.

61. Ibid., p. 88.

62. Cited in ibid., pp. 89–90.

63. Some of the literature, as preparation for putting a point of view, contains good summaries of the different positions: D. Sobek, *The Causes of War*, Cambridge: Polity, 2009 is an example.

64. Van Evera, 1998.

65. J. Black, *Why Wars Happen*, Chicago: Reaktion Books, 2005.

66. J. S. Mill, *System of Logic*, Bk 3, Ch. VIII.
67. See Fry, 2013, Ch. 27.

5 The Effects of War

1. Footnote on culturecide, Grayling, *Among the Dead Cities*, 2006, London: Bloomsbury, p. 21.
2. J. Ruskin lecture on war, delivered at the Royal Military Academy at Woolwich, December 1865.
3. J. S. Mill, 'The Contest in America', *Fraser's Magazine*, 1862.
4. B. Liddell Hart, *Strategy*, New York: Meridian, 2nd rev. edn, 1991, p. 368.
5. G. Braybon, *Women Workers in the First World War*, London: Routledge, 1981.
6. I. Morris, *War: What Is It Good For?*, London: Profile Books, 2014.
7. Ibid., Ch. 1, passim.
8. L. Keeley, *War Before Civilisation*, Oxford: Oxford University Press, 1996.
9. D. Fry (ed.), *War, Peace and Human Nature*, Oxford: Oxford University Press, 2013.
10. S. Pinker, *The Better Angels of Our Nature*, New York: Viking, 2011. See Norbert Elias, *The Civilising Process*, trans. E. Jephcott, Oxford: Blackwell, 1994 for an influential ur-version of the thesis about the increasing pacification of the world. It was first published in Germany in 1939 and its date and place of publication were among the reasons for the controversy that surrounded it when, in the 1960s, it became a target for criticism from those opposed to 'grand narratives' and Whig views of historical progress.
11. A good introduction to the relevant considerations is Pinker's TED talk in 2007 on the subject, available at https://www.ted.com/talks/steven_pinker_on_the_myth_of_violence. See also M. Eisner (ed.), *Violence in Evolutionary and Historical Perspective*, special issue of *British Journal of Criminology*, 51(4) (2011).
12. A. R. Gat and Z. Moaz, 'Global Change and the Transformation of War', in Gat and Moaz (eds), *War in a Changing World*, Ann Arbor, MI: University of Michigan Press, 2001, pp. 1–14.
13. M. White, *Atrocities: The 100 Deadliest Episodes in Human History*, New York: W. W. Norton, 2012, pp. 271, 578. One is here counting the casualties of the Chinese and Russian civil wars of the century, the bloody strife in the African continent, and others.

14. The figures given for the Balkans and Colombia are UNHCR estimates. See, e.g., its *Global Report* 2015, available at http://www.unhcr.org/uk/the-global-report.html.

15. Retrospectively it is possible to see an earlier dawning of awareness of war-induced psychological trauma; unexplained somatic disorders such as 'palpitations' or 'DAH' (disordered action of the heart) observed in soldiers in the Crimean War, and 'irritable heart' described by Jacob Mendes Da Costa in the American Civil War, were suspected to be psychogenic, and both acute post-combat exhaustion and a chronic form described as a kind of neurasthenia were observed in nineteenth-century war veterans. See E. Jones and S. Wessely, *Shell Shock to PTSD*, Hove: Psychology Press, 2005.

16. D. A. Grossman, *On Killing*, New York: Back Bay Books, 1996, pp. xxix, xxxiii, 4.

17. Ibid., p. xxxiii.

18. Ibid., pp. xii–xiii.

19. Ibid., p. xiv.

20. Ibid., p. 282.

21. Ibid., p. 285.

22. Ibid.

23. T. Tanielian and L. H. Jaycox (eds), *Invisible Wounds of War: Psychological and Cognitive Injuries, Their Consequences, and Services to Assist Recovery*, Santa Monica, CA: Rand Center for Military Health Policy Research, 2008, p. xxi.

24. The now classic examination of psychological medicine in the twentieth-century military sphere is Ben Shephard's *A War of Nerves: Soldiers and Psychiatrists in the Twentieth Century*, Cambridge, MA: Harvard University Press, 2001, which I had the pleasure of reviewing enthusiastically when it first appeared. The following account draws upon it.

25. There is a 'Shot at Dawn' memorial to them in the National Memorial Arboretum near Alrewas, Staffordshire.

26. D. Hunter, quoted in R. Bailey, 'The Second World War: Shellshock to Psychiatry', available at http://www.gresham.ac.uk/lecture/transcript/print/the-second-world-war-shellshock-to-psychiatry/.

27. G. M. Thomas, *Treating the Trauma of the Great War*, Baton Rouge, LA: Louisiana State University Press, 2009, p. 15.

28. Tanielian and Jaycox, 2008, p. 300.

29. Thomas, 2009, p. 73.

30. Shephard, 2001, p. xxii.

31. Jones and Wessely, 2005, p. 2.

6 Ethics, Law and War

1   J. Keegan, *A History of Warfare*, London: Hutchinson, 1993, p. 290.
2. Quoted in ibid., p. 291.
3. Augustine, *City of God*, Book XIX, Ch. 7.
4. Thomas Aquinas, *Summa Theologica*, Part II, Question 40.
5. Francisco de Vitoria, *De Jure Belli*, §60.
6. Francisco Suárez, *De Charitate* XIII, in *Extracts on Politics and Government*, trans. G. A. Moore, 1950, Chevy Chase, MD: Country Dollar Press, Sections 2, 3, 5, 8.
7. Ibid.
8. Hugo Grotius, *De Iure Belli ac Pacis*, 1625, Part II.
9. Ibid., Part III.
10. Ibid., Part III, XXI–XXV.
11. M. Walzer, *Just and Unjust Wars: A Moral Argument with Historical Illustrations*, 3rd edn, New York: Basic Books, 2000, Ch. 16.
12. A. C. Grayling, *Among the Dead Cities*, London: Bloomsbury, 2006.
13. M. Walzer, *Arguing About War*, New Haven, CT: Yale University Press, 2004, p. 12.
14. *A More Secure World: Our Shared Responsibility*, Report of the Secretary General's High-Level Panel on Threats, Challenges and Change, United Nations, 2004, Part 3, §207, available at http://www.un.org/en/peacebuilding/pdf/historical/hlp_more_secure_world.pdf.
15. In fact the mural might have been damaged invisibly by vibration shock, although the sandbagging – a large part of the miracle – protected surface damage from shrapnel and other flying debris.
16. K. Albutt et al., 'Stigmatisation and Rejection of Survivors of Sexual Violence in Eastern Democratic Republic of the Congo', *Disasters*, May 2016.
17. 'Atrocities Beyond Words: A Barbarous Campaign of Rape', *Economist*, 1 May 2008, available at http://www.economist.com/world/africa/displaystory.cfm?story_id=11294767.
18. A. Jones, 'A War on Women', *Los Angeles Times*, 17 January 2008, available at http://www.latimes.com/la-op-jones17feb17-story.html.
19. J. Holmes, 'Congo's Rape War', *Los Angeles Times*, 11 October 2007, available at http://www.latimes.com/news/la-oe-holmes 11oct11-story.html.
20. J. Gettleman, 'Rape Epidemic Raises Trauma of Congo War', *New York Times*, 7 October 2007, available at http://www.nytimes.com/2007/10/07/world/africa/07congo.html?ref—ultimedia&pagewanted=printWP.

21. A. Beevor, *The Fall of Berlin 1945*, New York: Penguin, 2003. Other estimates of the number of women who suffered rape put the figure at 2 million.

22. An organisation that seeks to keep women out of combat roles, the Center for Military Readiness cites the following in support of their view: that women are on average smaller and 'less aggressive' than men, with 50 per cent less upper body strength and 25 per cent less aerobic capacity, are not as accurate shooters as men, are twice as likely to suffer injuries requiring removal from active duty, are less good at negotiating physical obstacles, have less dense and therefore more friable bones – and are 'more nurturing because they have a better sense and understanding of motherhood'. M. Thompson, 'Women in Combat: *Vive a Différence*', *Time*, 25 January 2013, available at http://nation.time.com/2013/01/25/women-in-combat-vive-a-difference/.

23. E. M. Remarque, *All Quiet on the Western Front*, trans. A. W. Wheen, New York: Ballantine Books, 1987, p. 223.

7 The Future of War

1. I say 'his' here, but increasingly male exclusivity in combat roles is on the way out, as discussed in Chapter 6.

2. A. Damasio, *Descartes' Error*, New York: Putnam's, 1994.

3. Human Rights Watch, 'Losing Humanity: The Case Against Killer Robots', 2012, available at https://www.hrw.org/report/2012/11/19/losing-humanity/case-against-killer-robots.

4. US Department of the Navy, 'The Navy Unmanned Undersea Vehicle (UUV) Master Plan', 2004, quoted in ibid.

5. US Air Force Chief Scientist, 'Report on Technology Horizons: A Vision for Air Force Science & Technology During 2010–2030', 2010, quoted in ibid.

6. UK Ministry of Defence, *The UK Approach to Unmanned Aircraft Systems*, 2011, quoted in ibid.

7. US Navy Fact Sheet, quoted in ibid.

8. R. A. Clarke, *Cyber War*, New York: HarperCollins, 2010, p. 6.

9. T. Shanker, 'Cyberwar Nominee Sees Gaps in Law', *New York Times*, 14 April 2010.

Bibliography

Albutt, K., Kelly, J., Kabanga, J. and VanRooyen, M., 2016, 'Stigmatisation and Rejection of Survivors of Sexual Violence in Eastern Democratic Republic of the Congo'. *Disasters*, May.

Allen, B., 1996, *Rape Warfare*. Minneapolis: University of Minnesota Press.

Angell, N., 1910, *The Great Illusion*. New York: G. P. Putnam's Sons.

Archer, C. I., Ferris, J., Herwig, H. and Travers, T., 2008., *World History of Warfare*. Lincoln, NE: University of Nebraska Press.

Ardrey, R., 1966, *The Territorial Imperative*. New York: Atheneum.

Aron, R., 1968, *On War*. New York: Norton.

Beard, M., 2015, *SPQR: A History of Ancient Rome*. London: Profile Books.

Beevor, A., 2003, *The Fall of Berlin 1945*. New York: Penguin.

Bennett, M. et al., 2005, *Fighting Techniques of the Medieval World*. New York: Thomas Dunne Books.

Bicchieri, M. G. (ed.), 1972, *Hunters and Gatherers Today*. New York: Holt, Rinehart & Winston.

Black, J., 2002, *Warfare in the Western World, 1882–1975*. Bloomington, IN: Indiana University Press.

Black, J., 2004, *Rethinking Military History*. London: Routledge.

Black, J., 2005, *Why Wars Happen*. Chicago: Reaktion Books.

Blaney, G., 1988, *The Causes of War*, 3rd edn. New York: Free Press.

Bibliography

Bond, B., 1979, *Liddell Hart: A Study of His Military Thought*. London: Cassell.

Braybon, G., 1981, *Women Workers in the First World War*. London: Routledge.

Brent, P., 1976, *The Mongol Empire: Genghis Khan: His Triumph and His Legacy*. London: Weidenfeld & Nicolson.

Brown, M. E., 1998, *Theories of War and Peace*. Cambridge, MA: MIT Press.

Brown, S., 1988, *The Causes and Prevention of War*. New York: St Martin's Press.

Campbell, D. T., 1978, 'On the Genetics of Altruism and the Counterhedonic Components in Human Culture', in L. Wispe (ed.), *Altruism, Sympathy and Helping*. New York: Academic Press, pp. 39–57.

Clarke, R. A., 2010, *Cyber War*. New York: HarperCollins.

Corning, P. A., 1983, *The Synergism Hypothesis: A Theory of Progressive Evolution*. New York: McGraw Hill.

Cowley, R. and Parker, G. (eds), 2000, *The Readers' Companion to Military History*. New York: Houghton Mifflin.

Creasy, E., [1851] 1969, *The Fifteen Decisive Battles of the World*. New York: Heritage.

Creveld, M. van, 1991, *Technology and War: From 2000 BC to the Present*. New York: Free Press.

Damasio, A., 1994, *Descartes' Error: Emotion, Reason and the Human Brain*. New York: Putnam's.

Davies, N., 1996, *Europe: A History*. Oxford: Oxford University Press.

Dawes, J., 2013, *Evil Men*. Cambridge, MA: Harvard University Press.

Dawkins, R., 1976, *The Selfish Gene*. London: Oxford University Press.

Dobzhansky, T., 1962, *Mankind Evolving: The Evolution of the Human Species*. New Haven, CT: Yale University Press.

Douhet, G., 1942, *The Command of the Air*, trans. D. Ferrari. New York: Coward-McCann.

Ehrenreich, B., 1997, *Blood Rites: Origins and History of the Passions of War*. New York: Henry Holt.

Eisner, M. (ed.), 2011, *Violence in Evolutionary and Historical Perspective*, special issue of *British Journal of Criminology*, 51(4).

Elshtain, J. B., 1987, *Women and War*. Chicago: University of Chicago Press.

Emme, E. M. (ed.), 1959, *The Impact of Air Power: National Security and World Politics*. Princeton, NJ: Van Nostrand.

Bibliography

Evera, S. van, 1998, *Causes of War: Power and the Roots of Conflict*. Ithaca, NY: Cornell University Press.

Foley, R. T., 2007, *German Strategy and the Path to Verdun*. Cambridge: Cambridge University Press.

Freedman, L. (ed.), 1994, *War*. New York: Oxford University Press.

Freud, S., 1953, *Civilization, War and Death*, ed. J. Rickman. London: Hogarth Press and the Institute of Psycho-analysis.

Fry, D. (ed.), 2013, *War, Peace and Human Nature: The Convergence of Evolutionary and Cultural Views*. Oxford: Oxford University Press.

Gallie, W. B., 1978, *Philosophers of Peace and War*. Cambridge: Cambridge University Press.

Gallie, W. B., 1991, *Understanding War*. London: Routledge.

Galton, F., 1869, *Hereditary Genius*. London: Macmillan.

Galton, F., 1889, *Natural Inheritance*. London: Macmillan.

Gartzke, E., 2007, 'The Capitalist Peace'. *American Journal of Political Science*, 51(1), pp. 166–91. http://pages.ucsd.edu/~egartzke/ publications/gartzke_ajps_07.pdf.

Gat, A., 1989, *The Origins of Military Thought from the Enlightenment to Clausewitz*. Oxford: Oxford University Press.

Gat, A., 2008, *War in Human Civilization*. Oxford: Oxford University Press.

Gat, A. and Moaz, Z., 2001, 'Global Change and the Transformation of War', in A. Gat and Z. Moaz (eds), *War in a Changing World*. Ann Arbor: University of Michigan Press, pp. 1–14.

Glover, J., 1999, *Humanity: A Moral History of the Twentieth Century*. London: Jonathan Cape.

Goldstein, J. S., 2001, *War and Gender: How Gender Shapes the War System and Vice Versa*. Cambridge: Cambridge University Press.

Grayling, A. C., 2006, *Among the Dead Cities: Is the Targeting of Civilians in War Ever Justified?* London: Bloomsbury.

Grayling, A. C., 2008, *Towards the Light*. London: Bloomsbury.

Grayling A. C., 2016, *The Age of Genius*. London: Bloomsbury.

Grossman, D. A., 1996, *On Killing: The Psychological Cost of Learning to Kill in War and Society*. New York: Back Bay Books.

Gumplowicz, L., [1885] 1963, *Outlines of Sociology*, ed. I. L. Horowitz, trans. F. W. Moore. New York: Paine-Whitman.

Hamilton, W. D., 1964, 'The Genetic Theory of Social Behaviour'. *Journal of Theoretical Biology*, 7, pp. 1–16.

Hanson, V. D., 2009, *The Western Way of War*. Berkeley, CA: University of California Press.

Hinde, R. (ed.), 1991, *The Institution of War*. London: Macmillan.

Bibliography

Hinde, W., 1987, *Richard Cobden: A Victorian Outsider*. New Haven, CT: Yale University Press.

Holmes, R., 2001, *The Oxford Companion to Military History*. Oxford: Oxford University Press.

Howard, M., 1976. *War in European History*. New York: Oxford University Press.

Howard, M., 1983, *The Causes of Wars, and Other Essays*. Cambridge, MA: Harvard University Press.

Human Rights Watch, 2012, 'Losing Humanity: The Case Against Killer Robots'. https://www.hrw.org/report/2012/11/19/losing-humanity/case-against-killer-robots.

Jones, E. and Wessely, S., 2005, *Shell Shock to PTSD: Military Psychology from 1900 to the Gulf War*. Hove: Psychology Press.

Keegan, J., 1993, *A History of Warfare*. London: Hutchinson.

Keegan, J., 1999, *The Book of War*. New York: Viking Penguin.

Keeley, L., 1996, *War Before Civilisation: The Myth of the Peaceful Savage*. Oxford: Oxford University Press.

Keeley, L., 1997, 'Frontier Warfare in the Early Neolithic', in D. Martin and D. Frayer (eds), *Troubled Times: Violence and Warfare in the Past*. Amsterdam: Gordon and Breach, pp. 303–19.

Kenyon, K. M. and Holland, T. A., 1981, *Excavations at Jericho*, Vol. 3. London: British School of Archaeology at Jerusalem.

Keohane, R. (ed.), 1986, *Neorealism and its Critics*. New York: Columbia University Press.

Kim, H. J., 2013, *The Huns, Rome and the Birth of Europe*. Cambridge: Cambridge University Press.

Leatherman, J., 2011, *Sexual Violence and Armed Conflict*. Cambridge: Polity.

Levy, J. S., 1983, *War in the Modern Great Power System, 1495–1975*. Lexington: University Press of Kentucky.

Levy, J. S. and Thomson, W. R., 2010, *Causes of War*. Oxford: Wiley-Blackwell.

Levy, J. S. and Thomson, W. R., 2011, *The Arc of War: Origins, Escalation, and Transformation*. Chicago: University of Chicago Press.

Lewontin, R., Rose, S. and Kamin, L. J., 1984, *Not in Our Genes*. New York: Random House.

Liddell Hart, B., 1925, *Paris, or the Future of War*. London: Dutton.

Liddell Hart, B., 1941, *The Current of War*. London: Hutchinson.

Lorenz, K., 1996, *On Aggression*. London: Methuen.

Man, J., 2006, *Kublai Khan: From Xanadu to Superpower*. London: Bantam Press.

Maynard Smith, J., 1964, 'Group Selection and Kin Selection: A Rejoinder'. *Nature*, 201, pp. 1145–7.

Meilinger, P. S., 2003, *Airwar: Theory and Practice*. London: Cass.

Mertus, J., 2000, *War's Offensive on Women: The Humanitarian Challenge in Bosnia, Kosovo, and Afghanistan*. West Hartford, CT: Kumarian Press.

Meyer, M. et al., 2016, 'Nuclear DNA Sequences from the Middle Pleistocene Sima de los Huesos Hominins'. *Nature*, 531 (24 March), pp. 504–7.

Montagu, A., 1976, *The Nature of Human Aggression*. New York: Oxford University Press.

Morris, D., 1967, *The Naked Ape*. London: Jonathan Cape.

Morris, I., 2014, *War: What Is It Good For?* London: Profile Books.

Mousseau, M., 2009, 'The Social Market Roots of Democratic Peace'. *International Security*, 33(44), pp. 52–86.

Mousseau, M., Hegre, H. and Oneal, J. R., 2003, 'How the Wealth of Nations Conditions the Liberal Peace'. *European Journal of International Relations*, 9(2), pp. 277–314.

Mozarabic Chronicle of 754, trans. K. B. Wolf, in *Conquerors and Chroniclers of Early Medieval Spain*, trans. K. B. Wolf. Liverpool: Liverpool University Press, 2000, pp. 111–60.

Novikow, I. A., 1912, *War and Its Alleged Benefits*. New York: Holt.

Ore, T. E., 2000, *The Social Construction of Difference and Inequality: Race, Class, Gender and Sexuality*. Mountain View, CA: Mayfield.

Pape, R. A., 1996, *Bombing to Win: Air Power and Coercion in War*. Ithaca, NY: Cornell University Press.

Paret, P., 1993, *Understanding War: Essays on Clausewitz and the History of Military Power*. Princeton, NJ: Princeton University Press.

Parker, G. (ed.), 2008, *The Cambridge Illustrated History of Warfare: The Triumph of the West*. Cambridge: Cambridge University Press.

Parry, J. H., 1949, *Europe and the Wider World 1415–1715*. London: Hutchinson.

Pinker, S., 2011, *The Better Angels of Our Nature: Why Violence Has Declined*. New York: Viking.

Rapaport, A., 1989, *The Origins of Violence: Approaches to the Study of Conflict*. New York: Paragon House.

Reichberg, G. M., Syse, H. and Begby, E. (eds), 2006, *The Ethics of War: Classic and Contemporary Readings*. Oxford: Wiley-Blackwell.

Reisman, W. M. and Antoniou, C. T., 1994, *The Laws of War: A Comprehensive Collection of Primary Documents on International*

Laws Governing Armed Conflict. New Haven, CT: Yale University Press.

Remarque, E. M., 1987, *All Quiet on the Western Front*, trans. A. W. Wheen. New York: Ballantine Books.

Riley-Smith, J., 1973, *The Feudal Nobility and the Kingdom of Jerusalem, 1174–1277*. Macmillan: London.

Robertson, G., 2003, *Crimes Against Humanity: The Struggle for Global Justice*. New York: New Press.

Runciman, S. A., 1951, *History of the Crusades*. Cambridge: Cambridge University Press.

Sahlins, M., 2008, *The Western Illusion of Human Nature*. Chicago: Prickly Paradigm Press.

Saunders, J., 1971, *The History of the Mongol Conquests*. London: Routledge & Kegan Paul.

Sheehan, M., 1995, *The Balance of Power*. London: Routledge.

Shephard, B., 2001, *A War of Nerves: Soldiers and Psychiatrists in the Twentieth Century*. Cambridge, MA: Harvard University Press.

Sobek, D., 2009, *The Causes of War*. Cambridge: Polity.

Spencer, H., 1857, 'Progress: Its Law and Cause'. *Westminster Review*, Vol. 67.

Sousa, C. and Casanova, C., 2005/6, 'Are Great Apes Aggressive? A Cross-species Comparison'. *Antropologia Portuguesa*, 22/23, pp. 71–118.

Stoessinger, J. G., 1998, *Why Nations Go to War*. New York: St. Martin's Press.

Suarez, F., 1950, *De Charitate* XIII; *Extracts: Politics and Government from Defense of the Faith, Laws and God the Lawgiver, Tract on Faith [and] Tract on Charity*, trans. G. A. Moore. Chevy Chase, MD: Country Dollar Press.

Tanielian, T. and Jaycox, L. H. (eds), 2008, *Invisible Wounds of War: Psychological and Cognitive Injuries, Their Consequences, and Services to Assist Recovery*. Santa Monica, CA: Center for Rand Military Health Policy Research.

Thomas, G. M., 2009, *Treating the Trauma of the Great War: Soldiers, Civilians, and Psychiatry in France, 1914–1940*. Baton Rouge: Louisiana State University Press.

Thomas, W., 2001, *The Ethics of Destruction: Norms and Force in International Relations*. Ithaca, NY: Cornell University Press.

Thompson, M., 2013, 'Women in Combat: *Vive a Différence*'. *Time*, 25 January. http://nation.time.com/2013/01/25/women-in-combat-vive-a-difference/.

Bibliography

Thorson, T. L., 1970, *Biopolitics*. New York: Holt, Rinehart & Winston.

Tiger, L., 1969, *Men in Groups*. New York: Random House.

Tschanz, D. W., 1971, *History's Hinge: 'Ain Jalut*. http://archive.aramcoworld.com/issue/200704/history.s.hinge.ain.jalut.htm.

Turney-High, H. H., 1971, *Primitive War: Its Practice and Concepts*, 2nd edn. Columbia, SC: University of South Carolina Press.

United Nations, 2004, *A More Secure World: Our Shared Responsibility*, Report of the Secretary-General's High-level Panel on Threats, Challenges and Change. http://www.un.org/en/peacebuilding/pdf/historical/hlp_more_secure_world.pdf.

Waltz, K., 1959, *Man, the State, and War: A Theoretical Analysis*. New York: Columbia University Press.

Walzer, M., 2000, *Just and Unjust Wars: A Moral Argument with Historical Illustrations*, 3rd edn. New York: Basic Books.

Walzer, M., 2004, *Arguing About War*. New Haven, CT: Yale University Press.

Weatherford, J., 2004, *Genghis Khan and the Making of the Modern World*. New York: Random House.

Webster, C. and Frankland, N., 1961, *The Strategic Air Offensive Against Germany, 1939–1945*, Vol. IV. London: HMSO.

White, M., 2012, *Atrocities: The 100 Deadliest Episodes in Human History*. New York: Norton.

Wilson, E. O., 1975, *Sociobiology: The New Synthesis*. Cambridge, MA: Harvard University Press.

Wilson, E. O., 1978, *On Human Nature*. Cambridge, MA: Harvard University Press.

Wrangham, R. and Peterson, D., 1996, *Demonic Males: Apes and the Origins of Human Violence*. New York: Houghton Mifflin.

Wright, Q., 1983, *A Study of War*. Chicago: University of Chicago Press.

Index

Index

Index

Index

Index

Index

Index

Index

Index

Index